SO-CBG-963

a guide to JOB OPPORTUNITIES

THE OCCUPATIONAL OUTLOOK FOR BLUE COLLAR WORKERS

a guide to
JOB
OPPORTUNITIES

THE OCCUPATIONAL OUTLOOK FOR BLUE COLLAR WORKERS

Drake Publishers Inc   New York • London

Published in 1978 by
Drake Publishers, Inc.
801 Second Avenue
New York, New York 10017

Library of Congress Cataloging in Publication Data

United States. Bureau of Labor Statistics.
    A guide to job opportunities.

    Includes index.
    1. Vocational guidance—United States.
2. United States—Occupations. I. Title.
II. Title: The occupational outlook for blue
collar workers.
HF5382.5.U5U54   1978   331.7'02   78-8782
ISBN 0-8473-1786-2 pbk.

Printed in the United States of America

Contents

ow many kinds of jobs are there?

Several hundred occupations are described in this guide, al-
ough the total number of occupations in the U.S. economy
ay be counted in the thousands. Most occupations requiring
ng periods of education or training are not discussed. The
ain types of industrial and construction occupations are de-
ribed. The long-term job outlook for the Nation as a whole
discussed, too.

here should I look first?

Start with what you know about your own interests and abil-
ies. Do you like frequent contact with other people or do you
refer to spend a lot of time alone? Are you a good follower or
meone whose greatest rewards come from directing others in
work effort? The answers to these and similar questions can
elp you assess the personal traits and individual aptitudes that
fluence your job satisfaction and performance. It may be use-
il to discuss your personal needs and abilities with a counselor
ained in exploring human behavior. He or she is familiar with
sts and other methods for making this unique, personal assess-
ent.

The next step is to match your individual talents and goals
ith those demanded by various fields of work. Most career
usters in the *Guide* describe a variety of jobs in a single field
f work. Training and skill requirements within a particular
uster often vary a great deal.

If you know initially that the length or type of career train-
g open to you is restricted by your own financial limitations
r family obligations, you may want to narrow your job choices
those requiring high school.

You may already have a specific job or industry in mind. Or,
an important industry is located in your area, you may find
useful to read the *Guide* industry statement to learn about the
ifferent jobs in that industry and their varied training require-
ents and earnings potential.

hat will I learn?

Once you have chosen a place to begin — an occupation or
dustry you'd like to learn more about — you can use the *Guide*
find out what the job is like, what education and training are
ecessary, and what the advancement possibilities, earnings, and
mployment outlook are likely to be. Each section of the *Guide*
llows a standard format, making it easier to compare different
bs. What follows is a description of the type of information
resented in each statement, with a few words of explanation.

The **Nature of the Work** section describes the major duties
f workers in the occupation. It tells what workers do on the
b and how they do it. Although each job description is typi-
il of the occupation, duties are likely to vary by employer and
ze of employing organization, geographic location, and other
ctors. In some occupations, individual workers specialize in

certain tasks. In others they perform the entire range of work
in the occupation. Of course, job duties continually change as
technology advances, new industrial processes are developed,
and products or services change.

The **Places of Employment** section provides information on
the number of workers in an occupation and tells whether they
are concentrated in certain industries or geographic areas. Whether an occupation is large or small is important to a jobseeker because large occupations, even those growing slowly, offer more
openings than small ones because of the many workers who retire or die each year.

A few occupations are concentrated in certain parts of the
country. This information is included for the benefit of people
who have strong preferences about where they live — because
they do not wish to be separated from their families and friends,
for example. For most occupations, however, employment is
widely scattered and generally follows the same pattern as the
distribution of the population.

The **Training, Other Qualifications, and Advancement** section
should be read carefully because the decisions you make concerning preparation for an occupation represent a considerable
investment of time and money. Early and wise planning toward a career goal can save you unwarranted expenditures later.

Workers can qualify for jobs in a variety of ways, including
programs offered by postsecondary vocational schools, both public and private; home study courses; government training programs; experience or training obtained in the Armed Forces; apprenticeship and other formal training offered on the job or in
the classroom by employers; and high school courses. For each
occupation, the *Guide* identifies which of these routes of entry
is preferred. In many cases, alternative ways of obtaining training are listed as well. It is worth remembering that the level at
which you enter an occupation and the speed with which you
advance often are determined by the amount of training you
have.

Many occupations are natural stepping stones to others. The
world of work is dynamic and few workers spend their lives in
one or even two occupations. Some have several jobs over a
lifetime, changing careers when it is advantageous to do so. Frequently observed patterns of movement from one occupation
to another are discussed in the *Guide*. This type of information
can be useful in several ways.

It is helpful to know, for example, that skills gained working
at one job can make you more employable in another — perhaps
a job that is more desirable in terms of earnings or working conditions. On the other hand, it also is useful to know which jobs
offer the most opportunity for transferring to other work of a
similar nature.

In some cases moving from one occupation to another takes
more than the training or experience acquired on the job. Many
Guide statements describe the possibilities for advancement af-

ter additional training, and note any in-service programs that allow employees to gain needed skills while continuing to work part time. Certain occupations offer employment opportunities to persons with little or no previous work experience. The *Guide* includes many statements on such entry level jobs.

It is usually wise, however, to discuss the patterns of job transfer and advancement described in the *Guide* with counselors, local employers, and others who know about the particular job market where you want to work. Typical patterns of movement from one occupation to another may not apply in every employment setting.

All States have certification or licensing requirements for some occupations. Electricians and plumbers are examples of occupations that are licensed. If you are considering occupations that require State licensing, be sure to check the requirements in the State in which you plan to work.

An important factor in career choice is the extent to which a particular job suits your personality. Although it often is difficult for people to assess themselves, your counselor undoubtedly is familiar with tests that can help. Each statement in the *Guide* provides information which allows you to match your own unique personal characteristics — your likes and dislikes — with the characteristics of the job. For a particular job, you may need the ability to:

—make responsible decisions

—motivate others

—direct and supervise others

—work under close supervision

—work in a highly competitive atmosphere

—enjoy working with ideas and solving problems

—enjoy working with things — good coordination and manual dexterity are necessary

—work independently — initiative and self-discipline are necessary

—work as part of a team

—enjoy helping people

—derive satisfaction from seeing the physical results of your work

—work in a confined area

—perform repetitious work

—enjoy working outside, regardless of the weather.

The **Employment Outlook** section discusses prospective job opportunities. Knowing whether or not the job market is likely to be favorable is important in deciding whether to pursue a specific career. While your interests, your abilities, and your career goals are significant, you also need to know something about the availability of jobs in the fields that interest you most.

The employment outlook section of most *Guide* statements begins with a sentence about expected employment growth

through 1985. The occupation or industry is described as likely to grow about as fast as the average for all occupations or industries; faster than the average; or more slowly than the average (figure I). *Job opportunities in a particular occupation or industry usually are favorable if employment increases at least as rapidly as in the economy as a whole. Occupations or industries in which employment stays about the same or declines generally offer less favorable job prospects than those that are growing because the only openings are those due to deaths, retirements, and other separations from the labor force.*

Some *Guide* statements take note of the effect of fluctuations in economic activity. This information is valuable to people looking into long-range career possibilities at a time when the economy is in a recession. Persons understandably wonder: What will the economy be like when I enter the labor market? Will it be harder to find a job 5 or 10 years from now than it is today? The *Guide* gives information, wherever feasible, on occupations and industries whose levels of employment fluctuate in response to shifts in the economic climate. It is important to bear in mind that employment in many — but not all — occupations and industries is directly affected by an economic downturn. A sharp improvement in the outlook for these occupations and industries is likely as the economy picks up. However, other occupations and industries are less affected by short-term changes in economic activity. Other factors influence their growth or decline. These matters are explored in a number of *Guide* statements.

For some occupations, information is available on the supply of workers — that is, the number of people pursuing the type of education or training needed and the number subsequently entering the occupation. When such information is available, the *Guide* describes prospective job opportunities in terms of the expected demand-supply relationship. The prospective job situation is termed "excellent" when demand is likely to greatly exceed supply; "keen competition" when supply is likely to exceed demand. Other terms used in *Guide* statements are shown in Figure II.

Workers who transfer in to one occupation from another sometimes are a significant component of supply; similarly, those who transfer out may have a substantial effect on demand because their leaving usually creates a job opening. Although the information currently available on transfers among occupations is limited, some statements in the *Guide* discuss transfer patterns and their effect on the supply for certain occupations.

The information in this section should be used carefully. Getting a job may be difficult if the field is so small that openings are few or so popular that it attracts many more jobseekers than there are jobs. Getting a job also can be difficult in occupations and industries in which employment is declining, although this is not always the case. But even occupations that are small or overcrowded provide some jobs. So do occupations in which employment is growing very slowly or even declining, for there is a need to replace workers who leave the occupation. If the occupation is large, the number of job openings arising from replacement needs can be quite substantial. Machinists are an example of a large occupation that provides a significant number of job openings each year because workers leave. On the average, openings resulting from replacement needs are expected to account for nearly two-thirds of all job openings.

How reliable is the information on the outlook for employment over the next 10 years? No one can predict future labor market conditions with perfect accuracy. In every occupation and industry, the number of jobseekers and the number of job openings constantly changes. A rise or fall in the demand for a product or service affects the number of workers needed to produce it. New inventions and technological innovations create some jobs and eliminate others. Changes in the size or age distribution of the population, work attitudes, training opportunities, or retirement programs determine the number of workers available. As these forces interact in the labor market, some occupations experience a shortage, some a surplus, some a balance between jobseekers and openings. Methods used by economists to develop information on future occupational prospects differ, and judgments that go into any assessment of the future also differ. Therefore, it is important to understand what underlies each statement on outlook.

For every occupation and industry covered in the *Guide*, an estimate of future employment needs is developed. These estimates are consistent with a set of assumptions about the future of the economy and the country.

Finally, you should remember that job prospects in your community or State may not correspond to the description of the employment outlook in the *Guide*. For the particular job you are interested in, the outlook in your area may be better, or worse. The *Guide* does not discuss the outlook in local areas because the analysis is far too much for a centralized staff to handle. Such information has been developed, however, by many States and localities. The local office of your State employment service is the best place to ask about local-area employment projections. Names and addresses of these State and local information sources and suggestions for additional information on the job market are given in another section, **Where to Go for More Information**.

The **Earnings** section helps answer many of the questions that you may ask when choosing a career. Will the income be high enough to maintain the standard of living I want and justify my training costs? How much will my earnings increase as I gain experience? Do some areas of the country or some industries offer better pay than others for the same type of work?

Like most people, you probably think of earnings as money. But money is only one type of financial reward for work. Paid vacations, health insurance, uniforms, and discounts on clothing or other merchandise also are part of total earnings.

About 9 out of 10 workers receive money income in the form of a *wage* or *salary*. A wage usually is an hourly or daily rate of pay, while a salary is a weekly, monthly, or yearly rate. Most craft workers, operatives, and laborers are wage earners, while most professional, technical, and clerical workers are salary earners.

In addition to their regular pay, wage and salary workers may receive extra money for working overtime, or on a night shift or irregular schedule. In some occupations, workers also may receive tips or be paid a commission based on the amount of sales or services they provide to customers. Factory workers are sometimes paid a piece rate, which is an extra payment for each item they produce. For many workers, these types of pay amount to a large part of their total earnings.

Workers in some occupations earn self-employment income in addition to their wages or salaries. For example, electricians and carpenters often do small repair or remodeling jobs during evenings or weekends.

Besides money income, most wage and salary workers receive a variety of *fringe benefits* as part of their earnings on the job. Several are required by Federal and State law, including social security, workers' compensation, and unemployment insurance These benefits provide income to persons when they are not working because of old age, work-related injury or disability, or lack of suitable jobs.

Among the most common fringe benefits are paid vacations, holidays, and sick leave. In addition, many workers are covered by life, health, and accident insurance; participate in retirement plans; and are entitled to supplemental unemployment benefits. All of these benefits are provided — in part or in full — through their employers. Some employers also offer stock options and profit-sharing plans, savings plans, and bonuses.

Workers in many occupations receive part of their earnings in the form of goods and services, or *payments in kind*. They may receive free meals or housing.

Which jobs pay the most? This is a difficult question to answer because good information is available for only one type of earnings — wages and salaries — and for some occupations even this is unavailable. Nevertheless, the *Guide* does include some comparisons of earnings among occupations. Most statements indicate whether earnings in an occupation are greater than or less than the average earnings of workers who are not supervisors and work in private industry, but not in farming. This group represented about 60 percent of all workers in 1976 and had the most reliable earnings data currently available for comparison purposes.

Besides differences among occupations, many levels of pay exist within each occupation. Beginning workers almost always earn less than those who have been on the job for some time because pay rates increase as workers gain experience or do more responsible work.

Earnings in an occupation also vary by geographic location. Although it is generally true that earnings are higher in the North Central and Northeast regions than in the West and South, there are exceptions. You also should remember that those cities which offer the highest earnings are often those in which it is most expensive to live.

In addition, workers in the same occupation may have different earnings depending on the industry in which they work.

Because of these variations in earnings, you should check with a counselor or with local employers if you are interested in specific earnings information for occupations in your area.

The **Working Conditions** section provides information on factors that can affect job satisfaction because preferences for working conditions vary considerably among individuals. Some people, for example, prefer outdoor work while others prefer working indoors. Some people like the variety of shift work, and others want the steadiness of a 9-to-5 job. Following is a list of several working conditions that apply to some of the occupations in the *Guide*.

Overtime work. When overtime is required on a job, employees must give up some of their free time and need to be flexible in their personal lives. Overtime, however, does provide the opportunity to increase earning power.

Shift work. Evening or night work is part of the regular work schedule in some jobs. Employees who work on these shifts usually are working while most other people are off. Some persons prefer shift work, however, because they can pursue certain daytime activities, such as hunting, fishing, or gardening.

Environment. Work settings vary from clean, air-conditioned offices to places that are dirty, greasy, or poorly ventilated. By knowing the setting of jobs you find interesting, you can avoid an environment that you may find particularly unpleasant.

Outdoor work. Persons who work outdoors are exposed to all types of weather. This may be preferred to indoor work, however, by those who consider outdoor work more healthful.

Hazards. In some jobs employees are subject to possible burns, cuts, falls, and other injuries and must be careful to follow safety precautions.

Physical demands. Some jobs require standing, stooping, or heavy lifting. You should be sure that you have the physical strength and stamina required before seeking one of these jobs.

Considering working conditions when you make up your mind about a career can help you choose a job that brings you satisfaction and enjoyment.

How to Use the D.O.T. Numbers: The numbers in parentheses that appear just below the title of most *Guide* statements are D.O.T. code numbers. D.O.T. stands for Dictionary of Occupational Titles. Each job listed is classified by number according to the type of work performed, training required, physical demands, and working conditions. The D.O.T. index may be used as a cross-reference, making it easier to look up a particular occupation that is of interest.

The Outlook for Occupations

INDUSTRIAL PRODUCTION AND RELATED OCCUPATIONS

Cars, newspapers, radios, bathtubs, guided missiles, eating utensils, books, and pencil sharpeners all have at least one thing in common. They, and almost all other products that we use, are made by the millions of workers in industrial production and related occupations.

Most of these skilled and semiskilled blue-collar workers are employed in factories in the mass production of goods. Others work outside of manufacturing in a wide variety of activities ranging from showing motion pictures to shoeing horses.

Because mass production would not be possible without interchangeable parts, workers in the machining and foundry occupations play a basic role in the production process. These workers make the tools, dies, molds, cores, and other items that can be used to make hundreds or even thousands of identical parts. Assemblers may then put these parts together to make automobiles, television sets,

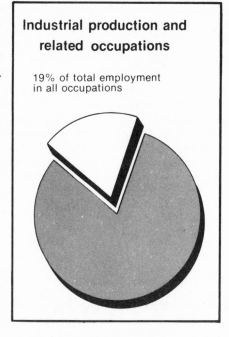

Industrial production and related occupations

19% of total employment in all occupations

and hundreds of other products. If the parts or finished products require painting, production painters do that

job. After the products are made, inspectors examine and test them to insure quality.

Other factory workers are not directly involved in the production process, but support it in some way. Stationary engineers, for example, operate soilers and other equipment used to heat and air-condition factories and other buildings, Millwrights move and install heavy machinery used in the production process and power truck operators move materials about the plant.

Printing is another type of mass production. Printing craft workers operate the machinery used to print newspapers, books, and other publications.

Industrial workers also are employed outside of manufacturing in a variety of activities. Automobile painters, for example, restore the finish on old and damaged cars. Photographic laboratory workers develop film and make prints and slides.

Most jobs in industrial production do not require a high school diploma. However, many employers prefer high school or vocational school graduates who have taken courses such as blueprint reading and machine shop.

Semiskilled workers, such as assemblers and power truck operators, ordinarily need only brief on-the-job training. Skilled workers, such as stationary engineers and machinists, require considerable training to qualify for their jobs. Many learn their trades on the job, but training authorities generally recommend completion of a 3- or 4-year apprenticeship program as the best way to learn a skilled trade.

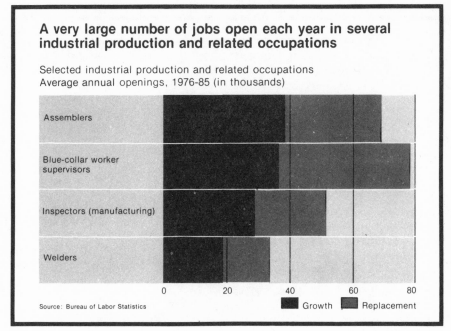

A very large number of jobs open each year in several industrial production and related occupations

Selected industrial production and related occupations
Average annual openings, 1976-85 (in thousands)

Source: Bureau of Labor Statistics   Growth   Replacement

FOUNDRY OCCUPATIONS

Many of the products that we use every day are made by casting or have parts that are made by casting. Casting is a method of forming metal into intricate shapes by pouring molten metal into carefully prepared molds and allowing it to solidify. Foundry workers produce metal castings for numerous industrial household products that range from machine tools and automobiles to bathtubs.

The *patternmaker*, the *molder*, and the *coremaker* each play an important part in the process. A *pattern-maker* makes a wood or metal model of the casting. A *molder* places it in a box and packs sand around the model to form a mold. If the casting is to have a hollow section, a *coremaker* makes a core of packed and hardened sand that is positioned in the mold before the molten metal is poured in.

In 1976, about 18,000 patternmakers, 53,000 molders, and 22,000 coremakers worked in the foundry industry. About three-fourths of them worked in shops that make and sell castings. The remainder worked in plants that make castings to use in their final products, such as plants operated by manufacturers of automobiles or machinery.

A high school education is the minimum requirement for an apprenticeship in patternmaking. Some highly skilled molding and coremaking jobs also may require a high school education, but an eighth grade education may be enough for entry into many molding and coremaking jobs.

The production and use of castings are expected to grow significantly through the mid-1980's. However, because of automation and other labsaving improvements in production methods, employment of patternmakers, coremakers, and molders is expected to increase only about as fast as the average for all occupations. In addition to those job openings that result from employment growth, other openings will arise from the need to replace experienced workers who die, retire, or transfer to other occupations. The number of openings may fluctuate from year to year because foundry employment is very sensitive to ups and downs in the economy.

Patternmakers, molders, and coremakers are discussed in detail in the following statements.

Sources of Additional Information

For details about training opportunities for patternmakers, molders, and coremakers, contact local foundries, the local office of the State employment service, the nearest office of the State apprenticeship agency, or the Bureau of Apprenticeship and Training, U.S. Department of Labor. Information also is available from the following organizations:

American Foundrymen's Society, Golf and Wolf Rds., Des Plaines, Ill. 60016.

International Molders' and Allied Workers' Union, 1225 E. McMillan St., Cincinnati, Ohio 45206.

PATTERNMAKERS

Nature of the Work

Foundry patternmakers are highly skilled craftworkers who make the patterns used in making molds for metal castings. Most of the workers in the occupation are *metal pattern-makers* (D.O.T. 600.280); a smaller number are *wood patternmakers* (D.O.T. 661.281). Some pattern-makers work with both metal and wood as well as with plaster and plastics.

Patternmakers work from blueprints prepared by engineers or drafters. They make a precise pattern for the product, carefully checking each dimension with instruments such as micrometers and calipers. Precision is important because any imperfections in the pattern will be reproduced in the castings made from it.

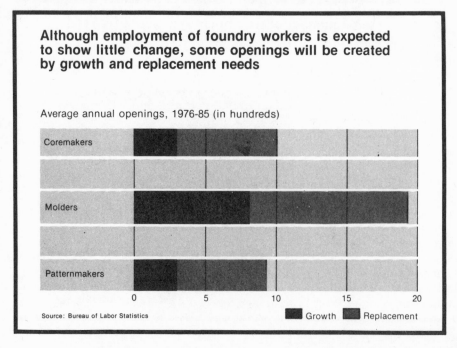

Although employment of foundry workers is expected to show little change, some openings will be created by growth and replacement needs

Average annual openings, 1976-85 (in hundreds)

Coremakers

Molders

Patternmakers

0   5   10   15   20

Source: Bureau of Labor Statistics   ■ Growth   ■ Replacement

Wood patternmakers select the wood stock, lay out the pattern, and saw each piece of wood to size. They then shape the rough pieces into final form with various woodworking machines, such as lathes and sanders, as well as many small handtools. Finally, they assemble the pattern segments by hand, using glue, screws, and nails.

Metal patternmakers prepare patterns from metal stock or from rough castings made from a wood pattern. To shape and finish the patterns, they use many metalworking machines, including lathes, drill presses, shapers, milling machines, power hacksaws, and grinders. They also use small handtools, such as files and rasps.

Training, Other Qualifications, and Advancement

Apprenticeship is the best means of qualifying as an experienced patternmaker. Because of the high degree of skill and the wide range of knowledge needed for patternmaking, it is difficult to learn the trade on the job, but in some instances skilled machinists have been able to transfer to metal patternmaking with additional on-the-job training or experience. High school courses in mechanical drawing, blueprint reading, and shop mathematics are helpful to persons interested in becoming patternmakers. In addition, vocational and technical school training in patternmaking, metalworking, and machining provide useful preparation for an apprentice, and may be credited toward completion of the apprenticeship.

The usual apprenticeship period for patternmaking is 5 years; however, a few apprenticeships last only 3 or 4 years. Each year at least 144 hours of classroom instruction usually are provided. Apprenticeship programs for wood and metal patternmaking are separate. Employers almost always require apprentices to have a high school education.

Apprentices begin by helping experienced patternmakers in routine duties. They make simple patterns under close supervision; as they progress, the work becomes increas-

ingly complex and the supervision more general. Patternmakers earn higher pay as their skill increases, and some become supervisors.

Patternmaking, although not strenuous, requires considerable standing and moving about. Manual dexterity is especially important because of the precise nature of the work. The ability to visualize objects in three dimensions also is important when reading blueprints.

Employment Outlook

Employment of foundry patternmakers is expected to increase only about as fast as the average for all occupations through the mid-1980's despite the anticipated large increases in foundry production. The increased use of metal patterns will allow production to increase faster than employment. Metal patterns, unlike wooden ones, can be used again and again, thus reducing the number of patterns that have to be made.

In addition to those openings created by employment growth, some job openings will arise because of the need to replace experienced patternmakers who retire, die, or transfer to other occupations. Most of these openings will be for metal patternmakers. The number of openings may fluctuate from year to year since the demand for foundry products is sensitive to changes in the economy.

Because patternmakers learn either basic metalworking or woodworking, they are prepared for jobs in related fields when patternmaking employment is not available. Wood patternmakers can qualify for woodworking jobs such as cabinetmaker, and metal patternmakers can transfer their skills to metalworking jobs such as machinist.

Earnings and Working Conditions

Patternmakers generally have higher earnings than other production workers in manufacturing. In January 1976, average straight-time hourly earnings of wood patternmakers ranged from $6 in gray iron and malleable iron foundries, to $6.25 in nonferrous foundries, according to a wage survey made by the National

Foundry Association. In comparison, all production workers in manufacturing industries averaged $5.19 an hour.

Patternmakers work indoors in well-lighted, well-ventilated areas. The rooms in which they work generally are separated from the areas where the casting takes place, so they are not exposed to the heat and noise of the foundry floor.

For sources of additional information, see the introductory section of this chapter.

MOLDERS

Nature of the Work

One of the oldest known methods of making metal products is by metal casting, or the process of pouring molten metal into a previously made mold and allowing the metal to harden in the shape of the mold. There are several different ways of making molds, but sand molding is the most common. In sand molding, molders make the mold by packing and ramming specially prepared sand around a pattern—a model of the object to be duplicated—in a box called a flask. A flask usually is made in two parts that can be separated to remove the pattern without damaging the mold cavity. When molten metal is poured into the cavity, it solidifies and forms the casting.

Technologically advanced molding machines that pack and ram the sand mechanically are now used to make most molds. Thus, most of the workers in this occupation are machine molders. *Machine molders* (D.O.T. 518.782) operate machines that speed up and simplify the making of large quantities of identical sand molds. Machine molders assemble the flask and pattern on the machine table, fill the flask with prepared sand, and operate the machine with levers and pedals. Many of these workers set up and adjust their own machines.

In a few foundries, hand molders

still construct the sand molds, using primarily manual methods. Power tools, such as pneumatic rammers, and handtools, such as trowels and mallets, are used to smooth the sand. Molds for small castings usually are made on the workbench by *bench molders* (D.O.T. 518.381); those for large and bulky castings are made on the foundry floor by *floor molders* (D.O.T. 518.381). An all-round hand molder makes many different types of molds. A less skilled molder specializes in a few simple types.

Training, Other Qualifications, and Advancement

Completion of a 4-year apprenticeship program, or equivalent experience, is needed to become a skilled hand molder. Workers with this training also are preferred for some kinds of machine molding, but in general a shorter training period is required in order to become a qualified machine molder. Some people learn molding skills informally on the job, but this way of learning the trade takes longer and is less reliable than apprenticeship.

An eighth grade education usually is the minimum requirement for apprenticeship. Many employers, however, prefer high school graduates.

Apprentices, under close supervision by skilled molders, begin with simple jobs, such as shoveling sand, and then gradually take on more difficult and responsible work, such as ramming molds, withdrawing patterns, and setting cores. They also learn to operate the various types of molding machines. As their training progresses, they learn to make complete molds. In addition, the apprentice may work in other foundry departments to develop all-round knowledge of foundry methods and practices. The apprentice usually receives at least 144 hours of classroom instruction each year in subjects such as shop arithmetic, metallurgy, and shop drawing.

Hand molders who do highly repetitive work that requires less skill usually learn their jobs during a brief training period. Trainees work with a molder to make a particular kind of mold. After 2 to 6 months, the trainee usually is capable of making a similar mold. Most machine molding jobs can be learned in 2 to 3 months on the job.

Physical standards for molding jobs are fairly high. Hand molders stand while working, must move about a great deal, and frequently must lift heavy objects. They need good vision and a high degree of manual dexterity. Molders may advance to a specialized molding job or eventually to a supervisory position.

Employment Outlook

Employment of molders is expected to increase about as fast as the average for all occupations through the mid-1980's. Although the demand for metal castings is expected to increase significantly, the trend to more machine molding, such as the sand slinging process, and other labor-saving innovations will allow large increases in production with only moderate employment growth. In addition to job openings created by employment growth, openings will arise from the need to replace experienced molders who retire, die, or transfer to other occupations. The number of openings, however, may fluctuate greatly from year to year because the demand for foundry products is sensitive to changes in the economy.

Earnings and Working Conditions

In January 1976, floor molders averaged $5.52 an hour and bench molders averaged $4.98, according to a wage survey made by the National Foundry Association. By comparison, production workers in all manufacturing industries averaged $5.19 an hour. Molders who were paid on an incentive basis generally had higher earnings.

Working conditions vary considerably from one foundry to another. Heat, fumes, and dust, have been greatly reduced in many plants by the installation of improved ventilation systems and air-conditioning; however, in many older foundries these still are problems.

Working in a foundry can be hazardous, and the injury rate is higher than the average for all manufacturing industries. Safety programs and safety equipment, such as metal-plated shoes, have helped reduce injuries at many foundries; however, molders must be careful to avoid burns from hot metal and to avoid cuts and bruises when handling metal parts and power tools.

For sources of additional information, see the introductory section of this chapter.

COREMAKERS

Nature of the Work

Coremakers prepare the "cores" that are placed in molds to form the hollow sections in metal castings. The poured metal solidifies around the core, so that when the core is removed the desired cavity or contour remains.

A core may be made either by hand or by machine. In both instances, sand is packed into a block of wood or metal in which a space of the desired size and shape has been hollowed out. After the core is removed from this box, it is hardened by baking or by another drying method. When hand methods are used, the coremaker uses mallets and other handtools to pack sand into the core box. Small cores are made on the workbench by *bench coremakers* (D.O.T. 518.381) and large ones are made on the foundry floor by *floor coremakers* (D.O.T. 518.381).

Machine coremakers (D.O.T. 518.885) operate machines that make sand cores by forcing sand into a core box. Some machine coremakers are required to set up and adjust their machines and do finishing operations on the cores. Others are primarily machine tenders. They are closely supervised and their machines are adjusted for them.

Training, Other Qualifications, and Advancement

Completion of a 4-year apprenticeship training program or the equivalent experience is needed to become a skilled hand coremaker. Apprenticeships also are sometimes required for the more difficult machine coremaking jobs. Apprenticeships in coremaking and molding often are combined.

Experienced coremakers teach apprentices how to make cores and operate ovens. Classroom instruction covering subjects such as arithmetic and the properties of metals generally supplements on-the-job training. Coremakers earn higher pay as their skill increases, and some may advance to supervisors.

An eighth grade education usually is the minimum requirement for coremaking apprentices; however, most employers prefer high school graduates, and some employers require apprentices to have graduated from high school. Some types of hand coremaking require a high degree of manual dexterity.

Employment Outlook

Although the production and use of metal castings are expected to increase substantially, employment of coremakers is expected to increase only about as fast as the average for all occupations through the mid-1980's, as the growing use of machine coremaking will allow large increases in production with only moderate employment growth. In addition to those job openings created by employment growth, other openings will arise because of the need to replace experienced coremakers who retire, die, or transfer to other occupations. The number of openings may fluctuate greatly from year to year since the demand for foundry products is sensitive to changes in the economy.

Earnings and Working Conditions

In January 1976, average hourly earnings of floor coremakers were $5.30; bench coremakers, $5.28; and machine coremakers, $5.31, according to a wage survey made by the National Foundry Association. By comparison, production workers in all manufacturing industries averaged $5.19 an hour. Coremakers who were paid on an incentive basis generally had higher earnings than those who were paid a straight hourly wage.

Working conditions vary considerably from one foundry to another. Heat, fumes, and dust, have been greatly reduced in many plants by the installation of improved ventilation systems and air-conditioning. Although the injury rate in foundries is higher than the average for manufacturing, coremaking is one of the least hazardous foundry jobs.

For sources of additional information, see the introductory section of this chapter.

performed, training, and earnings of these occupations are presented in the chapters that follow.)

MACHINING OCCUPATIONS

ALL-ROUND MACHINISTS

(D.O.T. 600.280, .281, and .381)

Nature of the Work

Machine tools are stationary, power-driven devices used to shape or form metal by cutting, impact, pressure, electrical techniques, or a combination of these processes. Most machine tools are named for the way in which they shape metal. For example, commonly used machine tools include boring machines, milling machines, lathes, drilling machines, and grinding machines. In 1976, over 1.1 million machinists, machine tool operators, tool-and-die makers, setup workers, and instrument makers used machine tools to make precise metal parts.

The most outstanding characteristic of machine tools is their precision of operation. For example, in this century the accuracy of machine tools has improved from a thousandth of an inch to about a millionth of an inch. A millionth of an inch is about 1/300th as thick as a human hair. This precision makes possible the production of thousands of iden-

tical parts which may easily be interchanged in the assembly or repair of final products. The interchangeability of parts, made possible by machine tools, is the most important requirement for the mass production of goods. As a result, nearly every product of American industry, from cornflakes to turbines, is made either using machine tools or using machines made with machine tools.

All-round machinists can operate most types of machine tools, whereas machine tool operators generally work with one kind only. Tool-and-die makers make dies (metal forms) for presses and diecasting machines, devices to guide drills into metal, and special gauges to determine whether the work meets specified tolerances. Instrument makers use machine tools to produce highly accurate instrument parts from metal and other materials. Setup workers adjust tools for semiskilled machine tool operators to run. (Detailed discussions of work

All-round machinists are skilled metal workers who can perform a wide variety of machining operations. They are able to set up and operate most types of machine tools used to make metal parts for cars, machines, and other equipment. Machinists also know the working properties of a variety of metals including steel, cast iron, aluminum, brass, and other metals. This knowledge of metals, plus their ability to work with machine tools, enables machinists to turn a block of metal into an intricate part meeting precise specifications.

All-round machinists plan and carry through all the operations needed to make a machined product. They also often are able to switch from making one product to another; as a result, variety is a major feature of all-round machinists' work.

Before they begin actually making a machined product, machinists usually consult blueprints or written specifications for the item. Using these, they are able to select tools and materials for the job and plan the cutting and finishing operations. They also make standard shop computations relating to dimensions of work and machining specifications. To be sure their work is accurate, they check it using precision instruments, such as micrometers, which measure to thousandths or even millionths of an inch. After completing machining operations, they may use hand files and scrapers to smooth rough metal edges before assembling the finished parts with wrenches and screwdrivers.

Like production machinists, all-round machinists who work in plant maintenance shops have a broad knowledge of mechanical principles and machining operations. These workers are responsible for repairing

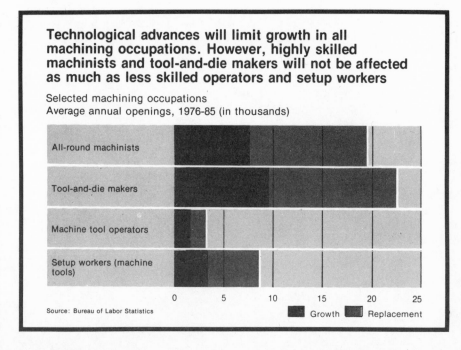

Technological advances will limit growth in all machining occupations. However, highly skilled machinists and tool-and-die makers will not be affected as much as less skilled operators and setup workers

Selected machining occupations
Average annual openings, 1976-85 (in thousands)

All-round machinists		
Tool-and-die makers		
Machine tool operators		
Setup workers (machine tools)		

0   5   10   15   20   25

Source: Bureau of Labor Statistics

■ Growth   ■ Replacement

parts or making new parts for machinery that has broken down. They sometimes also adjust and test the parts they have made or repaired for a machine.

Places of Employment

About 400,000 persons worked as machinists in 1976. Almost every factory using substantial amounts of machinery employed all-round machinists to maintain its mechanical equipment. Some all-round machinists made large quantities of identical parts such as automobile axle shafts in production departments of metalworking factories; others made limited numbers of varied products such as missile motor cases in machine shops.

Most all-round machinists worked in the following industries: machinery, including electrical; transportation equipment; fabricated metal products; and primary metals. Other industries employing substantial numbers of these workers were the railroad, chemical, food processing, and textile industries. The Federal Government also employed all-round machinists in Navy yards and other installations.

Although machinists work in all parts of the country, jobs are most plentiful in areas where many factories are located. Among the leading areas of employment are Los Angeles, Chicago, New York, Philadelphia, Boston, San Francisco, and Houston.

Training, Other Qualifications, and Advancement

A 4-year formal apprenticeship is the best way to learn the machinist trade, but some companies have training programs for single-purpose machines that require less than 4 years to complete. Many machinists do learn this trade on the job, however.

Persons interested in becoming machinists should be mechanically inclined and temperamentally suited to do highly accurate work that requires concentration as well as physical effort. Prospective machinists should be able to work independently. Although the work sometimes is

tedious and repetitious, all-round machinists frequently have the satisfaction of seeing the final results of their work.

A high school or vocational school education, including mathematics, physics, or machine shop training, is desirable. Some companies require experienced machinists to take additional courses in mathematics and electronics at company expense so that they can service and operate numerically controlled machine tools. In addition, equipment builders generally provide training in the electrical, hydraulic, and mechanical aspects of machine-and-control systems.

Typical machinist apprentice programs consist of approximately 8,000 hours of shop training and about 570 hours of related classroom instruction. In shop training, apprentices learn chipping, filing, hand tapping, dowel fitting, riveting, and the operation of various machine tools. In the classroom, they study blueprint reading, mechanical drawing, shop mathematics, and shop practices.

All-round machinists have numerous opportunities for advancement. Many become supervisors. Some take additional training and become tool-and-die or instrument makers. Skilled machinists may open their own shops or advance into other technical jobs in machine programming and tooling.

Employment Outlook

The number of all-round machinists is expected to increase at about the same rate as the average for all occupations through the mid-1980's. Growth in the demand for machined metal parts will cause most of the increase. In addition to openings created by growth in this large occupation, many openings will arise from the need to replace experienced machinists who retire, die, or transfer to other fields of work.

As population and income rise, so will the demand for machined goods, such as automobiles, household appliances, and industrial products. However, technological developments that increase the productivity of machinists are expected to keep

employment from rising as fast as the demand for machined goods.

Chief among these technological innovations is the expanding use of numerically controlled machine tools. These machines, which use computers to control various machining operations, significantly reduce the time required to perform machining operations.

Much of the employment growth will occur in the maintenance shops of manufacturing plants as industries continue to use a greater volume of complex machinery and equipment. More skilled maintenance machinists will be needed to prevent costly breakdowns in highly mechanized plants. Often the breakdown of just one machine can stop an entire production line for hours.

Earnings and Working Conditions

The earnings of machinists compare favorably with those of other skilled workers. Machinists employed in metropolitan areas had estimated average hourly earnings of $6.76 in 1976. Average hourly rates in 10 of the areas surveyed, selected to show how wage rates differ in various parts of the country, appear in the accompanying tabulation. Because machinists work indoors, they are able to work year round and in all

Area	Hourly rate
San Francisco—Oakland	$7.82
Detroit	7.61
New York	7.39
Houston	7.23
Chicago	7.19
Minneapolis—St. Paul	6.87
Atlanta	6.65
Dallas—Fort Worth	6.60
Boston	6.33
New Orleans	6.18

kinds of weather. As a result, their earnings are relatively stable. Many also receive numerous opportunities for overtime work.

Machinists must follow strict safety regulations when working around high-speed machine tools. Short-sleeved shirts, safety glasses, and other protective devices are required to reduce accidents. Most shops are clean and workplaces are well-lighted.

Many machinists are members of unions including the International Association of Machinists and Aerospace Workers; the International Union, United Automobile, Aerospace and Agricultural Implement Workers of America; the International Union of Electrical, Radio and Machine Workers; the International Brotherhood of Electrical Workers; and the United Steelworkers of America.

Sources of Additional Information

The National Machine Tool Builders Association, 7901 Westpark Dr., McLean, Va. 22101—whose members build a large percentage of all machine tools used in this country—will supply, on request, information on career opportunities in the machine tool industry.

The National Tool, Die and Precision Machining Association, 9300 Livingston Rd., Oxon Hill, Md. 20022, offers information on apprenticeship training, including recommended apprenticeship standards for tool and die makers certified by the U.S. Department of Labor's Bureau of Apprenticeship and Training.

The Tool and Die Institute, 777 Busse Highway, Park Ridge, Ill. 60068—a trade association—offers information on apprenticeship training in the Chicago area.

Many local offices of State employment services provide free aptitude testing to persons interested in becoming all-round machinists or tool and diemakers. In addition, the State employment service refers applicants for apprentice programs to employers. In many communities, applications for apprenticeship also are received by labor-management apprenticeship committees.

Apprenticeship information also may be obtained from the following unions (which have local offices in many cities):

International Association of Machinists and Aerospace Workers, 1300 Connecticut Ave. NW., Washington, D.C. 20036.

International Union, United Automobile, Aerospace and Agricultural Implement Workers of America, Skilled Trades Department, 8000 East Jefferson Ave., Detroit, Mich. 48214.

International Union of Electrical Radio and Machine Workers, 1126 16th St. NW., Washington, D.C. 20036.

INSTRUMENT MAKERS (MECHANICAL)

(D.O.T. 600.280)

Nature of the Work

Instrument makers (also called experimental machinists and modelmakers) are among the most skilled of all machining workers. They work closely with engineers and scientists to translate designs and ideas into experimental models, special laboratory equipment, and custom instruments. Experimental devices constructed by these craft workers are used, for example, to regulate heat, measure distance, record earthquakes, and control industrial processes. The parts and models may range from simple gears to intricate parts of navigation systems for guided missiles. Instrument makers also modify existing instruments for special purposes.

Instrument makers perform many tasks similair to those done by all-round machinists, tool-and-die makers, and setup workers. For example they may set up and use machine tools such as lathes and milling machines to fabricate metal parts for the instruments they make. In addition, they use handtools such as files and chisels to smooth rough metal parts. As in other types of machining work, accuracy is important. Like most machining workers, instrument makers measure finished parts to make sure they meet specifications, using a wide variety of precision measuring equipment, including micrometers, verniers, calipers, and dial indicators, as well as standard optical measuring instruments.

Unlike other skilled machining workers, instrument makers often are not given detailed instructions, such as blueprints, for their work. Instead, they may work from rough sketches or verbal instructions, or they may simply be given a concept to work with. As a result, their work often requires considerable imagination and ingenuity. In addition they must often work to finer tolerances than other machining workers. Sometimes specifications must not vary more than 10 millionths of an inch. To meet these standards, they use special equipment or precision devices, such as the electronic height gauge, which other machining workers seldom use. They also work with a wider variety of materials than other machining workers. These materials include plastics and rare metals such as titanium and rhodium.

In some instances, instrument makers work on instruments from start to finish. That is, they make all the parts, assemble them, and then test the finished product. However, in large shops, or where time is important, the work may be divided among a number of workers. Similarly, if an instrument has electrical or electronic components, electronic specialists may be consulted.

Places of Employment

Many of the approximately 6,000 instrument makers employed in 1976 worked for firms that manufactured instruments. Others were in research and development laboratories that make special devices for scientific research. The Federal Government employed many instrument makers.

The main centers of instrument making are located in and around a few large cities, particularly New York, Chicago, Los Angeles, Boston, Philadelphia, Washington, Detroit, Buffalo, and Cleveland.

Training, Other Qualifications, and Advancement

Some instrument makers advance from the ranks of machinists or skilled machine tool operators. These already skilled craft workers begin by doing the simpler instrument making tasks under close supervision. Usually 1 to 2 years or more of instrument shop experience are needed to qualify as instrument makers.

Other instrument makers learn their trade through apprenticeships that generally last 4 years. A typical 4-year program includes 8,000 hours of shop training and 576 hours of related classroom instruction. Shop training emphasizes the use of machine tools, handtools, and measuring instruments, and the working properties of various materials. Classroom instruction covers related technical subjects such as mathematics, physics, blueprint reading, chemistry, metallurgy, electronics, and fundamental instrument design. Apprentices must learn enough shop mathematics to plan their work and to use formulas. A basic knowledge of mechanical principles is needed in solving gear and linkage problems.

For apprenticeship programs, employers generally prefer high school graduates who have taken algebra, geometry, trigonometry, science, and machine shopwork. Further technical schooling in electricity, physics, machine design, and electronics often is desirable, and may make possible future promotions to technician jobs.

Persons interested in becoming instrument makers should have a strong interest in mechanical subjects and better than average ability to work with their hands. They must have initiative and resourcefulness because instrument makers often work with little or no supervision. Since instrument makers often face new problems, they must be able to develop original solutions. Frequently, they must visualize the relationship between individual parts and the complete instrument, and must understand the principles of the instrument's operation. Because of the nature of their jobs, instrument makers have to be very conscientious and take considerable pride in creative work.

As instrument makers' skills and knowledge improve, they may advance to more responsible positions. For example, they may plan and estimate time and material requirements for the manufacture of instruments or provide specialized support to professional personnel. Others may become supervisors and train less skilled instrument makers.

Employment Outlook

Employment in this very small occupation is expected to increase at about the same rate as the average for all occupations through the mid-1980's. Most openings, however, will occur as workers retire, die, or leave the occupation for other reasons. Overall, replacement needs will be small because there are so few workers in this field.

Some workers will be needed to make models of new instruments for mass production and also to make custom or special instruments, particularly in the expanding field of industrial automation. Also, more versatile and sensitive precision instruments can be expected to emerge from current research and development programs. Laborsaving technological innovations, however, will limit employment growth. Numerically controlled machine tools, for example, reduce the amount of labor required in machining operations.

Earnings and Working Conditions

Earnings of instrument makers compare favorably with those of other highly skilled metalworkers. In 1976, instrument makers generally earned about $7 an hour.

Instrument shops usually are clean and well-lighted, with temperatures strictly controlled. Instrument assembly rooms are sometimes known as "white rooms," because almost sterile conditions are maintained.

Serious work accidents are not common, but machine tools and flying metal particles may cause finger, hand, and eye injuries. Safety rules generally require the wearing of special glasses, aprons, tightly fitted clothes, and short-sleeved shirts.

Many instrument makers are union members. Among the unions representing them are the International Association of Machinists and Aerospace Workers; the International Brotherhood of Electrical Workers; and the International Union, United Automobile, Aerospace and Agricultural Implement Workers of America.

Sources of Additional Information

See the list under this same heading in the previous statement on all-round machinists.

MACHINE TOOL OPERATORS

(D.O.T. 602., 603., 604., 605., and 606.)

Nature of the Work

Machine tool operators use machine tools such as lathes, drill presses, milling machines, grinding machines, and punch presses to shape metal to precise dimensions. Although some operators can work with a wide variety of machine tools, most specialize in one or two types.

Operators fall into two broad skill categories—semiskilled and skilled. Semiskilled operators are essentially machine tenders who perform simple, repetitive operations that can be learned relatively quickly. Skilled operators can perform varied and complex machining operations. Both skilled and semiskilled operators have job titles related to the kind of machine they operate, such as milling machine operator and drill press operator.

Most machine tool operators fall into the semiskilled category. Their jobs vary according to the type of machine they work with; however, there are many tasks common to most machine tools. Typically, semiskilled operators place rough metal stock in a machine tool on which the speeds and operation sequence already have been set by skilled workers. By using special, easy-to-use gauges they watch the machine and make minor adjustments. However, they depend on skilled machining workers for major adjustments when their machine is not working properly.

The work of skilled machine tool operators is similar to that of all-round machinists, except that it usually is limited to only one type of machine and involves little or no hand fitting or assembly work. Skilled machine tool operators plan and set up the correct sequence of machining operations according to blueprints, layouts, or other instructions. They adjust speed, feed, and other controls, and select the proper cutting instruments or tools for each operation. Using micrometers, gauges, and other precision measuring instruments, they compare the completed work with the tolerance limits given in the specifications. They also may select cutting oils to keep the metal workpiece from getting too hot and lubricating oils to keep the machine tools running smoothly.

Places of Employment

More than 500,000 machine tool operators were employed in 1976. Most worked in factories that produce fabricated metal products, transportation equipment, and machinery in large quantities. Skilled machine tool operators also worked in production departments, maintenance departments, and toolrooms.

Machine tool operators work in every State and in almost every city in the United States. They are concentrated, however, in major industrial areas such as the Great Lakes Region. About one-fourth of all machine tool operators work in the Great Lakes cities of Detroit, Flint, Chicago, Cleveland, and Milwaukee. Among the other areas that have large numbers of these workers are Los Angeles, Philadelphia, St. Louis, and Indianapolis.

Training, Other Qualifications, and Advancement

Most machine tool operators learn their skills on the job. Beginners usually start by simply observing experienced operators at work. Later they learn to use measuring instruments and to make elementary computations needed in shopwork. When trainees first operate a machine, they are supervised closely by more experienced workers. After gaining some experience themselves, beginners often take over more of the duties associated with the tools they operate. For example, they may learn to adjust feed speeds and cutting edges, instead of calling upon other workers to perform these tasks. Some also may learn to read blueprints and plan the sequence of machining work.

Individual ability and effort largely determine the time required to become a machine tool operator. Most semiskilled operators learn their jobs in a few months, but becoming a skilled operator often requires 1 to 2 years. Some companies have formal training programs for new employees.

Although no special education is required for semiskilled jobs, persons seeking such work can improve their opportunities by completing courses in mathematics and blueprint reading. In hiring beginners, employers often look for persons with mechanical aptitude and some experience working with machinery. Physical stamina is important since much time is spent standing. Applicants should be able to work independently. They also should not mind working in a relatively small workspace. Although much of the work is tedious, many machine tool operators derive satisfaction from seeing the results of their work.

Skilled machine tool operators may become all-round machinists, tool-and-die makers, or advance to jobs in machine programming and maintenance.

Employment Outlook

Job opportunities for machine tool operators should be fairly plentiful in the years ahead. Employment in the occupation is expected to increase about as fast as the average for all occupations through the mid-1980's. In addition to openings arising from growth, many thousands of openings are expected to occur each year in this large occupation as operators retire, die, or transfer to other fields of work.

More machine tool operators will be needed as metalworking industries expand their output. However, the use of faster and more versatile automatic machine tools and numerically controlled machine tools will result in greater output per worker and tend to limit employment growth. Other factors that may slow growth in this occupation are the increasingly important new processes in metalworking, such as electrical discharge and ultrasonic machining, and the use of powdered metals that reduce the machining necessary for a final product.

Workers with thorough backgrounds in machining operations, mathematics, blueprint reading, and a good working knowledge of the properties of metals will be better able to adjust to the changing job requirements that will result from technological advances.

Earnings and Working Conditions

Machine tool operators are paid according to hourly or incentive rates, or on the basis of a combination of both methods. Highly skilled operators in metropolitan areas had estimated hourly earnings of $7.11 in 1976. This compares favorably with the average for nonsupervisory workers in private industry, except farming. Average hourly rates in 10 of the areas surveyed, selected to show how wage rates of machine tool operators differ in various parts of the country, appear in the accompanying tabulation.

Area	Hourly rate
Detroit	$7.89
Cleveland	7.30
Chicago	7.14
St. Louis	6.93
Baltimore	6.84
Cincinnati	6.34
Houston	6.30
Minneapolis—St. Paul	6.18
Dallas—Fort Worth	6.12
Boston	5.76

Most shops are clean and workplaces are well-lighted. Machine tool operators must use protective glasses to protect their eyes from flying metal particles. They cannot wear loose-fitting garments as these might get caught in the machine, injuring the operator or causing damage to the machine.

Most machine tool operators belong to unions, including the International Association of Machinists and Aerospace Workers; the International Union, United Automobile, Aerospace and Agricultural Implement Workers of America; the International Union of Electrical, Radio and Machine Workers; the International Brotherhood of Electrical Workers; and the United Steelworkers of America.

Sources of Additional Information

See the list under this same heading in the statement on all-round machinists.

SETUP WORKERS (MACHINE TOOLS)

(D.O.T. 600.380)

Nature of the Work

Machine tools used in shops that do machining in large volume usually are both very large and very complex. Setup workers, often called machine tool job setters, are skilled workers who specialize in preparing these tools for use. Most setup workers work on only one type of machine, such as a drill press or lathe; however, some set up several different kinds.

Before they begin preparing a machine for use, setup workers consult blueprints, written specifications, or job layouts. From these they can determine how fast the material to be machined should be fed into the machine, operating speeds, tooling, and the order in which the machine will perform its operations (operation sequence). They then select and install the proper cutting or other tools and adjust guides, stops, and other controls.

After setting up the machine, they usually make a trial run to be sure that it is running smoothly and producing parts that conform to specifications. When they are sure the machine is functioning properly, they explain to semiskilled operators how to run the machine and how to be sure that the machine's output meets specifications. They then turn the machine over to the semiskilled operators to begin production.

Places of Employment

In 1976, an estimated 60,000 setup workers were employed in factories that manufactured fabricated metal products, transportation equipment, and machinery. Most worked for large companies that employed many semiskilled machine tool operators. Setup workers usually are not employed in maintenance shops or in small jobbing shops.

Setup workers are found in every State. However, employment is concentrated in major industrial areas such as Los Angeles, Philadelphia, New York, Chicago, Detroit, and Cleveland.

Training, Other Qualifications, and Advancement

Setup workers must meet the same qualifications as all-round machinists. They must be able to operate one or more kinds of machine tools and select the sequence of operations so that metal parts will be made according to specifications. The ability to communicate clearly is important in explaining the machining operations to semiskilled workers. Setup workers may advance within a shop to supervisory jobs or transfer into other jobs, such as parts programmer.

Employment Outlook

Employment of setup workers is expected to increase about as fast as the average for all occupations through the mid-1980's. Although consumer and industrial demand for machined goods will grow, partly offsetting this will be greater productivity of setup workers due to the increasing use of numerically controlled machined tools. In these machine tools, cutting sequences, feed speeds, tool selection, and other operations are controlled by a computer. Most job opportunities will arise from the need to replace experienced workers who retire, die, or transfer to other occupations.

Earnings and Working Conditions

The earnings of setup workers compare favorably with those of other skilled machining workers. In 1976, setup workers in metropolitan areas had average earnings of about $7 an hour.

Because they work with high-speed machine tools that have sharp cutting edges, setup workers must follow certain safety practices. For example, they cannot wear loose-fitting clothes as these might get caught in the machine and they must wear safety goggles to protect their eyes from flying metal particles.

Many setup workers are members of unions, including the International Association of Machinists and Aerospace Workers; the International Union, United Automobile, Aerospace and Agricultural Implemen Workers of America; and the United Steelworkers of America.

Sources of Additional Information

See the list under this same heading in the statement on all-round machinists.

TOOL-AND-DIE MAKERS

(D.O.T. 601.280, .281, and .381)

Nature of the Work

Tool-and-die makers are highly skilled, creative workers whose products—tools, dies, and special guiding and holding devices—are used by other machining workers to mass-produce metal parts. Toolmakers produce jigs and fixtures (devices that hold metal while it is shaved, stamped, or drilled). They also make gauges and other measuring devices used in manufacturing precision metal parts. Diemakers construct metal forms (dies) to shape metal in stamping and forging operations. They also make metal molds for diecasting and for molding plastics. Tool-and-die makers also repair worn or damaged dies, gauges, jigs, and fixtures, and design tools and dies.

Compared with most other machining workers, tool-and-die makers have a broader knowledge of machining operations, mathematics, and blueprint reading. Like machinists, tool-and-die makers use almost every type of machine tool and precision measuring instrument. Because they work with all the metals and alloys commonly used in manufacturing, tool-and-die makers must be familiar with the machining properties, such as heat tolerance, of a wide variety of metals and alloys.

Places of Employment

More than 180,000 tool-and-die makers were employed in 1976. Most worked in plants that produce manufacturing, construction, and farm machinery. Others worked in automobile, aircraft, and other transportation equipment industries; small tool-and-die shops; and electrical machinery and fabricated metal industries.

Although tool-and-die makers are situated throughout the country, jobs are most plentiful in areas where many large factories are located. About one-fifth of all tool-and-die makers work in the Detroit and Flint, Chicago, and Los Angeles areas, which are major manufacturing centers for automobiles, machinery, and aircraft, respectively. Among the other areas that have large numbers of these workers are Cleveland, New York, Newark, Dayton, and Buffalo.

Training, Other Qualifications, and Advancement

Tool-and-die makers obtain their skills in a variety of ways including formal apprenticeship, vocational school, and on-the-job training. Formal apprenticeship programs, however, are probably the best way to learn the trade.

In selecting apprentices, most employers prefer persons with a high school or trade school education. Applicants should have a good working knowledge of mathematics and physics, as well as considerable mechanical ability, finger dexterity, and an aptitude for precise work. Some employers test apprentice applicants to determine their mechanical aptitudes and their abilities in mathematics.

Most of the 4 years of a tool-and-die apprenticeship are spent in practical shop training. Apprentices learn to operate the drill press, milling machine, lathe, grinder, and other machine tools. They also learn to use handtools in fitting and assembling tools, gauges, and other mechanical equipment, and study heat treating and other metalworking processes. Classroom training consists of shop mathematics, shop theory, mechanical drawing, tool designing, and blueprint reading. Several years of experience after apprenticeship are often necessary to qualify for more difficult tool-and-die work. Some companies have separate apprenticeship programs for toolmaking and diemaking.

Some machining workers become tool-and-die makers without completing formal apprenticeships. After years of experience as skilled machine tool operators or machinists, plus additional classroom training, they develop into skilled all-round workers who can make tools and dies.

Skilled tool-and-die makers have numerous paths for advancement. Some advance to supervisory and administrative positons in industry. Many tool-and-die makers become tool designers and others may open their own tool-and-die shops.

Employment Outlook

Employment of tool-and-die makers is expected to increase at about the same rate as the average for all occupations through the mid-1980's. Most openings, however, will occur as experienced tool-and-die makers retire, die, or transfer to other fields of work.

The long-range expansion in metalworking industries will result in a continued need for tools and dies. The growth of this occupation may be limited, however, by the use of electrical discharge machines and numerically controlled machines that have significantly changed toolmaking processes. Numerically controlled machining operations require fewer of the special tools and jigs and fixtures, and could increase the output of each tool-and-die maker.

The extensive skills and knowledge of tool-and-die makers can be acquired only after many years of experience. Because of this, tool-and-die makers are able to change jobs within the machining occupations more easily than other less skilled workers.

Earnings and Working Conditions

Tool-and-die makers are among the highest paid machining workers. In 1976, tool-and-die makers employed in metropolitan areas had estimated earnings of $7.21 an hour. This was about one and one-half times as much as the average for all nonsupervisory workers in private industry, except farming. Average hourly rates in 13 of the areas surveyed, selected to show how wage rates for tool-and-die makers differ in various parts of the country, appear in the accompanying tabulation.

Area	Hourly rate
San Francisco—Oakland	$8.87
Detroit	7.88
Chicago	7.72
Baltimore	7.61
Cleveland	7.18
Atlanta	7.07
Dallas—Fort Worth	7.00
Cincinnati	6.82
Boston	6.62
Houston	6.61
New York	6.45
Salt Lake City	6.17
Chattanooga	5.56

As with other machining workers, tool-and-die makers wear protective glasses when working around metal-cutting machines. Tool-and-die shops are usually safer than similar operations in production plants.

Many tool-and-die makers are members of unions, including the International Union, United Automobile, Aerospace and Agricultural Implement Workers of America; and the United Steelworkers of America.

Sources of Additional Information

See the list under this same heading in the statement on all-round machinists.

OTHER INDUSTRIAL PRODUCTION AND RELATED OCCUPATIONS

ASSEMBLERS

Nature of the Work

When Henry Ford began producing his automobile on an assembly line, modern mass production was born. Workers who before had built each automobile independently, now found themselves specializing in just one part of the job. Production became a team effort, with each worker performing a single task on every car rolling by on the line. Over the years, the assembly line spread to other industries, until today almost every manufactured item is produced in this way.

The workers who put together the parts of manufactured articles are called assemblers. Sometimes hundreds are needed to turn out a single finished product.

Many assemblers work on items that automatically move past their work stations on conveyors. In the automobile industry, for example, one assembler may start nuts on bolts by hand or with a hand tool, and the next worker down the line may tighten the nuts with a power wrench. These workers must complete their job within the time it takes the part or product to pass their work station.

Other assemblers, known as bench assemblers, do more delicate work. Some make subassemblies. These units are the intermediate steps in the production process; for example, steering columns for automobiles or motors for vacuum cleaners. Others make entire products. Assemblers in rifle manufacturing plants build complete rifles from a collection of parts and subassemblies and then test all the moving parts to be sure they function correctly. Bench work generally requires the ability to do precise and detailed work. Some electronics assemblers, for example, use tweezers, tiny cutters, and magnifying lenses to put together the small components used in radios and calculators.

Another group of assemblers, called floor assemblers, put together large machinery or heavy equipment on shop floors. School buses, cranes, and tanks are put together in this manner. Parts are installed and fastened, usually with bolts, screws, or rivets. Assemblers often use a power tool, such as a soldering iron or power drill, to get a proper fit.

A small number of assemblers are skilled workers who work with little or no supervision on the more complex parts of subassemblies, and are responsible for the final assembly of complicated jobs. A skilled assembler may have to wire the tubes for a television set or put together and test a calculator. Some work with the engineers and technicians in the factory, assembling products that these people have just designed. To test new ideas and build models, these workers must know how to read blueprints and other engineering specifications, and use a variety of tools and precision measuring instruments.

Places of Employment

About 1,100,000 assemblers worked in manufacturing plants in 1976. Almost two-thirds were in plants that made machinery and motor vehicles. More than half of all assemblers were employed in the heavily industrialized States of California, New York, Michigan, Illinois, Ohio, and Pennsylvania.

Training, Other Qualifications, and Advancement

Inexperienced people can be trained to do assembly work in a few days or weeks. New workers may have their job duties explained to them by the supervisor and then be placed under the direction of experienced employees. When new workers have developed sufficient speed and skill, they are placed "on their own" and are responsible for the work they do.

Employers seek workers who can do routine work at a fast pace. A high school diploma usually is not required.

For some types of assembly jobs applicants may have to meet special requirements. Some employers look for applicants with mechanical aptitude and prefer those who have taken vocational school courses such as machine shop. Good eyesight, with or without glasses, may be required for assemblers who work with small parts. In plants that make electrical and electronic products, which may contain many different colored wires, applicants often are tested for color blindness. Floor assemblers may have to lift and fit heavy objects, thus they should be physically fit.

As assemblers become more experienced they may progress to assembly jobs that require more skill and be given more responsibility. A few advance to skilled assembly jobs. Experienced assemblers who have learned many assembly operations and thus understand the construction of a product may become product repairers. These workers fix assembled articles that inspectors have ruled defective. Assemblers also may advance to inspector and a few are promoted to supervisor. Some assemblers become trainees in skilled trades jobs such as machinist.

Employment Outlook

Employment of assemblers is expected to grow faster than the average for all occupations through the mid-1980's, with thousands of openings each year. Most job openings, however, will result as workers retire, die, or leave the occupation.

More assemblers will be needed in manufacturing plants to produce goods for the Nation's growing economy. As population grows and personal income rises, the demand for consumer products, such as automobiles and household appliances, will increase. At the same time, business expansion will increase the demand for industrial machinery and equipment.

Most assemblers work in plants that produce durable goods, such as automobiles and aircraft, which are particularly sensitive to changes in business conditions and national defense needs. Therefore, even though employment is expected to grow, jobseekers may find opportunities scarce in some years.

Earnings and Working Conditions

Wage rates for assemblers ranged from about $3 to $7 an hour in 1976, according to information from a limited number of union contracts. Most assemblers covered by these contracts made between $4 and $6 an hour. Some assemblers are paid incentive or piecework rates, and therefore can earn more by working more rapidly.

The working conditions of assemblers differ, depending on the particular job performed. Bench assemblers who put together electronic equipment may work in a room that is clean, well lighted, and free from dust. Floor assemblers of industrial machinery may come in contact with oil and grease, and their working areas may be quite noisy from nearby machinery or tools that are used. Workers on assembly lines may be under pressure to keep up with the speed of the lines. Since most assemblers only perform a few steps in the assembly operation, assembly jobs tend to be more monotonous than other blue-collar jobs.

Work schedules of assemblers may vary at plants with more than one shift. Usually in order of seniority, workers can accept or reject a certain job on a given shift.

Many assemblers are members of labor unions. These include the International Association of Machinists and Aerospace Workers; the International Union of Electrical, Radio and Machine Workers; the International Union; United Automobile, Aerospace and Agricultural Implement Workers of America; the International Brotherhood of Electrical Workers; and United Steelworkers.

Source of Additional Information

Additional information about employment opportunities for assemblers may be available from local offices of the State employment service.

AUTOMOBILE PAINTERS

(D.O.T. 845.781)

Nature of the Work

Automobile painters make old and damaged motor vehicles "look like new." These skilled workers repaint older vehicles that have lost the luster of their original paint and make fender and body repairs almost invisible.

To prepare an automobile for painting, painters or their helpers remove the original paint or rust using air-or electric-powered sanders and a course grade of sandpaper. Before painting, they also must remove or protect areas which they do not want painted, such as chrome trim, headlights, windows, and mirrors. Painters or their helpers cover these areas with paper and masking tape.

When the car is ready, painters use a spray gun to apply primer coats to the automobile surface. After each coat of primer dries, they sand the surface until it is smooth before applying another coat. Final sanding may be uone by hand, using a fine grade of sandpaper. If the surface to be painted is not smooth, the paint job will be rough and uneven. Small nicks and scratches that cannot be removed by sanding are filled with automobile body putty.

Before painting repaired portions of an automobile, painters often have to mix paints to match the color of the car. This important part of the job can be very difficult when painting repaired parts of older cars because the original color often fades over the years.

Before applying paint, painters adjust the nozzle of the spray gun according to the kind of lacquer or enamel being used and, if necessary, they adjust the air-pressure regulator to obtain the correct pressure. If the spray gun is not adjusted properly, the paint may run or go on too thinly. To speed drying, they may place the freshly painted automobile under heat lamps or in a special infrared oven that is sealed to prevent dust and bugs from getting onto the fresh paint. After the paint has dried, painters or their helpers usually polish the newly painted surface.

Places of Employment

About 30,000 persons worked as automobile painters in 1976. Almost two-thirds worked in shops that specialize in automobile repairs. Most others worked for automobile and truck dealers. Some painters worked for organizations that maintained and repaired their own fleets of motor vehicles, such as trucking companies and buslines.

Painters are employed throughout the county, but are concentrated in metropolitan areas.

Training, Other Qualifications, and Advancement

Most automobile painters start as helpers and gain their skills informally by working with experienced painters. Beginning helpers usually perform tasks such as removing automobile trim, cleaning and sanding surfaces to be painted, and polishing the finished work. As helpers gain experience, they progress to more complicated tasks, such as mixing paint to achieve a good match and using spray guns to apply primer coats and painting small areas. Becoming skilled in all aspects of automobile painting usually requires 3 to 4 years of on-the-job training.

A small number of automobile painters learn through apprenticeship. Apprenticeship programs, which generally last 3 years, consist of on-the-job training supplemented by classroom instruction in areas such as shop safety practices, proper use of equipment, and general painting theory.

Persons considering this work as a career should have good health, keen eyesight, and a good color sense. Courses in automobile-body repair offered by high schools and vocational schools provide helpful experience. Completion of high school generally is not a requirement but may be an advantage, because to many employers high school graduation indicates that the person has at least some of the traits of a good worker, such as reliability and perseverance.

An experienced automobile painter with supervisory ability may advance to shop supervisor. Many experienced painters with the necessary funds open their own shops.

Employment Outlook

Employment of automobile painters is expected to increase about as fast as the average for all occupations through the mid-1980's. In addition to jobs created by growth, several hundred openings are expected to arise each year because of the need to replace experienced painters who retire or die. Openings also will occur as some painters transfer to other occupations.

Employment of automobile paintvrs is expected to increase primarily because more 4otor vehicles will be damaged in traffic accidents. As the number of vehicles on the road grows, accident losses will grow, even though better highways, lower speed limits, driver training courses, and improved bumpers and other safety features on new vehicles may slow the rate of growth.

Most persons who enter the occupation can expect steady work because the automobile repair business is not affected much by changes in economic conditions.

Job opportunities will be best in heavily populated areas. Many shops in small cities do not have enough business to hire trainees.

Earnings and Working Conditions

Painters employed by automobile dealers in 36 large cities had estimated average hourly earnings of $8.50 in 1976, compared to an average of $4.87 for all nonsupervisory workers in private industry, except farming. Skilled painters usually earn between two and three times as much as inexperienced helpers and trainees.

Many painters employed by automobile dealers and independent repair shops receive a commission based on the labor cost charged to the customer. Under this method, earnings depend largely on the amount of work a painter does and how fast it is completed. Employers frequently guarantee their commissioned painters a minimum weekly salary. Helpers and trainees usually receive an hourly rate until they become sufficiently skilled to work on a commission basis. Trucking companies, buslines, and other organizations that repair their own vehicles usually pay by the hour. Most painters work 40 to 48 hours a week.

Automobile painters are exposed to fumes from paint and paint-mixing ingredients. In most shops, however, the painting is done in special ventilated booths that protect the painters. Painters also wear masks to protect their noses and mouths. Painters must be agile because they often bend and stoop while working to reach all parts of the car.

Many automobile painters belong to unions, including the International Association of Machinists and Aerospace Workers; the International Union, United Automobile, Aerospace and Agricultural Implement Workers of America; the Sheet Metal Workers' International Association; and the International Brotherhood of Teamsters, Chauffeurs, Warehousemen and Helpers of America (Ind.). Most painters who are union members work for the larger automobile dealers, trucking companies, and buslines.

Sources of Additional Information

For more details about work opportunities, contact local employers, such as automobile-body repair shops and automobile dealers; locals of the unions previously mentioned; or the local office of the State employment service. The State employment service also may be a source of information about apprenticeship and other programs that provide training opportunities.

For general information about the work of automobile painters, write:

Automotive Service Industry Association, 230 North Michigan Ave., Chicago, Ill. 60601.

Automotive Service Councils, Inc., 188 Industrial Dr., Suite 112, Elmhurst, Ill. 60126.

BLACKSMITHS

(D.O.T. 356.381 and 610.381)

Nature of the Work

Years ago the village blacksmith was as vital to a community as the country doctor. No one else could repair a broken wagon wheel, shoe a horse, or forge a tool to suit a farmer's needs. Today, the blacksmith's work still is important in factories and mines where heavy metal equipment must be repaired, and at stables and racetracks. Power hammers and ready-made horseshoes have made much of the work easier, but the basic tasks remain largely the same.

The first thing a blacksmith must do when making or repairing anything made of metal is to heat it in a forge to soften it. Once the metal begins to glow red, it is ready for the blacksmith to pick it up with tongs, place it on the anvil, and begin to shape it using presses and power hammers. On repair jobs broken parts are rejoined by hammering them together. The blacksmith uses handtools such as hammers and chisels to finish the task at hand, often reheating the metal in the forge to keep it soft and workable.

Before a metal article can be used, it must be hardened. To complete this stage of the process, the blacksmith reheats the metal to a high temperature in the forge and then plunges it into a water or oil bath. However, metal hardened in this way is brittle and can break under stress. If strength is important, blacksmiths temper the metal instead. To do this, they heat the metal to a lower temperature than they use for hardening, keep it hot for some time, and then allow it to cool at room temperature.

Blacksmiths who specialize in shoeing horses are called farriers. Today, most farriers use ready-made horseshoes so that their primary job is to adjust shoes for a proper fit. On some occasions, however, they may have to make the shoes themselves. Racehorses need special care because they must withstand strenuous punishment to their legs and hooves. Improper shoeing can permanently damage a valuable horse. Farriers who shoe racehorses need to be able to recognize weaknesses in a horse's legs, and shoe it accordingly. Some horses, for example, need shoes that are thicker on the outside as compared to the inside edge in order to walk correctly. To shoe a horse, farriers begin by removing the old shoe with nail snippers and pincers. They examine the horse's hoof for bruises and then clean, trim, and shape the hoof. When the hoof is ready, they position and nail a shoe onto the hoof and finish by trimming the hoof flush to the new shoe.

Industrial occupations that are similar to blacksmith include forge and hammer operator, welder, and boilermaker.

Places of Employment

Of the approximately 10,000 blacksmiths employed in 1976, almost two-thirds worked in factories, railroads, and mines. The remainder worked in small shops, and most were self-employed. Blacksmiths work in all parts of the country—in rural communities as well as in large industrial centers.

Most farriers are self-employed and contract their services to horse trainers at racetrack stables and to owners of horses used for private or public recreation.

Training, Other Qualifications, and Advancement

Many beginners enter the occupation by working as helpers in blacksmith shops or large industrial firms that employ blacksmiths. Others enter through formal apprenticeship programs and transfer from related occupations such as forge operator or hammer operator. Apprenticeship programs usually last 3 or 4 years. The programs teach blueprint reading, proper use of tools and equipment, heat-treatment of metal, and forging methods. Most apprentices are found in large industrial firms rather than in small repair shops. Vocational school or high school courses in metalworking and blueprint reading are helpful to persons interested in becoming blacksmiths.

Many farriers learn their craft by assisting experienced farriers. Others may take a short course in horseshoeing lasting about 3 or 4 weeks before gaining experience on their own or as farriers' assistants. Courses in horseshoeing are taught in several colleges, as well as at private horseshoeing schools. Most of these are located in the Midwest. Persons considering enrolling at any school should talk to a farrier in their area concerning the school's performance in producing qualified farriers. At least 3 to 5 years of special training or experience are needed to obtain the skills necessary to shoe racehorses.

Farriers who wish to work at racetracks must pass a licensing examination. During the examination, they must demonstrate their knowledge of corrective shoeing techniques and the proper shoe to use depending on the condition of the horse's hoof or leg, and the condition of the racetrack. The examination is a performance test and does not require a written examination.

Blacksmiths must be in good physical condition. Pounding metal and handling heavy tools and parts require considerable strength and stamina. Farriers, of course, must have the patience to handle horses.

Opportunities for advancement are limited, especially for blacksmiths who work in small repair shops. However, blacksmiths may advance to be supervisors or inspectors in factories, or decide to open their own repair shops. Blacksmiths also may be able to transfer to related occupations such as forge, hammer, and press operators.

Farriers may open their own shops or travel from job to job with a portable forge, if one is needed. Those with sufficient skills to pass a licensing examination may find employment at racetracks.

Employment Outlook

Employment of blacksmiths is expected to decline through the mid-1980's. Forge shops are using machines to produce many of the metal articles that were formerly handmade by blacksmiths. In addition, welders are doing much of the metal repair work once done by blacksmiths. Nevertheless, some job openings will occur as experienced blacksmiths retire, die, or leave the occupation for other reasons.

Employment of farriers may increase slightly due to the growing popularity of horseracing and the increasing use of horses for recreational purposes. Since this is a small occupation, however, relatively few job openings will become available.

Earnings and Working Conditions

In union contracts covering a number of blacksmiths in steel plants and in the shipbuilding and petroleum industries, hourly pay ranged from $4 to $7.50 in 1976. Earnings of blacksmiths in railroad shops averaged $6.87 an hour in 1976. According to limited information, yearly earnings of farriers who shoed saddle horses averaged between $10,000 and $12,000 a year in 1976; those who shoed racehorses averaged around $15,000 a year.

Blacksmith shops tend to be hot and noisy, but conditions have improved in recent years because of large ventilating fans and less vibration from new machines. Blacksmiths are subject to burns from forges and heated metals and cuts and bruises from handling tools. Safety glasses, metal-tip shoes, face shields, and other protective devices have helped to reduce injuries.

The jobs of some farriers may be seasonal. During the summer months, when horses are ridden more often, farriers may work long hours and even on weekends. Also, those who specialize in shoeing racehorses often work at several different racetracks within their area and, therefore, must travel a great deal. In areas where horseracing is seasonal, they may have to move to another State during the off season.

Many blacksmiths are members of the International Brotherhood of Boilermakers, Iron Shipbuilders, Blacksmiths, Forgers and Helpers. Other unions representing blacksmiths include the United Steelworkers of America, the Industrial Union of Marine and Shipbuilding Workers of America, and the International Union of Journeymen Horseshoers.

Sources of Additional Information

For details about training opportunities in this trade, contact local blacksmith shops and local offices of the State employment service.

BLUE-COLLAR WORKER SUPERVISORS

Nature of the Work

In any organization, someone has to be boss. For the millions of workers who assemble television sets, service automobiles, lay bricks, unload ships, or perform any of thousands of other activities, a blue-collar worker supervisor is the boss. These supervisors direct the activities of other employees and frequently are responsible for seeing that millions of dollars worth of equipment and materials are used properly and efficiently. While blue-collar worker supervisors are most commonly known as foremen or forewomen, they also have many other titles. In the textile industry they are referred to as second hands; on ships they are known as boatswains; and in the construction industry they are often called overseers, straw bosses, or gang leaders.

Although titles may differ, the job of all blue-collar worker supervisors is similar. They tell other employees what jobs are to be done and make sure the jobs are done correctly. For example, loading supervisors at truck terminals assign workers to load trucks, and then check that the material is loaded correctly and that each truck is fully used. They may mark freight bills and keep charts to record the loads and weight of each truck. In some cases, supervisors also do the same work as other employees. This is especially true in the construction industry where, for example, bricklayer supervisors also lay brick.

Because they are responsible for the output of other workers, supervisors make work schedules and keep production and employee records. They use considerable judgment in planning and must allow for unforeseen problems such as absent workers and machine breakdowns. Teaching employees safe work habits and enforcing safety rules and regulations are other supervisory responsibilities. They also may demonstrate timesaving or laborsaving techniques to workers and train new employees.

In addition to their other duties, blue-collar worker supervisors tell their subordinates about company plans and policies; reward good workers by making recommendations for wage increases, awards, or promotions; and deal with poor workers by issuing warnings or recommending that they be fired or laid off without pay for a day or more. In companies where employees belong to labor unions, supervisors may meet with union representatives to discuss work problems and grievances. They must know the provisions of labor-management contracts and run their operations according to these agreements.

Places of Employment

About 1,445,000 blue-collar worker supervisors were employed in 1976. Although they work for almost all businesses and government agencies, over half work in manufacturing, supervising the production of cars, washing machines, or any of thousands of other products. Most of the rest work in the construction industry, in wholesale and retail trade, and in public utilities. Because employment is distributed in much the same way as population, jobs are located in all cities and towns.

Training, Other Qualifications, and Advancement

When choosing supervisors, employers generally look for experience, skill, and leadership qualities. Employers place special emphasis on the ability to motivate employees, maintain high morale, command respect, and get along with people. Completion of high school often is the minimum educational requirement, and 1 or 2 years of college or technical school can be very helpful to workers who want to become supervisors.

Most supervisors rise through the ranks—that is, they are promoted from jobs where they operated a machine, or worked on an assembly line, or at a construction craft. This work experience gives them the advantage of knowing how jobs should be done and what problems may arise. It also provides them with insight into management policies and employee attitudes towards these policies. Supervisors are sometimes former union representatives who are familiar with grievance procedures and union contracts. To supplement this work experience, larger companies usually have training programs to help supervisors make management decisions. Smaller companies often use independent training organizations or written training materials.

Although few blue-collar worker supervisors are college graduates, a growing number of employers are hiring trainees with a college or technical school background. This practice is most prevalent in industries with highly technical production processes, such as the chemical, oil, and electronics industries. Employers generally prefer backgrounds in business administration, industrial relations, mathematics, engineering, or science. The trainees undergo on-the-job training until they are able to accept supervisory responsibilities.

Supervisors with outstanding ability, particularly those with college education, may move up to higher management positions. In manufacturing, for example, they may advance to jobs such as department head and plant manager. Some supervisors, particularly in the construction industry, use the experience and skills they gain to go into business for themselves.

Employment Outlook

Employment of blue-collar worker supervisors is expected to increase at about the same rate as the average for all occupations through the mid-1980's. In addition, many job openings will arise as experienced supervisors retire, die, or transfer to other occupations.

Population growth and rising incomes will stimulate demand for goods such as houses, air conditioners, TV sets, and cars. As a result, more blue-collar workers will be needed to produce and sell these items, and more supervisors will be needed to direct their activities. Although most of these supervisors will continue to work in manufacturing, a large part of the increase in jobs will be due to the expansion of nonmanufacturing industries, especially in the trade and service sectors.

There is usually keen competition for supervisory jobs. Competent workers who possess leadership ability and have a few years of collge are the most likely to be selected.

Earnings and Working Conditions

In 1976, average annual earnings of blue-collar worker supervisors who worked full time were $15,149, compared with $12,946 for workers in all occupations. Supervisors usually are salaried. Their salaries generally are determined by the wage rates of the highest paid workers they supervise. For example, some companies keep wages of supervisors about 10 to 30 percent higher than those of their subordinates. Some supervisors may receive overtime pay.

Since supervisors are responsible for the work of other employees, they generally work more than 40 hours a week and are expected to be on the job before other workers arrive and after they leave. They sometimes do paperwork at home, such as making work schedules or checking employee time cards, and may find themselves worrying about job-related problems after work.

Working conditions vary from industry to industry. In factories, supervisors may get dirty around machinery and materials and have to put up with noisy factory operations.

Some supervisors who have limited authority may feel isolated, neither a member of the work force nor an important part of management. On the other hand, supervisors have more challenging and prestigious jobs than most blue-collar workers.

Sources of Additional Information

A bibliography of career literature on management occupations is available from:

American Management Association, 135 West 50th St., New York, N.Y. 10020.

BOILERMAKING OCCUPATIONS

Nature of the Work

Boilers, vats, and other large vessels that hold liquids and gases are essential to many industries. Boilers, for example, supply the steam that drives the huge turbines in electric utility plants and ships. Tanks and vats are used to process and store chemicals, oil, beer, and hundreds of other products. Layout workers and fitters help make the parts for these vessels, and boilermakers assemble them.

Layout workers (D.O.T. 809.381 and .781) follow blueprints in marking off lines on metal plates and tubes. These lines serve as guides to othe workers in the shop who cut the metal and then shape it on lathes or use other shaping tools such as grinders to produce the finished pieces. Layout workers use compasses, scales, gauges, and other devices to make measurements. Their measurements must be precise because errors may be difficult or impossible to correct once the metal is cut.

Before the boiler parts are assembled, *fitters* (D.O.T. 819.781) see that they fit together properly. These workers use bolts or temporary welds, called tackwelds, to hold the parts in place while they check the parts to see that they line up according to blueprints. Where alterations are necessary, fitters use grinders or cutting torches to remove excess metal, and welding machines to fill in small gaps. If large gaps appear, a new piece may have to be cut. Also, fitters use drills to line up rivet holes.

Small boilers may be assembled at the plant where they are made; however, once the pieces for a larger boiler or tank have been cut out and checked for a proper fit, they are transported to the shop or construction site where they are to be used. There, *boilermakers* (D.O.T. 805.281) assemble and erect the vessels using rigging equipment such as hoists and jacks to lift heavy metal parts into place, and then weld or rivet the parts together. After a boiler is completed, they test it for leaks or other defects.

Construction boilermakers also install auxiliary equipment on boilers and other vessels. For example, they install vapor barriers on open-top oil, gas, and chemical storage tanks to prevent fumes from polluting in the air. Boilermakers also install air pollution control equipment, such as precipitators and smoke scrubbers, in electric plants that burn high sulfur coal.

Boilermakers also do repair jobs. For example, boilers occasionally develop leaks. When they do, boilermakers find the cause of the problem, and then they may dismantle the boiler, patch weak spots with metal stock, replace defective sections with new parts, or strengthen joints. Installation and repair work usually must meet State and local safety standards.

Places of Employment

About 34,000 boilermakers, layout workers, and fitters were employed in 1976. Of these, several thousand boilermakers worked in the construction industry, mainly to assemble and erect boilers and other pressure vessels. Boilermakers also were employed in the maintenance and repair departments of iron and steel plants, petroleum refineries, railroads, shipyards, and electric powerplants. Large numbers worked in Federal Government installations, principally in Navy shipyards and Federal powerplants. Layout workers and fitters worked mainly in plants that make fire-tube and water-tube boilers, heat exchangers, heavy tanks, and similar products.

Boilermaking workers are employed throughout the country, but employment is concentrated in highly industrialized areas, such as New York, Philadelphia, Chicago, Pittsburgh, Houston, San Francisco, and Los Angeles.

Training, Other Qualifications, and Advancement

Many people have become boilermakers by working for several years as helpers to experienced boilermakers, but most training authorities agree that a formal apprenticeship is the best way to learn this trade. Apprenticeship programs usually consist of 4 years of on-the-job training, supplemented by about 150 hours of classroom instruction each year in subjects such as blueprint reading, shop mathematics, and welding. Apprentices often have to travel from one area to another, since there is not always work available in their locality.

Most layout workers and fitters are hired as helpers and learn the craft by working with experienced employees. It generally takes at least 2 years to become a highly skilled layout worker or fitter.

When hiring apprentices or helpers, employers prefer high school or vocational school graduates. Courses in shop, mathematics, blueprint reading, welding, and machine metalworking provide a useful background for all boilermaking jobs. Most firms require applicants to pass a physical examination because good health and the capacity to uo heavy work are necessary in these jobs. Mechanical aptitude and the manual dexterity needed to handle tools also are important qualifications.

Layout workers and fitters may become boilermakers or advance to shop supervisors. Boilermakers may become supervisors for boiler installation contractors; a few may go into business for themselves.

Employment Outlook

Employment in boilermaking occupations is expected to increase much wasterthan the average for all occupations through the mid–1980's. In addition to the job openings resulting from employment growth, other openings will arise each year as experienced workers retire, die, or transfer to other fields of work.

The construction of many new electric powerplants, especially nuclear plants, will create a need for additional boilers and will cause employment of boilermakers, layout workers, and fitters to increase.

The expansion of other industries that use boiler products, such as the chemical, petroleum, steel, and shipbuilding industries, will further increase the demand for these workers Also, as more laws are enacted to provide cleaner air, more boilermakers will be needed to install pollution control equipment.

Despite the expected overall increase in employment, most of the industries that purchase boilers are sensitive to economic conditions. Therefore, during economic downturns some boilermakers, fitters, and layout workers may be laid off, and others may have to move from one area of the country to another to find employment.

Earnings and Working Conditions

According to a national survey of workers in the construction industry, union wage rates for boilermakers averaged $10.03 an hour in 1976, compared with $9.47 for all building trades. Boilermakers employed in railroad shops averaged about $7 an hour in 1976.

Comparable wage data were not available for boilermakers employed in industrial plants. However, wage rates were available from union contracts that cover many boilermakers, layout workers, and fitters employed in fabricated plate work and the pe-

troleum and shipbuilding industries in 1976. Most of these contracts called for hourly rates ranging from about $5.50 to $10. Generally, layout workers earned more than boilermakers, and boilermakers earned more than fitters.

When assembling boilers or making repairs, boilermakers often work in cramped quarters and sometimes at great heights, since large boilers may be over 10 stories tall. Some work also must be done in damp, poorly ventilated places. Thus boilermaking is more hazardous than many other metalworking occupations. Employers and unions attempt to eliminate injuries by promoting safety training and the use of protective equipment, such as safety glasses and metal helmets.

Most boilermaking workers belong to labor unions. The principal union is the International Brotherhood of Boilermakers, Iron Shipbuilders, Blacksmiths, Forgers and Helpers. Other workers are members of the Industrial Union of Marine and Shipbuilding Workers of America; the Oil, Chemical and Atomic Workers International Union; and the United Steelworkers of America.

Sources of Additional Information

For further information regarding boilermaking apprenticeships or other training opportunities, contact local offices of the unions previously mentioned, local construction companies and boiler manufacturers, or the local office of the State employment service.

BOILER TENDERS

(D.O.T. 951.885)

Nature of the Work

Boiler tenders operate and maintain the steam boilers that power industrial machinery and heat factories, offices, and other buildings. They also may operate waste heat boilers that burn trash and other solid waste.

Boiler tenders control the mechanical or automatic devices that regulate the flow of air and fuel into the combustion chambers. They may, for example, start the pulverizers or stokers to feed coal into the firebox or start the oil pumps and heaters to ignite burners.

These workers may be responsible for inspecting and maintaining boiler equipment. This includes reading meters and gauges attached to the boilers to ensure safe operation. Sometimes boiler tenders make minor repairs, such as packing valves or replacing faulty indicators.

Boiler tenders also chemically test and treat water for purity. In this way, they prevent corrosion of the boiler and buildup of scale.

Boiler tenders often are supervised by stationary engineers who operate and maintain a variety of equipment, including boilers, diesel and steam engines, and refrigeration and air-conditioning systems.

Places of Employment

About one-half of the 73,000 boiler tenders employed in 1976 worked in factories. Plants that manufacture lumber, iron and steel, paper, chemicals, and stone, clay, and glass products are among the leading employers of boiler tenders. Public utilities also employ many of these workers. Many others worked in hospitals, schools, and Federal, State, and local governments.

Although boiler tenders are employed in all parts of the country, most work in the more heavily populated areas where large manufacturing plants are located.

Training, Other Qualifications, and Advancement

Some large cities and a few States require boiler tenders to be licensed. An applicant can obtain the knowledge and experience to pass the license examination by first working as a helper in a boiler room. Applicants for helper jobs should be in good physical condition and have mechanical aptitude and manual dexter-

ity. High school courses in mathematics, motor mechanics, chemistry, and blueprint reading also are helpful to persons interested in becoming boiler tenders.

There are two types of boiler tenders' licenses—for low pressure and high pressure boilers. Low pressure tenders operate boilers generally used for heating buildings. High pressure tenders operate the more powerful boilers and auxiliary boiler equipment used to power machinery in factories as well as heat large buildings, such as high-rise apartments. Both high and low pressure tenders, however, may operate equipment of any pressure if a stationary engineer is on duty.

Due to regional differences in licensing requirements, a boiler tender who moves from one State or city to another 4ay have to pass an examination for a new license. However, the National Institute for Uniform Licensing of Power Engineers is currently assisting many State licensing agencies in adopting uniform licensing requirements that would eliminate this problem by establishing reciprocity of licenses.

Boiler tenders may advance to jobs as stationary engineers. To help them advance, they sometimes supplement their on-the-job training by taking courses in chemistry, physics, blueprint reading, electricity, and air-conditioning and refrigeration. Boiler tenders also may become maintenance mechanics.

Employment Outlook

Employment of boiler tenders is expected to decline through the mid-1980's as more new boilers are equipped with automatic controls. Nevertheless, a few thousand openings will result each year from the need to replace experienced tenders who retire, die, or transfer to other occupations.

Earnings and Working Conditions

Boiler tenders had average hourly earnings of $6.20, according to a survey of 19 metropolitan areas in 1976. This was higher than the average for all nonsupervisory workers in

private industry, except farming. The average for tenders in individual areas ranged from $3.63 in Greenville, S.C., to $7.48 in Detroit, Mich.

Modern boiler rooms usually are clean and well-lighted. However, boiler tenders may have to work in awkward positions and be exposed to noise, heat, grease, fumes, and smoke. They also are subject to burns, falls, and injury from defective boilers or moving parts, such as pulverizers and stokers. Modern equipment and safety procedures, however, have reduced accidents.

The principal unions organizing boiler tenders are the International Brotherhood of Firemen and Oilers and the International Union of Operating Engineers.

Sources of Additional Information

Information about training or work opportunities in this trade is available from local offices of State employment services, locals of the International Brotherhood of Firemen and Oilers, locals of the International Union of Operating Engineers, and from State and local licensing agencies.

Specific questions about the nature of the occupation, training, and employment opportunities may be referred to:

National Association of Power Engineers, Inc., 176 West Adams St., Chicago, Ill. 60603.

International Union of Operating Engineers, 1125 17th St. NW., Washington, D.C. 20036.

For information concerning reciprocity of boiler tenders' licenses among various cities and States, contact:

National Institute for Uniform Licensing of Power Engineers, 176 West Adams St., Suite 1911, Chicago, Ill. 60603.

ELECTROPLATERS

(D.O.T. 500.380 and .781 through .886)

Nature of the Work

Electroplating is a commonly used

manufacturing process that gives metal or plastic articles a protective surface or an attractive appearance. Products that are electroplated include items as different as automobile bumpers, silverware, costume jewelry, and jet engine parts. In all cases, however, the object being plated is connected to one end of an electric circuit and placed in an appropriate solution. The other end of the electric circuit is connected to the plating material. By controlling the amount of electricity that flows from the plating material through the solution and to the object being plated, electroplaters control the amount of chromium, nickel, silver, or other metal that is applied to the final product.

Prior to electroplating any object, electroplaters study the job specifications which indicate the parts of the objects to be plated, the type of plating metal to be applied, and the desired thickness of the plating. Following these specifications, they prepare the plating solution by carefully adding the proper amounts and types of chemicals.

In preparing an article for electroplating, platers may first cover parts of it with lacquer, rubber, or tape to keep these parts from being exposed to the plating solution. They then either scour the article or dip it into a cleaning bath to remove dirt and grease before putting it into the solution.

Electroplaters must carefully inspect their work for defects such as minute pits and nodules. They may use a magnifying glass to examine the surface and micrometers and calipers to check the plating thickness.

Skill requirements and work performed vary by type of shop. All-round platers in small shops analyze solutions, do a great variety of plating, calculate the time and current needed for various types of plating, and perform other technical duties. They also may order chemicals and other supplies for their work. Platers in larger shops usually carry out more specialized assignments that require less extensive knowledge.

Places of Employment

About 36,000 people worked as electroplaters in 1976. About half of them worked in shops that specialized in metal plating and polishing for manufacturing firms and other customers. Virtually all of the remaining platers worked in plants that manufactured plumbing fixtures, cooking utensils, household appliances, electronic components, motor vehicles, and other metal products. The Federal Government employed a few platers for maintenance purposes at a number of military and civilian installations.

Electroplaters work in almost every part of the country, although most work in the Northeast and Midwest, near the centers of the metalworking industry. Large numbers 6f electroplaters work in Los Angeles, San Francisco, Chicago, New York, Detroit, Cleveland, Providence, and Newark.

Training, Other Qualifications, and Advancement

Most electroplaters learn the trade on the job by helping experienced platers. It usually takes at least 3 years to become an all-round plater. Platers in large shops usually are not required to have an all-round knowledge of plating, and can learn their jobs in much less time. However, workers who receive such limited training generally have difficulty in transferring to shops doing electroplating with metals outside their specialty.

A small proportion of electroplaters receive all-round training by working 3 or 4 years as an apprentice. Apprenticeship programs combine on-the-job training and related classroom instruction in the properties of metals, chemistry, and electricity as applied to plating. Apprentices do progressively more difficult work as their skill and knowledge increase. By the third year, they determine cleaning methods, do plating without supervision, make solutions, examine plating results, and direct helpers. Qualified platers may become supervisors. Some electroplaters who understand the chemical processes of electroplating and the chemical characteristics of metals, and who have an outgoing personality, may become sales representatives for metal products wholesalers or manufacturers. Electroplaters with the necessary capital may go into business for themselves.

A few people take a 1- or 2-year electroplating course in a junior college, technical institute, or vocational high school. In addition, many branches of the American Electroplaters Society give basic courses in electroplating. Persons who wish to become electroplaters will find high school or vocational school courses in chemistry, electricity, physics, mathematics, and blueprint reading helpful.

Employment Outlook

Employment of electroplaters is expected to grow more slowly than the average for all occupations through the mid-1980's. Besides employment growth, other openings will result from the need to replace experienced workers who retire, die, 6r leave the occupation for other reasons. Opportunities are expected to be favorable for individuals who want jobs as electroplaters.

Expansion of the metalworking industries and the electroplating of a broadening group of metals and plastics are expected to increase the need for electroplaters. However, employment growth will be somewhat restricted by the increasing application of automated plating equipment and water effluent standards established by the Environmental Protection Agency. Such standards will require plants to install equipment with additional water pollution controls to prevent pollution of streams and waters. This new non-polluting plating equipment will increase cost of electroplating and thus will reduce the demand for electroplated products and electroplaters.

Earnings and Working Conditions

Hourly wage rates for electroplaters ranged from $2.75 to $9.80 in 1976, according to the limited information available. During apprenticeship or on-the-job training, a worker's wage rate starts at about 60 to 70 percent of an experienced worker's rate and progresses to the full rate by the end of the training period. Electroplaters normally receive premium pay for working night shifts.

Occupational hazards associated with plating work include burns from splashing acids and inhalation of toxic fumes. Humidity and odor also are problems in electroplating plants. However, most plants have ventilation systems and other safety devices that have reduced occupational hazards. Protective clothing and boots provide additional protection. Electroplaters are on their feet most of their workday and do much reaching, lifting, bending and carrying. Generally, mechanical devices are used for lifting, but at times the worker must lift and carry objects weighing up to 100 pounds.

Some platers are members of the Metal Polishers, Buffers, Platers and Helpers International Union. Other platers have been organized by the International Union, United Automobile, Aerospace and Agricultural Implement Workers of America, and the International Association of Machinists and Aerospace Workers.

Sources of Additional Information

Information on the availability of apprenticeships or on-the-job training may be obtained from State employment offices and local union offices. Training opportunities may also be located by contacting manufacturing plants and job shops that do electroplating.

For more specific information about job opportunities and training, write to:

American Electroplaters Society, Inc., 1201 Lousiana Avenue Winter Park, Florida 23609.

National Association of Metal Finishers, 22 South Park, Montclair, N.J. 07042.

FORGE SHOP OCCUPATIONS

Forging is one of the oldest methods of working and shaping metals. The exceptional strength of forged metal parts makes this an often used method of forming products that must withstand heavy wear. Many machine tools such as wrenches and drill bits are forged because they are subjected to constant stress and pressure.

The simplest forging method is hand forging done by a blacksmith. Modern forge shops, however, substitute heavy power equipment and dies (tools that shape metal) for the blacksmith's hammer and anvil. In this way, products can be forged in much greater quantity. Five employees operating a large forging machine can turn out more forgings in an hour than five blacksmiths can make in a year.

Most forgings are steel; but aluminum, copper, brass, bronze, and other metals also are forged. Nonferrous forgings are useful in many critical applications, for example, aircraft landing gear. Some of the advantages of nonferrous metal forgings are corrosion resistance and a lighter weight to strength ratio.

Forged products may be as small and lightweight as a key, or they may be as bulky and heavy as a piece of industrial machinery.

Nature of the Work

Before metal can be shaped, it must be heated in intensely hot furnaces (forges) until it is soft. Workers place the heated metal between two metal dies that are attached to power presses or hammers. With tremendous force, the hammers or presses pound or squeeze the metal into the desired shape. To finish the forging, other workers remove rough edges and excess metal and perform other finishing operations such as heat treating and polishing.

Two kinds of dies are used. The open die is flat and similar to the blacksmith's hammer, and is used when only a limited quantity of forgings or large-size, simple-shaped forgings are needed. The impression, or closed die, has a cavity shaped to the form of the metal part, and is used to produce large quantities of identical forgings.

Basic forge-shop equipment consists of various types of hammers, presses, dies, upsetters, and furnaces.

Forge-shop workers also use handtools, such as hammers and tongs, to help mold and shape parts to fit exact specifications. Measuring devices such as rules, scales, and calipers are needed to inspect the finished products.

Descriptions of some major forge-shop production occupations follow.

Hammersmiths (D.O.T. 612.381) direct the operation of open die power hammers. They follow blueprints and interpret drawings and sketches so that the part being forged will meet specifications. Hammersmiths determine how to position the metal under the hammer and which tools are needed to produce desired angles and curves. They decide the amount of hammer force and if and when the metal needs additional heating.

Hammersmiths head crews of four or more workers. A typical crew includes a hammer driver or hammer runner who regulates the force of the forging blow; a crane operator who transfers the metal from the furnace to the hammer and properly places it under the hammer; and a heater who controls the furnace that heats the metal to correct temperatures. The rest of the crew consists of one or more helpers to assist as needed.

The duties of *hammer operators* (D.O.T. 610.782), who operate impression die power hammers, are similar to those just described for hammersmiths. Generally the parts forged by closed die hammers are more intricate and detailed, thus these operators are highly skilled. With the assistance of a crew of helpers and heaters, hammer operators set and align dies in the hammers. They correctly position the metal under the hammer, control the force of the forging blow, and determine if and when the metal needs additional heating to make it easier to shape the metal to that of the die impression.

Press operators (D.O.T. 611.782 and .885) control huge presses equipped with either impression or open dies. These machines press and squeeze hot metal rather than hammer or pound it, and the operators regulate machine pressure and move the hot metal between the dies. They also may control the metal heating operations. Some operators set up the dies in the presses, using instruments such as squares and micrometers to make sure these are in place. Their skills are very similar to those of hammersmiths or hammer operators.

With the help of heaters and several helpers, *upsetters* (D.O.T. 611.782) operate machines that shape hot metal by applying horizontal pressure. The heads of nails and bolts, for example, are made by upset forging.

Heaters (D.O.T. 619.782) control furnace temperatures. They determine when the metal has reached the correct temperature by observing the metal's color and the furnace's temperature gauge. Using tongs or mechanical equipment, they transfer the hot metal from the furnace to hammers or presses. Some heaters clean furnaces.

Inspectors (D.O.T. 612.281) examine forged pieces for accuracy, size, and quality. They use tools such as gauges, micrometers, squares, and calipers to measure the exact dimensions of the forgings. Machines that test strength and hardness and electronic testing devices also may be used.

Die sinkers (D.O.T. 601.280) make the impression dies for the forging hammers and presses. Working from a blueprint, drawing, or template, these skilled workers make an outline of the object to be forged on two matching steel blocks. They measure and mark the object's shape in the blocks to form the impression cavity by using milling machines and other machine tools such as EDM (electrical discharge machinery) and ECM (electrical chemical machinery). Using handtools such as scrapers and grinders, and measuring tools such as calipers and micrometers, die sinkers smooth and finish the die cavity to fit specifications. Finally, a sample is prepared from the finished cavity and is checked against specifications.

Many forge-shop workers clean and finish forgings. For example, *trimmers* (D.O.T. 617.885) remove excess metal with presses equipped with trimming dies. *Grinders* (D.O.T. 705.884) remove rough edges with power abrasive wheels. *Sandblasters* or *shotblasters* (D.O.T. 503.887) operate sandblasting or shotblasting equipment that cleans and smoothes forgings. *Picklers* (D.O.T. 503.885) dip forgings in an acid solution to remove surface scale and reveal any surface defects. *Heat treaters* (D.O.T. 504.782) heat and cool forgings to harden and temper the metal.

Places of Employment

In 1976, about 71,000 production workers were employed in forge shops. About three-fourths of these worked in shops that make and sell forgings. The remainder worked in plants that use forgings in their final products, such as plants operated by manufacturers of automobiles, farm equipment, and handtools.

Although forge-shop workers are found in all areas, they are concentrated near steel-producing centers that provide the steel for forgings, and near metalworking plants that are the major users of forged products. Large numbers of forge-shop workers are employed in and around the cities of Detroit, Chicago, Cleveland, Los Angeles, and Pittsburgh.

Training, Other Qualifications, and Advancement

Most forge-shop workers learn their skills on the job. They generally join hammer or press crews as helpers or heaters, and progress to other jobs as they gain experience. Advancement to hammersmith, for example, requires several years of on-the-job training and experience.

Some forge shops offer apprenticeship training programs for skilled jobs such as diesinker, heat treater, hammer operator, hammersmith, and press operator. These programs usually last 4 years, and offer classroom training and practical experience in metal properties, power hammer and furnace operation, handtool use, and blueprint reading.

Training requirements for inspectors vary. Only a few weeks of on-the-job training are necessary for those who examine forgings visually or use only simple gauges. Others who inspect forgings that must meet exact specifications may need some background in blueprint reading and mathematics, and may be given several months of training.

Employers usually do not require a high school diploma, but graduates may be preferred. Persons interested in more skilled forge-shop jobs should complete high school and take mathematics (especially geometry), drafting, and shopwork.

Although cranes are used to move very large objects, forge-shop workers must be strong enough to lift and move heavy forgings and dies. They also need stamina and endurance to work in the heat and noise of a forge shop.

Employment Outlook

Employment of forge-shop production workers is expected to increase more slowly than the average for all occupations through the mid-1980's. Some new jobs will become available because of growth, but most openings will arise from the need to replace experienced workers who or transfer to other fields of work.

Employment will grow because of expansion in industries that use forgings, particularly automobile and energy-related industries. The expansion of nuclear power plant construction will cause a great demand for forged piping and fittings. Likewise, many forged drilling bits and other forged products will be needed for oil drilling and coal mining operations. However, employment will not keep pace with forge shop production because improved forging techniques and equipment will result in greater output per worker.

Employment in some forge shops is sensitive to changes in economic conditions. In shops that make automobile parts, for example, employment fluctuates with changes in the demand for new cars; thus, jobs in these shops may be plentiful in some years, scarce in others.

Earnings and Working Conditions

Average hourly earnings of forge-shop production workers are higher than the average for all manufacturing production workers. In 1976, production workers in iron and steel forging plants averaged $6.86 an hour, compared to $5.19 an hour for production workers in all manufacturing industries.

Forge-shop occupations are more hazardous than most manufacturing occupations. However, improvements in machinery and shop practices have reduced some noise and vibration. For example, many forge shops have heat deflectors and ventilating fans to reduce heat and smoke. Also, labor and management cooperate to encourage good work practices through safety training and the required use of protective equipment such as face shields, ear plugs, safety glasses, metal-toed shoes, helmets, and machine safety guards.

Most forge-shop workers are union members. Many are members of the International Brotherhood of Boilermakers, Iron Shipbuilders, Blacksmiths, Forgers and Helpers. Others are members of the United Steelworkers of America; the International Union, United Automobile, Aerospace and Agricultural Implement Workers of America; the International Association of Machinists and Aerospace Workers; and the International Die Sinkers' Conference (Ind).

Sources of Additional Information

For information on employment opportunities in forging, contact local offices of the State employment service, personnel departments of forge shops, locals of the labor organizations listed above, or:

The Forging Industry Association, 55 Public Square, Cleveland, Ohio 44113.

The Open Die Forging Institute, 102 Pageant Ave., Rogers, Ark. 72756.

FURNITURE UPHOLSTERERS

(D.O.T. 780.381)

Nature of the Work

Whether restoring a treasured antique or simply giving an old living room couch a facelift, upholsterers combine artistic flair and skill to recondition sofas, chairs, and other upholstered furniture. These craft workers repair or replace fabrics, springs, padding, and other parts that are worn or damaged. (Workers employed in the manufacture of upholstered furniture are not included in this statement.)

The tasks involved in upholstering any piece of furniture are basically the same, although each job is unique in some ways because of differences in furniture construction. As the first step, upholsterers usually place the furniture on padded wooden benches or some other type of support so that they may work at a convenient level. Using hammers and tack pullers, they remove tacks holding the old fabric to the wooden frame. After stripping the old fabric, they remove the burlap and padding that cover the springs. Upholsterers examine the springs and remove broken or bent ones. If the nylon or cotton webbing—which hold the springs in place—is worn, upholsterers remove all the springs and all the webbing.

To rebuild the furniture, upholsterers may reglue loose sections of the frame and refinish exposed wooden parts. They then tack webbing to one side of the frame, stretch it tight, and tack it to the opposite side. Other webbing is woven across the first and attached to the frame in a similar fashion to form a mat. After putting springs on the mat so they compress evenly, upholsterers sew or staple each spring to the webbing or frame and tie each spring to the ones next to it. Burlap then is stretched over the springs, cut and smoothed, and tacked to the frame. To form a smooth rounded surface over the springs and frame, upholsterers cover all surfaces of the furniture with foam rubber, cotton pads, or other filling material. After sewing the padding to the burlap, they cover it with heavy cloth and tack the cloth to the frame. Finally, upholsterers put the new fabric cover, which has been cut to size and temporarily stitched together for fitting, on the furniture. After checking that the cover fits tightly and smoothly—or noting where adjustments are necessary—they remove the cover and sew it together. To complete the job, upholsterers put the cover back on the furniture; sew or tack on fringe, buttons, or other ornaments; and make pillow covers.

Upholsterers use a variety of handtools including tack and staple removers, pliers, hammers, and hand or power shears. They use special tools such as webbing stretchers and upholstery needles. They also use sewing machines.

Sometimes upholsterers pick up and deliver furniture. Those who own and manage shops order supplies and equipment and keep business records.

Places of Employment

About 27,000 people worked as furniture upholsterers in 1976. Over three-fourths of all furniture upholsterers own and operate, or work in small upholstery shops. These shops generally have less than three workers. Some upholsterers are employed by furniture stores. A few work for businesses, such as hotels, that maintain their own furniture.

Upholsterers work in all parts of the country. However, employment is concentrated in metropolitan areas, where the large population provides the greatest demand for the upholsterer's services.

Training, Other Qualifications, and Advancement

The most common way to enter this trade is to start as a helper in an upholstery shop and learn on the job. Helpers learn by upholstering furniture under the direction of experienced workers. Much time and practice are needed to learn complex tasks such as measuring and cutting the new fabric and sewing and attaching it to the frame with a minimum of waste. Usually about 3 years of on-the-job training are required to become a fully skilled upholsterer.

Inexperienced persons may get valuable training from vocational or high school courses in upholstery. However, additional training and experience in a shop are usually required before these workers can qualify as skilled upholsterers. In a few large cities, locals of the Upholsterers' International Union of North America run formal apprenticeship programs that last from 3 to 4 years. The programs place graduates of local vocational schools in upholstery shops where they receive on-the-job training.

Persons interested in becoming upholsterers should have good manual dexterity, coordination, and be able to do occasional heavy lifting. An eye for detail, good color sense, patience, and a flair for creative work are helpful in making upholstered furniture as attractive as possible.

The major form of advancement for upholsterers is opening their own shop. It is easy to open a shop because only a small investment in handtools is needed. However, the business is extremely competitive, so operating a shop successfully is difficult.

Employment Outlook

Little or no change is expected in employment of upholsterers through the mid-1980's. Most job openings will arise because of the need to replace experienced workers who retire, die, or transfer to other occupations.

More upholstered furniture will be used as population, personal income, and business expenditures grow. However, the demand for upholsterers will be limited because more people are buying less expensive furniture and replacing rather than reupholstering it.

Earnings and Working Conditions

Hourly wages for experienced furniture upholsterers ranged from $4.25 to $8 in 1976. Some highly skilled upholsterers earned over $10 an hour. Wages for inexperienced trainees ranged from $2.50 to $4 an hour. Upholsterers generally work 40 hours a week.

Working conditions in upholstery shops vary—many shops are spacious, adequately lighted, well-ventilated, and well-heated; others are small and dusty. Upholsterers stand while they work and do a considerable amount of stooping and bending and some heavy lifting.

Upholsterers usually buy their own handtools; employers provide power tools.

Some upholsterers are members of the Upholsterers' International Union of North America.

Sources of Additional Information

For more details about work opportunities for upholsterers, contact local upholstery shops or the local office of the State employment service.

INSPECTORS (MANUFACTURING)

Nature of the Work

Most products—including the things we eat, drink, wear, and ride in—are checked by inspectors sometime during the manufacturing process to make sure they are of the desired quality. Inspectors also check the quality of the raw materials and parts that make up finished goods.

A variety of methods are used to make certain that products meet specifications. Inspectors may taste-test a soft drink or examine a jacket for flaws, imperfections, or defects. They may use tools such as micrometers, protractors, gauges, and magnifying glasses to make sure that airplanes are assembled properly. Inspectors frequently make simple calculations to measure parts and examine work orders or blueprints to verify that products conform to standards.

Semiskilled inspectors usually work under close supervision, whereas skilled inspectors generally have more responsibility and less supervision. For example, skilled inspectors usually have authority to accept or reject most products, and often analyze the reasons for faulty construction and recommend corrective action. Skilled inspectors also may know how to use a wider variety of complex testing instruments.

Some inspectors make minor repairs and adjustments, such as filing a rough edge or tightening a bolt, and grade products for quality. In many plants, when the number of rejected items rises above a certain proportion, inspectors notify their supervisors.

Places of Employment

About 692,000 inspectors were employed in 1976. Two-thirds worked in plants that produced durable goods such as machinery, transportation equipment, electronics equipment, and furniture. Others worked in plants that produced goods such as textiles, apparel, and leather products.

Inspectors worked in every part of the country, although they were concentrated in the industrialized States. Almost two-thirds were found in Ohio, New York, Michigan, Illinois, Pennsylvania, California, New Jersey, North Carolina, and Indiana.

Training, Other Qualifications, and Advancement

Inspectors generally are trained on the job for a brief period—from a few hours or days to several months, depending upon the skill required.

Employers look for applicants who have good health and eyesight—with or without glasses—and who can follow directions and concentrate on details. Applicants should be able to get along with people since inspectors occasionally work as part of a team. A few large companies give preemployment tests to check skills such as the ability to work with numbers. Some employers may hire applicants who do not have a high school diploma but who have qualifying aptitudes or related experience. Other employers prefer experienced workers for inspection jobs. Many inspectors acquire the necessary skills and experience by working at various production line jobs, especially assembling.

Some semiskilled inspectors—particularly in metalworking industries—who take courses, such as blueprint reading and shop mathematics, may advance to skilled inspectors. After acquiring sufficient experience and knowledge, a few become quality control technicians or supervisors.

Employment Outlook

Employment of inspectors is expected to increase faster than the average for all occupations through the mid-1980's, with thousands of openings each year. As population and personal incomes grow, most manufacturing industries are expected to increase their output, and thus employment in the long run. This business growth will create a need for more industrial machinery and equipment. Additionally, the growing complexity of manufactured products should result in a need for more inspectors. Many openings will result as workers retire, die, or transfer to other occupations.

Inspectors seeking jobs in companies that produce durable goods, which are particularly sensitive to changes in business conditions, may find jobs scarce in some years, plentiful in others.

Earnings and Working Conditions

Wages for inspectors ranged from $2.70 to $7.02 an hour in 1976, according to information from a limited number of union contracts. Most inspectors covered by these contracts earned between $3.50 and $5.50 an hour.

Working conditions vary considerably for inspectors. For example, some have well lighted, air-conditioned workplaces in an aircraft or missile plant; others, who work on the production floor of a machinery or metal fabricating plant, often are exposed to high temperatures, oil, grease, and noise.

Many inspectors are members of labor unions, including the International Union, United Automobile, Aerospace and Agricultural Implement Workers of America; the International Association of Machinists and Aerospace Workers; the International Union of Electrical, Radio and Machine Workers; the International Brotherhood of Electrical Workers; United Steelworkers; and the Allied Industrial Workers of America.

Sources of Additional Information

Information about employment opportunities in this field may be available from State employment service offices.

The American Society for Quality Control certifies quality technicians. They also publish a careers booklet called "Careers in the Quality Sciences," which describes the occupation of inspector and includes information on quality engineering and management careers as well. For information about the test required for certification, or for a free copy of the booklet, write to:

American Society for Quality Control, 161 West Wisconsin Ave., Milwaukee, Wis. 53203.

MILLWRIGHTS

(D.O.T. 638.281)

Nature of the Work

With the coming of the Industrial Revolution, machines replaced many handcrafted items and new and bigger factories became necessary. The textile industry in England was one of the first to use machinery to mass produce its goods. The workers who planned and built these textile mills, and set up the equipment that was needed, were called millwrights. The occupation gradually expanded to other factories, and today the millwright installs all types of machinery in almost every industry.

The millwright is a skilled craftworker who may perform any or all of the tasks involved in preparing machinery for use in a plant. This often includes construction of concrete foundations or wooden platforms on which heavy machines are mounted. As they either personally prepare or supervise the construction of these structures, millwrights must know how to read blueprints and work with various building materials.

Millwrights also may have to dismantle existing equipment, for instance when it becomes obsolete or to make better use of factory space. Wrenches, hammers, pliers, metal cutting torches, and other hand and power tools are used to loosen and disassemble parts.

To aid in moving machinery, the millwright may use any number of rigging devices. For example, to install a new oven in a food processing plant, millwrights may use a hoist or a small crane to move the oven from the truck on which it arrived to a conveyor which would carry it into the plant. Then it may be lifted, with the aid of a crowbar for leverage, onto a dolly and taken to a foundation for proper positioning.

In assembling machinery, millwrights fit bearings, align gears and wheels, attach motors and connect belts to prepare a machine for use. Mounting and assembling a piece of equipment requires tools similar to those used in the dismantling process. When precision leveling is necessary, many measuring devices must be used. To set up automatic pinsetting equipment in a bowling alley, for example, plumb bobs—or weights which determine perpendicularity—must be attached. Millwrights also use squares to test right angles and calipers to measure diameter and thickness.

Many of the millwright's duties also are performed by industrial machinery repairers. (See industrial machinery repairers.) This includes preventative maintenance, such as keeping machinery regularly oiled and greased, and fixing or replacing worn parts.

Millwrights employed by contract installation and construction companies do a variety of installation work. Those employed in factories usually specialize in installing the particular types of machinery used by their employers. They also may maintain plant equipment such as conveyors and cranes.

Places of Employment

Most of the estimated 96,000 millwrights employed in 1976 worked for manufacturing companies; the majority were in transportation equipment, metal, paper, lumber, and chemical products industries. Others worked for contractors in the construction industry. Machinery manufacturers employed a small number to install equipment in customers' plants.

Millwrights work in every State. However, employment is concentrated in heavily industrialized areas such as Detroit, Pittsburgh, Cleveland, Buffalo, and the Chicago-Gary area.

Training, Other Qualifications, and Advancement

Some millwrights start as helpers to skilled workers and learn the trade informally on the job. This process generally takes 6 to 8 years. Others learn through formal apprenticeship programs which last 4 years. Apprenticeship programs include training in dismantling, moving, erecting, and repairing machinery. Helpers also may work with concrete and receive instruction in related skills such as carpentry, welding, and sheet-metal work. Classroom instruction is given in shop mathematics, blueprint reading, hydraulics, electricity, and safety.

Applicants for apprentice or helper jobs must be at least 17 years old. Some employers prefer to hire high school or vocational school graduates. Courses in science, mathematics, mechanical drawing, and machine shop practice are useful. Because millwrights often put together and take apart complicated machinery, mechanical aptitude is important. Strength and ability also are important, because the work requires a considerable amount of lifting and climbing.

Employment Outlook

Employment of millwrights is expected to increase about as fast as the average for all occupations through the mid-1980's. Employment will increase as new plants are built, as existing plant layouts are improved, and as increasingly complex machinery is installed and maintained. Besides job openings from

employment growth, thousands of openings will arise annually as experienced millwrights retire, die, or transfer to other occupations.

Earnings and Working Conditions

According to a survey of metropolitan areas, hourly wages for millwrights averaged $7.25 in 1976—more than one-third higher than the average wage for all nonsupervisory workers in private industry, except farming. Earnings for millwrights in 11 areas that represent various regions of the country appear in the accompanying tabulation:

Area	Hourly rate
Indianapolis	$7.81
Detroit	7.63
Houston	7.33
Baltimore	7.30
Cincinnati	7.21
Chicago	6.99
St. Louis	6.90
Minneapolis—St. Paul	6.75
New York	6.68
New Orleans	6.11

Millwrights employed by factories ordinarily work year round. Those employed by construction companies and companies that manufacture and install machinery may experience periods of unemployment; however, they usually are compensated with a higher hourly wage rate. Frequently these millwrights must travel.

The work of millwrights involves some hazards. For example, there is the danger of being struck by falling objects or machinery that is being moved. There also is the danger of falling from high workplaces, for millwrights must often climb up walkways and platforms to install equipment. In addition, millwrights are subject to usual shop hazards such as cuts and bruises. Accidents have been reduced by the use of protective devices such as safety belts and hats.

Most millwrights belong to labor unions, among which are the International Association of Machinists and Aerospace Workers; United Brotherhood of Carpenters and Joiners of America (construction millwrights);

United Steelworkers of America; International Union, United Automobile, Aerospace and Agricultural Implement Workers of America; United Paperworkers International Union; the International Union of Electrical, Radio and Machine Workers; and the International Brotherhood of Firemen and Oilers.

Sources of Additional Information

For further information on apprenticeship programs, write to the Apprenticeship Council of your State's labor department, local offices of your State employment service, local firms that employ millwrights or:

United Brotherhood of Carpenters and Joiners of America, 101 Constitution Ave. NW., Washington, D.C. 20001.

OPHTHALMIC LABORATORY TECHNICIANS

(D.O.T. 711.381 and 713.884)

Nature of the Work

Ophthalmic laboratory technicians (also called *optical mechanics*) make eyeglasses ordered by dispensing opticians, eye physicians (ophthalmologists), and optometrists. The two types of ophthalmic laboratory technicians are surfacer (or lens grinder) and bench technician (or finisher). In small laboratories, one person may perform the tasks of both a surfacer and a finisher. Starting with standard size lens blanks, which large optical firms mass-produce, they set up and operate machines to grind and polish eyeglass lenses according to prescription specifications. Surfacers use precision instruments to measure the lenses and make sure that they fit the prescription. In large laboratories, work is divided into separate operations which are performed mainly by workers who operate power grinding and polishing machines.

Bench technicians mark and cut lenses and smooth their edges to fit frames. They then assemble the lenses and frame parts into finished glasses. Bench technicians use special tools, such as lens cutters and glass drills, as well as small files, pliers, and other handtools. They also use automatic edging machines to shape lens edges and precision instruments to detect imperfections. In large laboratories, the duties of bench technicians are divided into several operations which are performed mainly by semiskilled workers.

Places of Employment

About 22,000 persons worked as ophthalmic laboratory technicians in 1976. Most ophthalmic laboratory technicians work in ophthalmic laboratories. Some work for retail optical dispensaries or other stores that sell prescription lenses. A few work for eye physicians or optometrists who dispense glasses directly to patients.

Ophthalmic laboratory technicians are found in every State. However, employment is concentrated in large cities and in populous States.

Training, Other Qualifications, and Advancement

The vast majority of all ophthalmic laboratory technicians learn their skills on the job. At first, technician trainees do simple jobs such as processing lenses through a grinding machine. As they gain experience, they progress to other operations such as lens cutting and eyeglass assembly. When the trainees have acquired experience in all types of work, which usually takes about 3 years, they are considered all-round optical mechanics. Some technicians specialize in one type of job, such as surfacing or bench work. The training time required to become a specialist is less than that needed to become an all-round technician.

High school graduates also can prepare to become a technician through 3- to 4-year formal apprenticeship programs. Apprentices with exceptional ability may complete their training in a shorter period. Most training authorities agree that technicians who learn as apprentices have more job opportunities and more opportunities for advancement than those without such training.

Apprentices are generally trained to be either ophthalmic surfacers or finishers. All apprentices receive instruction in optical mathematics and optical physics. Ophthalmic surfacers receive training in lens grinding and ophthalmic finishers learn to assemble eyeglasses into frames and to do frame repair.

Some technicians receive training while in the Armed Forces or by attending vocational schools which offer 9-month full-time optical technician courses. Graduates from these types of programs generally need additional on-the-job training.

Employers prefer applicants for entry jobs as ophthalmic laboratory technicians to be high school graduates who have had courses in the basic sciences. A knowledge of physics, algebra, geometry, and mechanical drawing is particularly valuable. Interest in and ability to do precision work are essential.

Some States require licenses for ophthalmic laboratory technicians. To obtain a license, the applicant generally must meet certain minimum standards of education and training, and must also pass either a written or practical examination, or both. For specific requirements, the licensing boards of individual States should be consulted.

Ophthalmic laboratory technicians can become supervisors and managers. Some technicians become dispensing opticians, although the trend is to train specifically for optician jobs. Some technicians, especially those receiving their training in both shop and dispensing work, may go into business for themselves.

Employment Outlook

Employment of ophthalmic laboratory technicians is expected to increase faster than the average for all occupations through the mid-1980's. In addition to the job openings from employment growth, some openings will arise from the need to replace experienced workers who retire, die, or leave the occupation for other reasons.

More technicians will be needed due to the rising demand for eyeglasses. The demand for eyeglasses is expected to increase as a result of increases in population and a greater awareness of the need for eyeglasses. State programs to provide eye care for low-income families, union health insurance plans, and Medicare also will stimulate demand. Moreover, the growing variety of frame styles and colors may encourage individuals to buy more than one pair of glasses.

Earnings and Working Conditions

Hourly wage rates for ophthalmic technicians ranged from $4.60 to $7.50 in 1976, based on information from a small number of union contracts.

Apprentices start at about 60 percent of the skilled worker's rate; their wages are increased periodically so that upon completion of the apprenticeship program, they receive the beginning rate for experienced workers.

Most ophthalmic laboratory technicians work a 5-day, 40-hour week.

Work surroundings of the ophthalmic technician are pleasant, well-lighted, and well-ventilated, but noisy because of the power-grinding and polishing machines.

Some ophthalmic laboratory technicians are members of unions. The principal union in this field is the International Union of Electrical, Radio and Machine Workers (AFL-CIO).

Sources of Additional Information

A list of schools offering courses for people who wish to become ophthalmic laboratory technicians is available from:

National Academy of Opticianry, 514 Chestnut St., Big Rapids, Mich. 49307.

National Federation of Opticianry Schools, 300 Jay St., Brooklyn, N.Y. 11202.

For general information about the occupation, contact:

International Union of Electrical, Radio and Machine Workers, 1126 16th St. NW., Washington, D.C. 20036.

Opticians Association of America, 1250 Connecticut Ave. NW., Washington, D.C. 20036.

PRODUCTION PAINTERS

Nature of the Work

Almost every metal or wood product manufactured gets a coating of paint or other finish before it leaves the factory. Automobiles, for example, usually receive rust preventative, primer, and paint totaling at least 10 coats. Even pencils are dipped in paint several times before they are packed into boxes.

The workers who apply the varnish, lacquer, paint, and other finishes used in factories are called production painters. Because they generally work on assembly lines, production painters' skills are different from those of painters who repair damaged cars in body shops and from those who paint newly constructed buildings. Most production painters use sprayguns to apply finishes; while the rest operate automatic painting machinery, such as spraying machines, dipping tanks, and tumbling barrels. Since painters may spray hundreds of identical items a day, the work may become repetitive.

Painters mix the paint at the beginning of the process. They first figure areas to be covered, and then follow directions to blend paint to its correct color and thickness. These steps require simple arithmetic involving decimals and fractions. Viscosity meters are used to make sure the paint is the right consistency, for if it is too thick or too thin, the paint has to be mixed over. Pressure of the spray gun nozzles and spray pattern controls also must be adjusted properly to ensure that the paint is evenly applied.

Besides spraying, painters are responsible for other duties on the production line. If an object is to be multi-colored, masking tape must be applied to keep colors from overlapping. Production painters who operate machinery set up the painting equipment at the beginning of the shift and are responsible for keeping it running. Other machines used in the painting process may also be operated by the painters. For example, washing tanks are used to clean items prior to painting and baking ovens dry the painted articles. At the end of the shift, painters must clean spray guns and other equipment used, such as mixing paddles or gauges which check paint consistency.

An increasing number of production lines use automatic painting machinery. Here, production painters are necessary to check for imperfections and to paint parts of an article that the machine misses. For example, some modern applicators cannot paint inside surfaces, such as the interior of a bucket. Painters use spray guns to paint these areas. As production lines become more automated, painters must learn to handle all types of modern painting machinery, such as electrostatic applicators and powder-type painting systems.

Places of Employment

About 104,000 production painters were employed in 1976. About two-thirds of the total worked in plants that made automobiles, machinery, furniture and other wood products, or manufactured metal products such as cans, tinware, and handtools. Although production painters are scattered geographically, large numbers are employed in industrialized States. A fourth of all furniture painters were employed in North Carolina and Pennsylvania, while one-third of all automobile painters worked in Michigan—over half of these in Detroit. Over a quarter of the painters employed by companies making machinery and metal products worked in Ohio and Illinois.

Training, Other Qualifications, and Advancement

Because no formal apprenticeship or training program exists, new production painters acquire their skills on the job. Inexperienced workers often start off loading and unloading items from conveyor lines. After they become familiar with the production process and as openings arise, they may be taught new painting skills. They usually learn the work by watching and helping experienced painters. Training varies from a few days to several months. Some modern painting processes, such as those used to apply powdered coatings, demand more skill than others and thus a correspondingly longer training period. As painters gain experience they can advance to higher skill categories, assume more responsibility, and receive higher wages.

Production painters usually have to stand for long periods of time to do their job. Although they seldom have to lift heavy objects, the production line nature of the job demands good physical condition, since the painters may be exposed to fumes or have to bend or stoop in their work. For example, to paint the underside or top of an object, such as a car, may require reaching or crouching. Good eyesight is an asset to distinguish colors and check that paint has been applied evenly. High school graduation is generally not required for entry level positions, but a diploma or its equivalent may be needed to advance to higher skill levels.

Opportunities for advancement are limited, although a small number of production painters become supervisors.

Employment Outlook

Employment of production painters is expected to increase at about the same rate as the average for all occupations through the mid-1980's. Many job openings also will result as experienced workers retire, die, or transfer to other occupations.

Most manufacturing industries are expected to increase their output in the years ahead. Demand for consumer products, such as automobiles and furniture, will increase as population and personal income grow.

Business growth will create a need for more industrial machinery and equipment. Employment of painters, however, is not expected to keep pace with manufacturing output because increased use of automatic painting processes and other labor-saving innovations should raise output per worker.

Most production painters work in plants that produce durable goods, such as automobiles, where employment is particularly sensitive to changes in general economic and business conditions. Therefore, these painters may be subject to occasional layoffs.

Earnings and Working Conditions

Hourly wage rates for production painters ranged from $2.63 to $6.12 in 1976, based on information from a limited number of union contracts. Most painters covered by these contracts earned between $4 and $5 per hour.

Because painters are exposed to fumes from paint and paint-mixing ingredients, they may wear masks which cover the nose and mouth. Many wear coveralls to protect their clothes. They also may need earplugs, since noisy factory conditions often exist. When painting large objects, such as a car or refrigerator, they may have to work in awkward and cramped positions.

Among unions organizing production painters are the International Union, United Automobile, Aerospace and Agricultural Implement Workers of America; International Association of Machinists and Aerospace Workers; and the United Steelworkers of America

Sources of Additional Information

More facts about job opportunities in this field may be available from local offices of the State employment service. General information on production painters may be obtained from:

Materials Marketing Associates, Inc., Shepard-Benning Building, 520 Pleasant, St. Joseph, Mich. 49085.

Federation of Societies for Coatings Technology, 1315 Walnut St., Philadelphia, Pa. 19107.

WELDERS

(D.O.T. 810. through 819.887)

Nature of the Work

Welding consists of joining pieces of material, usually metal, by fusing or bonding them together. It is the most common method of permanently connecting metal parts that go into the construction of automobiles, spacecraft, ships, household appliances, construction equipment, and thousands of other products. Beams and steel reinforcing rods in bridges, buildings, and roads frequently are joined by welding. In addition, a growing number of plastic parts are welded to make a variety of products.

Welding processes differ in the way heat is created and applied to the parts being joined. In arc welding, the most frequently used process, heat is created as electricity flows across a gap from the tip of the welding electrode to the metal. In resistance welding, heat is created by resistance to the flow of current through the metal. In gas welding, the combustion of burning gases melts the metal. As part of many welding processes, filler materials, called welding electrodes or welding rods, are melted and added to the joint to give it greater strength. When the heat is removed, the metal and filler material solidify and join the parts. It is the welder's job to control the heat and the weld pool size and to add the filler material so that together they form a strong joint.

Since welding processes differ and are used for a wide variety of purposes, the equipment used and the skill levels of welders vary. Jobs vary from those of highly skilled manual welders who can use gas and electric arc welding equipment in more than one position and who can plan their work from drawings or other specifications to those of unskilled welding ma-

chine tenders who simply press a button to start the welding machine. Skilled welders know the material characteristics and properties of steel, aluminum, and other metals and can weld joints in all positions. For example, maintenance welders, pipe welders, and many of the welders who construct ships are skilled welders.

Ship welders join the steel plates, beams, and pipes used to build ships. Some welded joints are on the floor, some are on the wall, and some are overhead. All must be carefully welded to insure that the ship will not break apart in rough seas.

Ship welders generally use arc welding equipment, although gas equipment also is used in many areas. After reading instructions or specifications to learn which materials and welding method to use and obtaining supplies from the storage area, ship welders are ready to begin work. When employing shielded metal arc welding they use a rod in a holder attached to an electric cable coming from a welding power supply. The other power supply cable is attached to the metal being welded which completes the electrical circuit and controls are adjusted to provide the correct amount of welding current. When the power is turned on they "strike an arc" by briefly touching the rod to the metal to start the electricity flowing and then pulling the rod back to create a small gap which the current must jump. If the distance between the rod and the metal is correct, an arc will jump across the space; the heat from the electric arc melts the rod and the metal. Welders control the arc movement along the joint. As the rod melts and becomes shorter they move the holder closer to the metal to keep the correct arc length. When the rod becomes very short, it is discarded and replaced with a new one.

Maintenance welders repair tools, machines, and equipment—for example, a leaking pipe. In such cases, welders may bring their equipment to the job. Gas welding is used in many cases because electrical power may not be available and the torch, hoses, and tanks of gas are portable.

After examining the pipe and preparing the break for repair—usually by grinding—maintenance welders select the proper welding filler rod for the job. Next, they light the torch and adjust regulators on the tanks of fuel gas, such as acetylene, hydrogen, etc., and oxygen to obtain the right gas mixtures and flame. With the filler rod in one hand and the torch in the other, they heat the edges of the break and apply the heat. As the metal begins to melt, the welders periodically melt the end of the filler rod in the hot, liquid metal while they carefully move the torch and rod along the crack to complete the repair. Welders must be careful to keep the torch at the right distance from the metal in order to apply the heat correctly and to add filler material, as needed, to fill the crack.

Not all welders have the skills required of shipbuilding or maintenance welders. For example, less skilled workers use semiautomatic arc welding equipment to speed up the job of welding automobile frames. Semiautomatic equipment consists of a welding gun that welders must manipulate but which automatically supplies the proper amount of arc heat and filler material to the joint. In this case, assembly lines bring car frames to welders and put them in place. Welders then position their welding guns on the parts to be welded and operate a switch on the handle which automatically "strikes an arc". They guide the arc to complete one or two joints before the assembly line takes the frame to another worker. Like other welders, they are responsible for the soundness of the joint. However, they need less skill because all parts they weld are identical and each is welded in the same position.

If the factory is large, and many identical parts are to be welded, the company may save money by using automatic welding machines. Such machines may be used, for example, in making automobile mufflers and washing machines. The workers who operate these machines need little knowledge of welding and are frequently called welding machine operators to distinguish them from more skilled, manual welders. Welding machine operators place the parts to be joined in holders on the machine. To complete the weld, operators simply push a button. The machine then clamps the part in place and rotates it, as necessary, to complete the welding cycle. After the welding cycle is finished, operators remove the welded parts and load the machine again.

Closely related to welders are cutters. Cutters use the heat from burning gases or an electric arc to cut and trim metal rather then join it. Some cutters operate electrically or mechanically controlled machines that automatically follow the proper guideline.

Places of Employment

About 660,000 welders and flame cutters were employed in 1976, including a relatively small number of cutters who used both flame and arc-cutting equipment. Almost two-thirds of all welders help manufacture durable goods; for example, boilers, bulldozers, trucks, ships, and heavy machinery. Most of the rest repair metal products or help construct bridges, large buildings, and pipelines.

Welders are concentrated in the manufacturing centers of the Great Lakes States. About one-third work in Pennsylvania, Ohio, Michigan, Indiana, and Illinois. Because of the widespread use of welding, the rest are distributed much the same as the population is with large numbers working in New York, Texas, Wisconsin, and California.

Training, Other Qualifications, and Advancement

Generally, it takes several years of training to become a skilled welder. Some of the less skilled jobs, however, can be learned on the job in a few months. Some welding machine operators, for example, learn to operate a machine in a few hours and become completely qualified in a week.

Beginners often start in simple production jobs where the type and thickness of the metal and the position of the welding operation rarely change. As the need arises, supervisors or experienced workers teach new employees how to weld different types of metals, and how to weld vertical and overhead joints. Many large companies conduct programs to train people as welders. After completing the course, individuals are offered jobs. A few companies offer employees welder apprenticeship programs that last several years, including classroom and on-the-job training.

Persons planning careers as welders or cutters need manual dexterity, good eyesight, and good eye-hand coordination. They should be able to concentrate on detailed work for long periods, and should be free of any physical disabilities that would prevent them from bending, stooping, and working in awkward positions. Most employers prefer applicants who have high school or vocational school training in welding. Courses in shop mathematics, mechanical drawing, blueprint reading, physics, and chemistry also are helpful.

New developments are requiring new skills of welders. This is particularly true in fields such as atomic energy or aerospace manufacturing, which have high standards for the reliability of welds. Before being assigned to work on buildings, bridges, pipelines, or other jobs where the strength of the weld is highly critical, welders may be required to pass an examination of their welding skills given by an employer or government agency. Welders who pass such examinations generally are referred to as "certified welders."

Promotion opportunities for welders are good. Some welding machine operators learn skilled welding jobs; skilled welders may be promoted to welding inspectors, technicians, or supervisors. Experienced workers who have obtained college training on the properties of metals often become welding engineers and are in great demand to develop new application for welding. A small number of experienced welders open their own welding repair shops.

Employment Outlook

Job opportunities for welders should be very good in the years ahead. Employment in this large field is expected to increase faster than the average for all occupations through the mid-1980's. The faster increase will be caused by the generally favorable long run outlook for metalworking industries and by the greater use of welding in particular. In addition to openings created by employment growth, many jobs should arise each year because of the need to replace experienced welders who retire, die, or transfer to other occupations. Job opportunities may vary from year to year, however, because employment of welders in the manufacturing and construction industries fluctuates with ups and downs in the economy.

Increases in population and income are expected to stimulate demand for cars, buildings, heavy machinery, appliances, and thousands of other products that welders help make. Employment of welders also is expected to increase as welding replaces other methods of joining metals. Welding generally is cheaper than other methods of joining metal parts, and it is being used more frequently in the manufacturing and construction industries.

Earnings and Working Conditions

National wage data on welders are not available. However, the limited data available indicate that welding machine operators earned from $3.93 to $5.10 in 1976. Welders in the construction industry earned $6 to $12 an hour, depending on location.

Welders and cutters use protective clothing, safety shoes, goggles, helmets with protective lenses, and other devices to prevent burns and eye injuries. Although lighting and ventilation usually are adequate, welders occasionally work in the presence of toxic gases and fumes created when some metals melt. They are often in contact with rust, grease, and dirt on metal surfaces. Welding machine operators are largely free from the hazards associated with manual welding. A face shield or goggles generally offer adequate protection to these workers.

Many welders are union members. However, because welding also is done by other craft workers, for example by pipefitters, and only recently has received recognition as a distinct craft, welders belong to many different unions. Among these are the International Association of Machinists and Aerospace Workers; the International Brotherhood of Boilermakers, Iron Shipbuilders, Blacksmiths, Forgers and Helpers; the International Union, United Automobile, Aerospace and Agricultural Implement Workers of America; the United Association of Journeymen and Apprentices of the Plumbing and Pipe Fitting Industry of the United States and Canada; and the United Electrical, Radio and Machine Workers of America (Ind.).

Sources of Additional Information

For further information on training and work opportunities for welders, contact local employers or the local office of the State employment service. For general information about welders, write to:

The American Welding Society, 2501 NW. 7th St., Miami, Fla. 33125.

International Union, United Automobile, Aerospace and Agricultural Implement Workers of America, 8000 East Jefferson Ave., Detroit, Mich. 48214.

CONSTRUCTION OCCUPATIONS

Construction craft workers represent the largest group of skilled workers in the Nation's labor force. Altogether, there were 3.3 million employed in 1976—about 3 out of every 10 skilled workers.

The more than two dozen skilled construction trades vary greatly in size. Several major trades—carpenter, painter, operating engineer, plumber, and electrician—each had more than 200,000 workers; carpenters alone numbered more than 1 million, about one-third of all construction craft workers. In contrast, only a few thousand each were employed in trades such as marble setter, terrazzo worker, and stonemason.

What are the Construction Trades?

Workers in the construction trades build, repair, and modernize homes and all kinds of buildings. They also work on a variety of other structures, including highways, airports, and missile launching pads.

Construction work may be divided into three categories: structural, finishing, and mechanical. In general, each trade falls in one of these categories: *Structural work*: Carpenter, operating engineer (construction machinery operator), bricklayer, iron worker, cement mason, stonemason, and boilermaker. *Finishing work*: Lather, plasterer, marble setter, terrazzo worker, painter, paperhanger, glazier, roofer, floor covering installer, and insulation worker. *Mechanical work*: Plumber, pipefitter, construction electrician, sheetmetal worker, elevator constructor, and millwright.

Most construction trades are described individually later in this chapter. Boilermakers and millwrights are described elsewhere.

Places of Employment

Most jobs are with contractors in the construction industry. The vast majority of construction contractors are small—generally employing fewer than 10 people. A few large contractors, however, employ thousands. Large numbers of construction trade workers are employed in other industries, such as mining and manufacturing, mainly to do maintenance and repair work. Chemical manufacturers, for example, need plumbers and pipefitters to maintain the complex pipe networks in their processing plants. Government agencies employ construction trade workers to maintain highways, buildings, and sanitation systems.

Many construction trade workers are self-employed and contract with homeowners and businesses for small jobs. Self-employment is most common in paperhanging, painting, and floor covering work, but it also is found in other trades.

Employment in the construction trades is distributed geographically in much the same way as the Nation's population. Thus, the highest concentration generally is in industrialized and highly populated areas.

Training, Other Qualifications, and Advancement

Most training authorities recommend formal apprenticeship training as the best way to acquire the all-round skills in the construction trades. Apprenticeship is a prescribed period of on-the-job training, supplemented by related classroom instruction that is designed to familiarize apprentices with the materials, tools, and principles of their trade. Formal apprenticeship agreements are registered with a State apprenticeship agency or the U.S. Department of Labor's Bureau of Apprenticeship and Training.

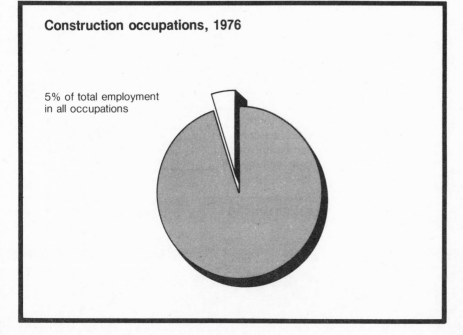

Construction occupations, 1976

5% of total employment in all occupations

Although apprenticeship provides the most thorough training, many people acquire construction skills informally by working as laborers and helpers and observing experienced craft workers. Some acquire skills by attending vocational or trade schools or by taking correspondence school courses.

Apprentices generally must be at least 18 years old and in good physical condition. A high school or vocational school education, or its equivalent, including courses in mathematics and mechanical drawing, is desirable. Courses in construction trades, such as carpentry and electricity, also are recommended. Often, applicants are given tests to determine their aptitudes. For some trades, manual dexterity, mechanical aptitude, and an eye for proper alignment of materials are important.

The formal apprenticeship agreement generally calls for 3 to 4 years of on-the-job training and 144 hours or more of related classroom instruction each year. On the job, most instruction is given by a particular craft worker to whom the apprentice is assigned.

Classroom instruction varies among the construction trades, but usually includes courses such as history of the trade, characteristics of materials, shop mathematics, and basic principles of engineering.

In most communities, the apprenticeship programs are supervised by joint apprenticeship committees composed of local employers and local union representatives. The committee determines the need for apprentices in the community and establishes minimum standards of education, experience, and training. Whenever an employer cannot provide all-round instruction or relatively continuous employment, the committee transfers the apprentice to another employer. Where specialization by contractors is extensive—for instance, in electrical work—customarily the committee rotates apprentices among several contractors at intervals of about 6 months.

In areas where these committees have not been established, the apprenticeship agreement is solely between the apprentice and the employer or employer group. Many

people have received valuable training under these programs but they have some disadvantages. No committee is available to supervise the training offered and settle differences over the terms and conditions of training. What the apprentice learns depends largely on the employer's business prospects and policies. If the employer lacks continuous work or does only a restricted type of work, the apprentice cannot develop all-round skills.

In many localities, craft workers—most commonly electricians and plumbers—are required to have a license to work at their trade. To qualify for these licenses, they must pass an examination to demonstrate a broad knowledge of the job and of State and local regulations.

Construction trades craft workers may advance in a number of ways. Many become supervisors. In most localities, small jobs are run by "working supervisors" who work at the trade along with members of their crews. On larger jobs, the supervisors do only supervisory work. Craft workers also can become estimators for contractors. In these jobs, they estimate material requirements and labor costs to enable the contractor to bid on a particular project. Some craft workers advance to jobs as superintendents on large projects. Others become instructors in trade

and vocational schools or sales representatives for building supply companies. A large number of craft workers have become contractors in the homebuilding field.

Starting a small contract construction business is easier than starting a small business in many other industries. Only a moderate financial investment usually is needed, and it is possible to conduct a fairly substantial business from one's home. However, the contract construction field is very competitive, and the rate of business failure is high among small contractors.

Employment Outlook

Employment in the construction trades is expected to increase faster than the average for all occupations through the mid-1980's. In addition to employment growth, many job openings will result each year from the need to replace experienced workers who transfer to other fields of work, retire, or die.

However, since construction activity is sensitive to changes in the Nation's economy, the number of openings may fluctuate sharply from year to year.

Over the long run, construction activity is expected to grow substantially. The anticipated increases in population and households, and the

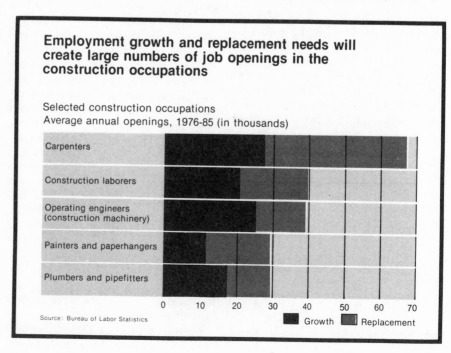

Employment growth and replacement needs will create large numbers of job openings in the construction occupations

Selected construction occupations
Average annual openings, 1976-85 (in thousands)

Carpenters

Construction laborers

Operating engineers (construction machinery)

Painters and paperhangers

Plumbers and pipefitters

0   10   20   30   40   50   60   70

Source: Bureau of Labor Statistics

■ Growth   ■ Replacement

relatively low level of housing construction in the early 1970's, are expected to create strong pressure for new housing. Among other factors that will stimulate construction activity are higher levels of personal income and a rise in spending for new industrial plants and equipment. Also, there will be a growing demand for alteration and modernization work on existing structures, as well as for maintenance and repair work on highway systems, dams, bridges, and similar projects.

The increase in employment is not expected to be as great as the expansion in construction activity. Continued technological developments in construction methods, tools and equipment, and materials will raise output per worker. One important development is the growing use of prefabricated units at the job site. For example, preassembled outside walls and partitions can be lifted into place in one operation.

The rates of employment growth will differ among the various construction trades. Employment growth is expected to be fastest for cement masons and for insulation workers. Trades that will have the slowest growth rates are plasterers and sheet-metal workers.

Earnings and Working Conditions

Average hourly wage rates of unionized workers in the construction trades are about twice the hourly wage rate for nonsupervisory and production workers in private industry, except farming. Wage rates for apprentices usually start at 50 percent of the rate paid to experienced workers and increase at 6-month to 1-year intervals until the full rates are achieved upon the completion of training. The following table shows union hourly averages for selected construction trades in large cities surveyed in 1976.

	Hourly rate
Plumbers	$10.47
Electricians	10.33
Bricklayers	9.91
Carpenters	9.84
Plasterers	9.48
Painters	9.24

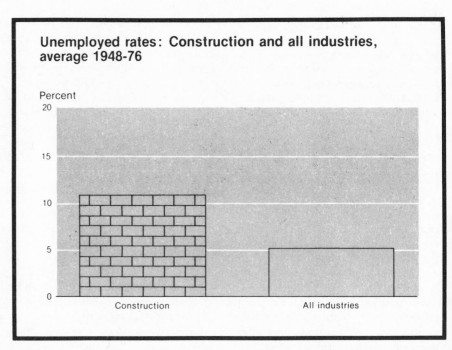

Unemployed rates: Construction and all industries, average 1948-76

Except for a few trades such as electricians, elevator constructors, plumbers and pipefitters, yearly earnings for experienced workers and their apprentices generally are lower than hourly rates would indicate because the number of hours that they work a year can be adversely affected by poor weather and fluctuations in construction activity.

Traditionally, winter is the slack period for construction activity, particularly in colder regions. Some workers, such as laborers and roofers, may not work for several months. However, not only cold but also rain may slow—even stop—work on a construction project. Also, because the construction trades are so dependent on one another—particularly on large projects—work delays or strikes in one trade can delay or stop the work of another. The accompanying chart shows that the unemployment rate in the construction industry is about twice that of workers as a whole.

Construction work frequently requires prolonged standing, bending, stooping, and working in cramped quarters. Exposure to weather is common since much of the work is done outdoors or in partially enclosed structures. Many people prefer construction work because it permits them to be outdoors.

Because construction workers may need to work with sharp tools, amidst the clutter of materials, while standing on temperary scaffolding, and in bad weather, they are more prone to injury than workers in other jobs. Indeed, the construction industry has the highest injury and illness rate of all industries. However, employers increasingly are placing an emphasis on safe working conditions and are stressing safe work habits—practices that reduce the risk of injuries.

The construction trades offer especially good opportunities for young people who are not planning to go to college, but who are willing to spend several years in learning a skilled occupation. Construction workers can find job opportunities in all parts of the country. Their hourly wage rates generally are much higher than those of most other manual workers. As previously noted, construction trade workers with business ability have greater opportunities to open their own businesses than workers in most other skilled occupations.

A large proportion of construction workers are members of trade unions affiliated with the Building and Construction Trades Department of the AFL-CIO.

Sources of Additional Information

Information about opportunities for apprenticeship or other training can be obtained from local construction firms and employer associations, the local office of the State employment service or State apprenticeship agency, or the local office of the Bureau of Apprenticeship and Training, U.S. Department of Labor. Many apprenticeship programs are supervised by local union-management committees. In these instances, an apprentice applicant may apply directly to the coordinator of the committee.

For additional information on jobs in the construction trades, contact:

American Federation of Labor and Congress of Industrial Organizations, Building and Construction Trades Department, 815 16th St. NW., Washington, D.C. 20006.

Associated General Contractors of America, Inc., 1957 E St. NW., Washington, D.C. 20006.

National Association of Home Builders, 15th and M Sts. NW., Washington, D.C. 20005.

For the names of labor organizations and trade associations concerned with specific trades, see the discussions of individual building trades that follow.

BRICKLAYERS, STONEMASONS, AND MARBLE SETTERS

(D.O.T. 861.381 and .781)

Nature of the Work

Bricklayers, stonemasons, and marble setters work in closely related trades, each producing attractive, durable surfaces. Bricklayers build walls, partitions, fireplaces, and other structures with brick, cinder block, and other masonry materials. They also install firebrick linings in industrial furnaces.

Stonemasons build stone walls as well as set stone exteriors and floors. They work with two types of stone—natural cut, such as marble, granite, and limestone; and artificial stone made from cement, marble chips, or other masonry materials. Because stone is expensive, stonemasons work mostly on high-cost buildings, such as offices, hotels, and churches.

Marble setters install marble which provides very decorative and highly durable surfaces. Marble setters, like stonemasons, work mostly on high-cost buildings. The marble they use usually is cut and polished before it is sent to the job site.

In putting up a wall, bricklayers first build the corners at each end of the wall, using plumblines and a level. A line then is stretched from corner to corner as a guide for each course or layer of brick. Bricklayers spread a bed of mortar (cement mixture) with a trowel (a flat metal tool), place the brick on the mortar bed, and then tap it into place. As blueprints specify, they cut bricks with a hammer and chisel to fit around windows, doors, and other openings. Mortar joints are finished with jointing tools to leave a neat and uniform appearance. Bricklayers also may weld metal supports for bricks.

Bricklayers are assisted by hod carriers, or helpers, who supply them with bricks and other materials, mix mortar, and set up and move scaffolding. (See the statement on construction laborers that appears elsewhere.)

Stonemasons often work from a set of drawings in which each stone has been numbered for identification. Helpers may locate and bring the prenumbered stones to the masons. A derrick operator using a hoist may be needed to lift large pieces into place.

When building a stone wall, masons set the first layer of stones into a shallow bed of mortar. They align the stones with plumblines and levels, and tap them into position with a wood mallet. Masons build the wall by alternating layers of mortar and stone. As the work progresses, they fill the joints between stones with mortar using a pointed metal tool to smooth the mortar to an attractive finish. To hold stones in place, stonemasons sometimes position pieces of metal within the wall by welding or bolting them together. After positioning the rocks, they cover the metal with mortar. Finally, for a clean appearance, masons wash the stone with a mild acid solution to remove dirt and dry mortar.

When setting stone floors, masons trowel a thin layer of mortar over the surface. They then hand set the stone in the mortar, leaving the surface of the stone exposed. To finish, workers trowel the joints and wash the stone.

To cut stone into various shapes and sizes, masons find the grain of each piece of stone and use a special hammer to strike it along a predetermined line. Valuable pieces often are cut with a saw that has a special blade.

Setting marble is very much like setting stone. Marble setters prepare a fine mixture of cement, sand, and water—called mortar—then trowel a thin layer of it onto the surface. For floors and for walls where the holding strength of mortar alone is sufficient, setters—following instructions from blueprints—often hand set each marble piece into the mortar, leaving the face of the marble exposed. For heavy pieces, workers employ a hoist to lift and position the marble. To secure heavy pieces on walls, setters use bolts in addition to mortar. Once the marble pieces are positioned and secured, setters mortar and trowel the joints and clean the marble's surface.

In addition to construction work, marble setters do repair work. They fill and cover holes and cracks in marble with mortar prepared and finished to look like the marble. They also polish and replace marble. When pieces are too large, setters cut them to size using a special saw.

Bricklayers, stonemasons, and marble setters primarily use handtools—including trowels, brick and stone hammers, wood or rubber mallets, and chisels. For exacting cuts of brick, stone, or marble, they use high-powered electric saws equipped with special cutting blades.

Places of Employment

About 175,000 bricklayers, stonemasons, and marble setters were employed in 1976; most were bricklayers. Workers in these crafts were employed primarily by special trade, building, or general contractors. A relatively small number of bricklayers work for government agencies or businesses that do their own construction and alteration.

Workers in these trades are employed throughout the country, but are concentrated in metropolitan areas. In cities that are too small to have a demand for full-time stonemasons or marble setters, bricklayers will install stone or marble as a sideline.

About 1 out of 7 bricklayers, stonemasons, and marble setters is self-employed—a proportion higher than that in most building crafts. Many of the self-employed specialize in contracting on small jobs such as patios, walks, and fireplaces.

Training, Other Qualifications, and Advancement

Most bricklayers as well as some stonemasons and marble setters pick up their skills informally by working as helpers or hod carriers and by observing and learning from experienced workers. The remainder learn their skills through apprenticeship, which provides the most thorough training.

Individuals who learn the trade informally usually become bricklayers. They start with carrying materials, moving scaffolds, and mixing mortar. However, it takes several months to a year before they are taught to spread mortar and lay brick. They begin with simple patterns and progress to more complex designs. Learning to set stone or marble might take several years.

Apprenticeships for bricklayers, stonemasons, and marble setters usually are sponsored by local union-management committees. The apprenticeship program requires 3 years of on-the-job training, in addition to 144 hours of classroom instruction each year in subjects such as blueprint reading, mathematics, layout work, and sketching. Apprentices learn the general applications of brick, stone, and marble.

Apprentices start by carrying materials and mixing mortar. Within 2 or 3 months, they learn to align, lay, and clean brick. Apprentices eventually learn to work with stone and marble. After apprenticeship, they usually specialize in one of the three trades.

Applicants for apprenticeships must be at least 17 years old. Apprentice and helper applicants should be in good physical condition.

A high school or vocational school education is preferable, as are courses in mathematics, mechanical drawing, and shop.

Experienced workers can advance to supervisory positions or become estimators. They also can open contracting businesses of their own.

Employment Outlook

Employment of bricklayers is expected to increase about as fast as the average for all occupations through the mid-1980's. In addition to the job openings that result from employment growth, many openings will arise as experienced bricklayers retire, die, or leave the occupation for other reasons.

As population and business growth create a need for new homes, factories, offices, and other structures, the demand for bricklayers will grow. Stimulating this growth will be the increasing use of brick for decorative work on building fronts and in lobbies and foyers. The use of brick, particularly for interior load-bearing walls, is growing and will add to overall employment needs.

Over the long run, job openings for bricklayers are expected to be plentiful; however, the number of openings may fluctuate from year to year because employment in this trade is sensitive to ups and downs in construction activity. For any given year, opportunities usually are best during the spring and summer when construction activity picks up.

Employment of stonemasons and marble setters is not expected to change significantly through the mid-1980's. Stone and marble have lost popularity as building materials because they have become much more expensive than materials such as brick and concrete. Nevertheless, a small number of jobs will become available due to the need to replace stonemasons and marble setters who retire, die, or leave the occupations.

Earnings and Working Conditions

Hourly wage rates were $9.90 for bricklayers, $10.05 for stonemasons, and $9.60 for marble setters, according to a 1976 survey of union wage rates in metropolitan areas. These rates are about twice the average wage of nonsupervisory and production workers in private industry, except farming. However, yearly earnings for workers in these trades generally are lower than hourly rates would indicate because the annual number of hours they work can be adversely affected by poor weather and fluctuations in construction activity.

In each trade, apprentices start at about 50 percent of the wage rate paid to experienced workers. The rate increases as they gain experience.

The work of bricklayers, stonemasons, and marble setters sometimes is strenuous because it involves moderately heavy lifting and prolonged standing and stooping. Most of the work is performed outdoors.

A large proportion of bricklayers, stonemasons, and marble setters are members of the Bricklayers, Masons and Plasterers' International Union of America.

Sources of Additional Information

For details about apprenticeships or other work opportunities in these trades, contact local bricklaying, stonemasonry, or marble setting contractors; a local of the union listed above; a local joint union-management apprenticeship committee; or the nearest office of the State employment service or State apprenticeship agency.

For general information about the work of either bricklayers or stonemasons, contact:

International Union of Bricklayers and Allied Craftsmen, International Masonry Apprenticeship Trust, 815 15th St. NW., Washington, D.C. 20005.

Information about the work of bricklayers also may be obtained from:

Associated General Contractors of America, Inc., 1957 E St. NW., Washington, D.C. 20006.

Brick Institute of America, 1750 Old Meadow Rd., McLean, Va. 22101.

CARPENTERS

(D.O.T. 860.281 through .781)

Nature of the Work

Carpenters, the largest group of building trades workers, are employed in almost every type of construction activity. Their work is commonly divided into two broad categories—"rough" carpentry and "finish" carpentry. Skilled carpenters are able to do both types of work.

Carpenters build according to instructions obtained from supervisors, blueprints, or both. In rough work, they erect the wood framework in buildings, including subfloors, partitions, floor joists, and rafters. In addition, they install heavy timbers used in the building of docks, railroad trestles, and similar heavy installations. Rough carpentry also includes the building of forms to enclose concrete until it is hardened, the making of chutes for pouring concrete, and the erecting of scaffolds and temporary buildings on the construction site. In all cases, carpenters must use materials and building techniques that conform to local building codes.

In finish work, which begins after the rough work is complete, carpenters install molding, wood paneling, cabinets, window sash, door frames, doors, and hardware and complete other finish work. Finish carpentry also includes building stairs and laying floors. Carpenters who do finish work must consider the appearance as well as the structural accuracy of the work. For example, they use a mitre-box saw to cut moldings so joints will not be noticed, and hide nails or screws with putty for a neat appearance.

As part of their job, carpenters also saw, fit, and assemble plywood, wallboard, and other materials. They use nails, bolts, wood screws, or glue to fasten materials. They may also install linoleum, asphalt tile, and similar soft floor coverings. Carpenters use handtools such as hammers, saws, chisels, planes, and power tools such as portable power saws, drills, and rivet guns.

Because of the wide scope of work in the trade, carpenters tend to concentrate on only one type of work. For example, some carpenters specialize in erecting new houses; others specialize in laying hardwood floors. Specialization is more common in large metropolitan areas; in smaller communities and in rural areas, carpenters ordinarily do all types of carpentry and also may install glass, put in insulation, and paint.

Places of Employment

About 1,010,000 carpenters were employed in 1976, of whom about one in five was self-employed. Most carpenters work for contractors and homebuilders who construct new buildings and other structures or who alter, remodel, or repair buildings; some carpenters alternate between wage employment for contractors and self-employment on small jobs. Most other carpenters work for government agencies, utility companies, manufacturing firms, or other large organizations.

Carpenters work throughout the country and, because of their versatility, are much less concentrated geographically than any other construction occupation.

Training, Other Qualifications, and Advancement

Most training authorities recommend the completion of an apprenticeship program as the best way to learn carpentry. A large number of workers in this trade, however, have acquired their skills informally (for example, by working as carpenters' helpers).

The apprenticeship program, sponsored by the local joint committee of contractors and unions, usually consists of 4 years of on-the-job training, in addition to a minimum of 144 hours of related classroom instruction each year. On the job, apprentices learn elementary structural design and become familiar with the common systems of frame and concrete form construction. They also learn to use the tools, machines,

equipment, and materials of the trade. In addition, they learn the many carpentry techniques, such as laying out, form building, framing, finishing, and welding.

Apprentices receive classroom instruction in drafting and blueprint reading, mathematics for layout work, and the use of woodworking machines. Both in the classroom and on the job they learn the relationship between carpentry and the other building trades, because the work of the carpenter is basic to the construction process.

Other informal on-the-job programs are provided by local contractors and usually are shorter and less thorough than apprenticeships. The degree of training and supervision in these programs depends principally on the size of the contractor. A small contractor who specializes in homebuilding may provide training in only one area—for example, rough framing. In contrast, a large general contractor may provide training in several areas.

Persons interested in carpentry should obtain the all-round training given in apprenticeship programs. Carpenters with such training will be in much greater demand and will have better opportunities for advancement than those who can do only the relatively simple, routine types of carpentry.

Apprenticeship applicants generally must be at least 17 years old. A high school or vocational school education is desirable, as are courses in carpentry, shop, mechanical drawing, and general mathematics. Good physical condition, a good sense of balance, and lack of fear of working on high structures are important assets. Applicants should also have manual dexterity and the ability to solve arithmetic problems quickly and accurately. In addition, they should be able to work closely with others. Required tests, designed to help measure an applicant's aptitude for carpentry, are given by local joint committees.

Carpenters may advance to carpenter supervisors or to general construction supervisors. Carpenters usually have greater opportunities than most other construction workers to become general construction supervisors since they are involved with the entire construction process. Some carpenters are able to become contractors and employ others.

Employment Outlook

Job opportunities for carpenters should be plentiful over the long run. Because of the large number of people employed in this field, replacement needs are high. Besides the job openings that result from the need to replace carpenters who retire, die, or leave their job for other reasons, many openings will be created by employment growth.

Employment of carpenters is expected to grow about as fast as the average for all occupations through the mid-1980's. Population and business growth will lead to a demand for more houses and other structures, thus increasing the demand for carpenters. More carpenters also will be needed for alteration and maintenance work. However, because construction activity is sensitive to ups and downs in the economy, the number of job openings may fluctuate greatly from year to year.

Earnings and Working Conditions

According to a survey of metropolitan areas in 1976, union wage rates for carpenters averaged $9.85 an hour, or about twice the average rate for production and nonsupervisory workers in private industry, except farming. Annual earnings, however, may not be as high as the hourly rates would indicate, because carpenters lose some worktime due to poor weather and occasional unemployment between jobs.

Hourly wage rates for apprentices usually start at about 50 percent of the rate paid to experienced carpenters and increase by about 5 percent at 6-month intervals.

As in other building trades, the carpenter's work is active and sometimes strenuous, but exceptional physical strength is not required. However, prolonged standing, as well as climbing and squatting, often are necessary. Carpenters risk injury from slips or falls, from contact with sharp or rough materials, and from the use of sharp tools and power equipment. Many people like carpentry because they can work outdoors.

A large proportion of carpenters are members of the United Brotherhood of Carpenters and Joiners of America.

Sources of Additional Information

For information about carpentry apprenticeships or other work opportunities in this trade, contact local carpentry contractors, a local of the union mentioned above, a local joint union-management apprenticeship committee, or the nearest office of the State employment service or State apprenticeship agency.

For general information on apprenticeship in this trade, contact:

Associated General Contractors of America, Inc., 1957 E St. NW., Washington, D.C. 20006.

United Brotherhood of Carpenters and Joiners of America, 101 Constitution Ave. NW., Washington, D.C. 20005.

CEMENT MASONS AND TERRAZZO WORKERS

(D.O.T. 844.884, 852.884, and 861.781)

Nature of the Work

Cement masons mix, pour, and finish concrete for many types of construction projects. The projects range from finishing of small jobs, such as patios and floors, to work on huge dams and miles of concrete highways. On small projects, a mason, assisted by one or two helpers, may do all of the masonry work; on large projects, a crew of several masons and many helpers may be employed. Among other tasks, cement masons may color concrete surfaces, expose aggregate in walls and sidewalks, or fabricate concrete beams, columns, and panels.

Terrazzo workers create attractive walkways, floors, patios, and panels by exposing marble chips and other fine aggregates on the surface of finished concrete. However, much of the preliminary work of terrazzo workers is the same as that for cement masons.

In preparing a site for pouring concrete, cement masons make sure the forms for molding the concrete are set for the desired pitch and depth and are properly aligned. Masons direct the pouring of the concrete and supervise laborers who use shovels or special rakes to place and spread the concrete. Masons then guide a "straightedge" (a long, straight piece of wood or similarly shaped piece of metal) back and forth across the top of the forms to level the freshly poured concrete and to show low spots, where concrete is added and leveled again.

Immediately after leveling the cement, masons carefully press a "darby" (a long, straight 1 inch by 4 inch piece of wood with smooth, rounded edges and a handle) with sweeping motions over the surface of the concrete, forcing heavy particles under and smoothing the top.

After darbying, masons wait until heavy particles in the cement settle to the bottom and excess water works its way to the surface. When the excess water evaporates and the concrete is firm but workable, masons complete their work.

Finishers first press an edger gently between the forms and the concrete, and guide it carefully along the edge and the surface. This produces slightly rounded edges and helps prevent them from chipping or cracking.

For joints, finishers use a flat tool that has a smooth ridge protruding from the center. At specified markings, workers make joints or grooves that help prevent unsightly cracks on the surface.

Next, finishers rub a float—a small and smooth, rectangular piece of wood—over the entire surface, carefully avoiding edges and joints. Floating embeds the heavier material deeper into the concrete, removes most imperfections, and brings the lighter material—mortar—to the surface.

As the final step, masons sweep the mortar with a trowel (a flat, metal tool) back and forth over the surface to create a smooth finish. On some jobs, electrically powered trowels may be used.

Masons also produce other finishes. For a coarse, non-skid finish, masons brush the surface with a broom or stiff bristled brush. For a pebble-like finish, they embed gravel chips into the surface, leaving the tops of the chips exposed. They wash any excess cement from the exposed chips with a mild acid solution for a neat appearance. For color, they sprinkle on a dye which they brush and trowel into the surface.

For concrete surfaces, such as columns, ceilings, and wall panels, that will remain exposed after forms are stripped, concrete finishers locate and correct any defects. First, they chisel away high spots and loose cement and smooth them out with a rubbing brick. They then fill the defects with a rich cement mixture, and either float or trowel a smooth, uniform finish.

Some cement masons specialize in laying a mastic coat (a fine asphalt mixture) over concrete, particularly in buildings where sound-insulated or acid-resistant floors are specified.

Cement masons must know their materials and be familiar with various chemical additives which speed or slow the setting time. Because of the effects of heat, cold, and wind on the drying time of cement, masons must be able to recognize by sight and touch what is occurring in the cement mixture so that they can prevent structural defects.

Attractive, marble-chipped terrazzo requires three layers of materials. First, either cement masons or terrazzo workers build a solid, level concrete foundation that is 3 inches to 4 inches deep.

After the forms are removed from the foundation, workers apply a 1 inch deep mixture of sandy concrete. When this layer becomes tacky, terrazzo workers partially embed metal dividing strips into the concrete wherever there is to be a joint or change of color in the terrazzo. Before this layer dries, workers make sure the tops of the strips are level with one another. The ferrule strips become a network of rigid dividers for terrazzo panels, allowing for unique design and color variation between panels. They also help prevent cracks from developing in the finished terrazzo.

For the final layer, terrazzo workers blend a fine concrete mixture which may be color dyed. They pour this mixture into each of the panels, then hand trowel each panel until level with the tops of the ferrule strips. While the mixture is wet, workers toss marble chips of various colors into each of the panels. To completely embed the marble chips, workers roll a lightweight roller over the entire surface.

When the terrazzo is thoroughly dry, workers grind it with a terrazzo grinder(somewhat like a disc-type floor polisher, only much heavier). The surface is ground until even with the top of the ferrule strips. Pits and holes are filled and steel troweled for a smooth, level surface. When the surface is dry, terrazzo workers clean, polish, and seal it for a rich, lustrous finish.

Places of Employment

About 71,000 cement masons and terrazzo workers were employed in 1976. Cement masons work for general contractors who construct entire projects, such as highways or large buildings, and for contractors who do only concrete work. Some masons install composition resilient floors for specialty floor contractors. A small number of masons are employed by municipal public works departments, public utilities, and manufacturing firms that do their own construction work. Most terrazzo workers work for special trade contractors who install decorative floors and wall panels.

One out of 10 cement masons and terrazzo workers is self-employed, about the same proportion as in other building trades. Most masons specialize in small jobs, such as driveways, sidewalks, and patios; most terrazzo workers, in floors.

Training, Other Qualifications, and Advancement

Cement masons and terrazzo workers learn their trade either through on-the-job training as helpers or through 2-year or 3-year apprenticeship programs. About one-third of all cement masons worked as construction laborers before becoming cement masons.

On-the-job training programs, almost all of which are available to cement mason trainees, provide informal instruction from experienced workers. Helpers learn to handle the tools, equipment, machines, and materials of the trade. They begin with simple tasks, such as spreading and using a straightedge on freshly poured concrete. As they advance, assignments become more complex, and usually within a year helpers are doing finishing work.

Two-year and 3-year apprenticeship programs, usually sponsored by local union-contractor agreements, also provide on-the-job training in addition to 144 hours of classroom instruction each year. In the classroom, apprentices learn applied mathematics, blueprint reading, and safety. Three-year apprentices receive special instruction in layout work and estimating.

When hiring helpers and apprentices, employers prefer high school graduates who are at least 18 years old, in good physical condition, and licensed to drive. High school courses in shop mathematics and blueprint reading or mechanical drawing provide a helpful background.

Experienced cement masons or terrazzo workers may advance to supervisors or contract estimators, or may open concrete contracting businesses.

Employment Outlook

Employment of cement masons and terrazzo workers is expected to grow much faster than the average for all occupations through the mid-

1980's. As population and the economy grow, more masons will be needed to help build apartments, offices, factories, and other structures. The greater use of concrete as a building material also will add to the demand for these workers. Prestressed concrete columns, for example, are being used increasingly in place of steel columns for large buildings. Besides the job openings created by employment growth, many openings will arise as experienced masons retire, die, or transfer to other fields of work. For terrazzo workers, most, if not all, openings will arise from replacement needs.

While the employment outlook is expected to be favorable over the long run, the number of job openings may fluctuate from year to year because construction activity is sensitive to ups and downs in the economy.

Earnings and Working Conditions

Union cement masons and terrazzo workers in metropolitan areas had estimated average wages of $9.35 an hour in 1976, about twice the average wage for nonsupervisory and production workers in private industry, except farming. Union masons generally have higher wage rates than nonunion masons. Apprentices usually start at 50 to 60 percent of the rate paid to experienced cement masons or terrazzo workers.

Annual earnings for cement masons, terrazzo workers, and apprentices generally are lower than hourly rates would indicate because the annual number of hours they work can be adversely affected by poor weather and fluctuations in construction activity.

Cement masons usually receive premium pay for hours worked in excess of the regularly scheduled workday or workweek. They often work overtime, because once concrete has been poured the job must be completed.

Mason or terrazzo work is active and strenuous. Since most finishing is done on floors or at ground level, workers must stoop, bend, and kneel. Because some jobs are outdoors, worktime is lost due to rain and freezing weather. In some cases, however, concrete and terrazzo can be poured year round by using heated, temporary shelters made of sheet plastic.

A large proportion of cement masons and terrazzo workers are union members. They belong either to the Operative Plasterers' and Cement Masons' International Association of the United States and Canada, or to the Bricklayers, Masons and Plasterers' International Union of America.

Sources of Additional Information

For information about apprenticeships and work opportunities, contact local cement finishing contractors; locals of unions previously mentioned; a local joint union-management apprenticeship committee; or the nearest office of the State employment service or apprenticeship agency.

For general information about cement masons and terrazzo workers, contact:

Associated General Contractors of America, Inc., 1957 E St. NW., Washington, D.C. 20006.

International Union of Bricklayers and Allied Craftsmen, 815 15th St. NW., Washington, D.C. 20005.

Operative Plasterers' and Cement Mason International Association of the United States and Canada, 1125 17th St. NW., Washington, D.C. 20036.

CONSTRUCTION LABORERS

(D.O.T. 801.887, 809.887, 842.887, 844.887, 850.887, 851.887, 852.887, 853.887, 859.884 and .887, 860.884 and .887, 861.884 and .887, 862.884 and .887, 865.887, 866.887, 869.887, and 892.883)

Nature of the Work

Construction laborers work on all types of construction projects—houses, highways, dams, airports, missile sites. They are usually the first workers to arrive on a construction project—assisting in site preparation—and the last to leave. Laborers under the direction of other trade workers provide much of the routine physical labor on construction and demolition projects. They erect and dismantle scaffolding, set braces to support the sides of excavations, and clean up rubble and debris. Laborers also help unload and deliver materials, machinery, and equipment to carpenters, masons, and other construction workers.

On alteration and modernization jobs, laborers tear out the existing work. They perform most of the work done by wrecking and salvage crews during the demolition of buildings.

When concrete is mixed at the worksite, laborers unload and handle materials and fill mixers with ingredients. Whether the concrete is mixed on-site or hauled in by truck, laborers pour and spread the concrete and spade or vibrate it to prevent air pockets. In highway paving, laborers clean the right-of-way, grade and help prepare the site, and set the forms into which wet concrete is poured. They cover new pavement with straw, burlap, or other materials to keep it from drying too rapidly.

Some construction laborers have job titles that indicate the kinds of work they do. Bricklayers' tenders and plasterers' tenders, both commonly known as hod carriers, help bricklayers and plasterers by mixing and supplying materials, setting up and moving portable scaffolding, and providing many other services. Hod carriers must be familiar with the work of bricklayers and plasterers and know the materials and tools they use. Some hod carriers also help cement masons.

Another group of laborers, pipelayers, lay sewer and other large, nonmetal pipe and seal connections with concrete and other materials.

Recent years have seen much mechanization of the laborers' tasks. Thus, in their traditional work, laborers now may operate such things as motorized lifts and ditch-diggers of the "walk-behind" variety, various kinds of small mechanical hoists, as well as laser beam equipment to align and grade ditches and tunnels.

Although some construction laborers' jobs require few skills, many jobs require training and experience, as well as a broad knowledge of construction methods, materials, and operations. Rock blasting, rock drilling, and tunnel construction are examples of work in which "know-how" is important. Laborers who work with explosives drill holes in rock, handle explosives, and set charges. They must know the effects of different explosive charges under varying rock conditions to prevent injury and property damage. Laborers do almost all the work in the boring and mining of a tunnel, including operations that would be handled by workers in other trades if the job were located above ground.

Places of Employment

About 715,000 construction laborers were employed in 1976. Most of them worked for construction contractors, for State and city public works and highway departments, and for public utility companies.

Training, Other Qualifications, and Advancement

Little formal training is needed to get a job as a construction laborer. Generally, applicants must be at least 18 years old and in good physical condition. Most new employees transfer from other occupations, such as truckdriver, farm laborer, or janitor.

Beginners' jobs are usually of the simplest type, such as unloading trucks and digging ditches. As workers gain experience, job assignments become more complex.

Many tasks require skills too complex for on-the-job training. As a result, contractors and unions have established 4- to 8-week formal training programs in many States to teach basic construction concepts, safety practices, and machinery operation.

After several years of experience and training, many laborers advance to craft jobs, such as carpenter, bricklayer, or cement mason.

Employment Outlook

Employment of construction laborers is expected to grow about as fast as the average for all occupations through the mid-1980's. In addition to openings created by occupational growth, job openings will result from the need to replace workers who retire, die, or leave the occupation for other reasons. On the average, tens of thousands of job openings will become available each year. Because employment of laborers is sensitive to the ups and downs in construction activity, however, the annual number of openings may fluctuate.

Over the long run, growth in population and economic activity will spur construction. Laborers will be needed to meet the demand for moving materials, mixing and pouring concrete, and helping craft workers, particularly on large projects such as dams, highways, high rise buildings, and bridges.

Earnings and Working Conditions

Union wage rates for construction laborers averaged $7.50 an hour in 1976, compared with $4.87 an hour for production and nonsupervisory workers in private industry, except farming.

Annual earnings for construction laborers generally are lower than hourly rates would indicate because the annual number of hours they work can be adversely affected by poor weather and fluctuations in construction.

Construction work is physically strenuous, since it requires frequent bending, stooping, and heavy lifting. Much of the work is performed outdoors. Many construction laborers are members of the Laborers' International Union of North America.

Sources of Additional Information

For information about work opportunities, contact local building or construction contractors, a local of the Laborers' International Union of North America, or the local office of the State employment service.

For general information about the work of construction laborers, contact:

Laborers' International Union of North America, 905 16th St. NW., Washington, D.C. 20006.

Laborers'-Associated General Contractors' Education and Training Program, 1730 Rhode Island Ave., Suite 909, Washington, D.C. 20036.

DRYWALL INSTALLERS AND FINISHERS

(D.O.T. 840.887 and 842.884)

Nature of the Work

Developed as a substitute for wet plaster, drywall consists of a thin wall of plaster sandwiched between two pieces of heavy paper. It is used today for walls and ceilings of most new homes because it saves both time and money compared to traditional construction using plaster.

Two new occupations have emerged in response to the widespread use of this construction material: drywall installers and drywall finishers. Installers fasten drywall panels to the framework inside houses and other buildings. Finishers do touchup work to get the panels in shape for painting.

Drywall panels are manufactured in standard sizes—for example, 4 feet by 12 feet. Thus, installers must measure and cut some pieces to fit in small spaces, such as above and below windows. They also saw holes in the panels for electric outlets, air-conditioning units, and plumbing. After making these alterations, installers apply glue to the wooden framework, press the panels against it, and nail them down. An installer usually is assisted by a helper because large panels are too heavy and cumbersome for one person to handle.

Some installers specialize in hanging drywall panels on metal framework in offices, schools, and other large buildings. Following plans that indicate the location of rooms and hallways, they saw metal rods and channels to size, bolt them together to make floor-to-ceiling frames, and attach the drywall panels to the frames with screws. The workers also erect suspended ceilings. They hang metal bands from wires that are embedded in the concrete ceiling. The installers run the bands horizontally across the room, crisscrossing them to form rectangular spaces for the ceiling panels.

After the drywall has been installed, finishers fill joints between panels with a quick-drying paste. Using the wide, flat tip of a special knife, and brushlike strokes, they spread the paste into and along each side of the joint. Before the paste dries, workers use their knives to press a perforated paper tape into the paste and to scrape away excess paste. When the first application of paste is dry, finishers apply another to fill any depressions and to make a smooth surface. Nail and screw heads also are covered with this compound. Finishers sand these patched areas to make them as smooth as the rest of the wall surface. They also repair nicks and cracks caused by the installation of air-conditioning vents and other fixtures. Some finishers specialize in sanding, taping, or repair work.

Places of Employment

About 45,000 persons worked as drywall installers and finishers in 1976. Most worked for contractors that specialize in drywall construction; others worked for contractors that do all kinds of construction.

Installers and finishers are employed throughout the country, but are concentrated in urban areas. In many small towns, carpenters install drywall and painters finish it.

Training, Other Qualifications, and Advancement

Persons who become drywall installers or finishers usually start as helpers and learn most of their skills on the job. Some employers, in cooperation with unions, offer special programs which supplement on-the-job training with a few hours of classroom instruction each week. Each program lasts about 2 years.

Installer helpers start by carrying materials, holding panels, and cleaning up debris. Within a few weeks, they are taught to measure, cut, and install panels. Eventually, they become experienced installers, capable of working quickly and without help.

Finish helpers begin with taping joints and touching up nail holes and scratches. They soon learn to install corner guards and to conceal openings around pipes. Near the end of their training, they learn to estimate costs of installing and finishing drywall.

Employers prefer high school graduates who are in good physical condition, but applicants with less education frequently are hired. High school or trade school courses in carpentry provide a helpful background for drywall work. Installers must be good at simple arithmetic.

After qualifying as an installer or finisher, a person who has leadership ability may become a supervisor within a few years. Some workers start their own drywall contracting businesses.

Employment Outlook

Employment of drywall workers is expected to grow much faster than the average for all occupations through the mid-1980's due to an increase in construction activity. Besides the workers hired to fill openings arising from this increased demand, many will be hired to replace those who retire, die, or take jobs in other occupations. Because construction activity fluctuates, however, the number of new workers needed may vary greatly from year to year.

Most job openings will be in metropolitan areas. Building contractors in small cities may not have enough business to hire full-time drywall workers.

Earnings and Working Conditions

According to limited information, drywall installers and finishers earned from $6.50 to $9 an hour in 1976. By comparison, all nonsupervisory and production workers in private industry, except farming, averaged $4.87 an hour.

Many contractors pay installers and finishers according to the amount of work they complete—for example, from 3 to 5 cents for each square foot of panel installed. In a day, the average drywall worker installs 35 to 40 panels, each 4 feet by 12 feet.

A 40-hour week is standard for installers and finishers, but they sometimes work longer. Those who are paid hourly rates receive premium pay for overtime. Unlike many construction workers, installers and finishers work indoors and do not lose time and pay when the weather is bad.

As in other construction trades, drywall work sometimes is strenuous. Installers and finishers spend most of the day on their feet, either standing, bending, stooping, or squatting. Installers have to lift and maneuver heavy panels. Hazards include the possibility of falls from ladders and injuries from power tools.

Some installers are members of the United Brotherhood of Carpenters and Joiners of America, and some finishers are members of the International Brotherhood of Painters and Allied Trades.

Sources of Additional Information

For details about job qualifications and training programs, write to:

International Association of Wall and Ceiling Contractors/Gypsum Drywall Contractors International, 1711 Connecticut Ave. NW., Washington, D.C. 20009.

National Joint Painting, Decorating, and Drywall Apprenticeship and Training Committee, 1709 New York Ave. NW., Washington, D.C. 2006.

ELECTRICIANS (CONSTRUCTION)

(D.O.T. 821.381, 824.281, and 829.281 and .381)

Nature of the Work

Heating, lighting, power, air-conditioning, and refrigeration components all operate through electrical systems that are assembled, installed, and wired by construction electricians. These workers also install electrical machinery, electronic equipment and controls, and signal and communications systems.

Construction electricians follow blueprints and specifications for most installations. To install wiring in factories and offices, they may bend, fit, and fasten conduit (pipe or tubing) inside partitions, walls, or other concealed areas. Workers also fasten to the wall small metal boxes that will house electrical devices such as switches.

To complete circuits between outlets and switches, they then pull insulated wires or cables through the conduit. They work carefully to avoid damaging any wires or cables. In lighter construction, such as housing, plastic-covered wire usually is used rather than conduit. In any case, electricians connect the wiring to circuit breakers, transformers, or other components. Wires are joined by twisting ends together with pliers and covering the ends with special plastic connectors. When additional strength is desired, they may use an electric "soldering gun" to melt metal onto the twisted wires then cover them with durable, electrical tape. When the wiring is finished, they test the circuits for proper connections and grounding.

For safety, electricians follow National Electrical Code specifications and procedures and, in addition, must comply with requirements of State, county, and municipal electrical codes.

Electricians generally furnish their own tools, including screwdrivers, pliers, knives, and hacksaws. Employers furnish heavier tools, such as pipe threaders, conduit benders, and most test meters and power tools.

Places of Employment

Most of the 260,000 construction electricians employed in 1976 worked for electrical contractors. Many others were self-employed contractors. Construction electricians are employed throughout the country, but are concentrated in in-dustrialized and urban areas.

Training, Other Qualifications, and Advancement

Most training authorities recommend the completion of a 4-year apprenticeship program as the best way to learn the electrical trade. Compared to most other construction trades, electricians have a higher percentage of apprentice-trained workers. However, some people learn the trade informally by working for many years as electricians' helpers. Many helpers gain additional knowledge through trade school or correspondence courses, or through special training in the Armed Forces.

Apprenticeship programs are sponsored through and supervised by local union-management committees. These programs provide 144 hours of classroom instruction each year in addition to comprehensive on-the-job training. In the classroom, apprentices learn blueprint reading, electrical theory, electronics, mathematics, and safety and first-aid practices. On the job, under the supervision of experienced electricians, apprentices must demonstrate mastery of electrical principles. At first, apprentices drill holes, set anchors, and set up conduit. In time and with experience, they measure, bend, and install conduit, as well as install, connect, and test wiring. They also learn to set up and draw diagrams for entire electrical systems.

Beginners who are not apprentices can pick up the trade informally in a variety of ways. For example, some begin working in manufacturing plants piecing together electrical components. Others start in maintenance where they learn about circuit breakers, fuses, switches, and other electrical devices. Later, they change jobs and broaden their knowledge by working as helpers for experienced electricians. While learning to install conduit, connect wires, and test circuits, helpers are also taught good safety practices.

All applicants should be in good health and have at least average physical strength. Good color vision is important because workers frequently must identify electrical wires by color. Also important are agility and dexterity. Applicants for apprentice positions must be at least 18 years old and usually must be a high school or vocational school graduate with 1 year of algebra. Courses in electricity, electronics, mechanical drawing, science, and shop provide a good background.

To obtain a license, which is necessary for employment in some cities, an electrician must pass an examination which requires a thorough knowledge of the craft and of State and local building codes.

Experienced construction electricians can advance to supervisors, superintendents, or contract estimators for contractors on construction jobs. Many electricians start their own contracting businesses. In most large urban areas, a contractor must have an electrical contractor's license.

Employment Outlook

Employment of construction electricians is expected to increase faster than the average for all occupations through the mid-1980's. As population and the economy grow, more electricians will be needed to install electrical fixtures and wiring in new and renovated homes, offices, and other buildings. In addition to jobs created by employment growth, many openings will arise as experienced electricians retire, die, or leave the occupation for other reasons.

While employment in this field is expected to grow over the long run, it n.ay fluctuate from year to year due to ups and downs in construction activity. When construction jobs are not available, however, electricians may be able to transfer to other types of electrical work. For example, they may find jobs as maintenance electricians in factories or as electricians in shipbuilding or aircraft manufacturing.

Earnings and Working Conditions

According to a survey of metropolitan areas, union wage rates for electricians averaged $10.33 an hour in 1976. This was about twice the average wage of nonsupervisory and production workers in private industry, except farming. Because the seasonal nature of construction work affects electricians less than workers in most building trades, their annual earnings also tend to be higher.

Apprentice wage rates start at from 40 to 50 percent of the rate paid to experienced electricians and increase periodically.

Construction electricians are not required to have great physical strength, but they frequently must stand for long periods and work in cramped quarters. Because much of their work is indoors, electricians are less exposed to unfavorable weather than are most other construction workers. They risk electrical shock, falls from ladders and scaffolds, and blows from falling objects. However, safety practices have helped to reduce the injury rate.

A large proportion of construction electricians are members of the International Brotherhood of Electrical Workers.

Sources of Additional Information

For details about electrician apprenticeships or other work opportunities in this trade, contact local electrical contractors; a local chapter of the National Electrical Contractors Association; a local union of the International Brotherhood of Electrical Workers; a local union-management apprenticeship committee; or the nearest office of the State employment service or State apprenticeship agency. Some local employment service offices screen applicants and give aptitude tests.

For general information about the work of electricians, contact:

International Brotherhood of Electrical Workers, 1125 15th St. NW., Washington, D.C. 20005.

National Electrical Contractors Association, 7315 Wisconsin Ave. NW., Washington, D.C. 20014.

National Joint Apprenticeship and Training Committee for the Electrical Industry, 9700 E. George Palmer Hwy., Lanham, Md. 20801.

ELEVATOR CONSTRUCTORS

(D.O.T. 825.381 and 829.281)

Nature of the Work

Elevator constructors, also called elevator mechanics, assemble and install elevators, escalators, and similar equipment. In new buildings, they install equipment during construction. In older buildings, they replace earlier installations with new equipment. Once the equipment is in service, they maintain and repair it. Installation or repair work usually is performed by small crews consisting of skilled elevator constructors and their helpers.

When installing a new elevator, mechanics first prepare the elevator shaft—a vertical opening that passes through the floors of a building and allows the elevator to move up and down. They remove any obstructions such as wood or metal crossmembers and, at the bottom of the shaft, they may erect forms, then mix and pour concrete for a foundation.

So the elevator will move up and down safely and smoothly, workers erect a strong steel frame within the shaft. For the frame, they bolt heavy steel guide rails to the walls along the shaft as well as to the steel supports fastened to the walls around the shaft at each floor.

To install electrical wires and controls, mechanics secure special metal tubing to the shaft's walls, running it from floor to floor. Workers then pull plastic-covered electrical wires through the tubing, which helps protect the wires. Next, they install circuit breakers and switches—usually at each floor and at the main control panel. Finally workers fasten the wires to the switches and test for proper connections.

Next, mechanics assemble the elevator car at the bottom of each shaft. "Footings" of the car frame are set into the grooves of the heavy steel guide rails; the frame parts are bolted or welded together. Workers then install the car's platform, walls, ceiling, and doors.

For each elevator, workers install a hoist. This giant, electrically powered spool simultaneously winds and unwinds a heavy steel cable that connects the elevator car at one end to its counterweight at the other. As a result, the car and its counterweight move in opposite directions to assist in each other's movement. While the hoist winds the cable from one side, pulling the car upward, it also unwinds the cable on the other side, causing the counterweight to descend. As the weight descends, it helps to pull the car swiftly and smoothly upward.

With the car assembled and the hoist installed, workers connect the necessary electrical wires to the car. These will carry signal instructions for the car's operation.

Next, at the elevator entrances on each floor, mechanics bolt metal door frames to the concrete, metal, or wood ceilings, floors, and walls. The frames support the grooved metal tracks along which the doors open and close. After setting the doors in the frames, workers connect and test the wires that help to operate the doors.

Finally, after the connections have been tested, the cables secured, and the guide rails greased, the entire system is checked for proper operation.

Elevator constructors employ similar work techniques when constructing escalators. These electrically powered stairs rotate around huge oval tracks that run from floor to floor. Unlike elevators, which run according to specific signals, escalators run continuously. Consequently, while elevators need sophisticated circuits and many wires, escalators only need one electric wire. Workers simply connect the wire from a switch to the motor that drives the giant bicycle-like chain and rotates the stairs.

Alteration work is similar to new installation because all elevator equipment except the old rail, car frame, platform, and counterweight is generally replaced. Elevator mechanics inspect elevator and escalator installations periodically and, when necessary, adjust cables and lubricate or replace parts.

Alteration work on elevators is important because of the rapid rate of innovation and improvement in elevator engineering.

To install and repair modern elevators, most of which are electrically controlled, elevator constructors must have a working knowledge of electricity, electronics, and hydraulics. They also must be able to repair electric motors as well as control and signal systems. Because of the variety of their work, they use many different handtools, power tools, and testing n.eters and gauges.

Places of Employment

Most of the estimated 20,000 elevator constructors in 1976 were employed by elevator manufacturers to do installation, modernization, and repair work. Some are employed instead by small, local contractors who specialize in elevator maintenance and repair. Still others work for government agencies or business establishments that do their own elevator maintenance and repair.

Training, Other Qualifications, and Advancement

Almost all elevator constructors learn their skills through on-the-job training supplemented by classroom instruction. On the job, trainees are assigned initially to experienced elevator mechanics. Beginning tasks include carrying materials and tools, bolting rails to walls, and assembling cab parts. Eventually, tasks become more complex and require greater knowledge and skill. For example, electrical wiring requires a knowledge of local and national electrical codes and of electrical theory. Later on, trainees learn to test elevators and adjust them for maximum performance. In the classroom, trainees learn electrical and electronic theory, mathematics, applications of physics, and safety techniques.

Generally, training advancement depends upon the trainee's ability and level of experience. The average trainee usually qualifies as a helper after 6 months of experience and usually becomes a fully qualified elevator constructor within 4 years. Some States and cities require elevator constructors to pass a licensing examination.

Applicants for trainee positions must be at least 18 years old and have a high school or vocational school education; courses in electricity, mathematics, and physics can provide a useful background. Applicants also must pass an aptitude test before training begins. Good physical condition and a high degree of mechanical aptitude are important.

Some constructors advance to jobs as supervisors or elevator inspectors. A relatively small number go into the elevator contracting business.

Employment Outlook

Employment in this small occupation is expected to increase faster than the average for all occupations through the mid-1980's. Growth in the number of high-rise apartment and commercial buildings will create job openings in elevator construction, as will the need to replace experienced workers who retire, die, or stop working for other reasons. The total number of job openings will be limited, however, because of the relatively small size of the occupation.

Earnings and Working Conditions

In 1976, union elevator constructors in metropolitan areas had estimated average wages of $10.30 an hour or twice the average wage paid to production and nonsupervisory workers in private industry, except farming. Hourly wage rates for trainees start at about 50 percent of the rate paid to experienced elevator mechanics and increase periodically.

Unlike most other construction trades, elevator contructors usually work year round. When construction of new buildings declines, the construction of new elevators and escalators declines, but the demand for the repair and maintenance of older elevators and escalators increases.

Elevator construction involves lifting and carrying heavy equipment and parts, but this is usually done by helpers. Most of the work takes place indoors and at great heights. Workers are exposed to the dangers of falls and electrical shocks.

Most elevator constructors are

members of the International Union of Elevator Constructors.

Sources of Additional Information

For further details about work opportunities as a helper in this trade, contact elevator manufacturers, elevator construction or maintenance firms, or a local of the union mentioned above. In addition, the local office of the State employment service may have information about opportunities in this trade.

For general information about the work of elevator constructors, contact:

International Union of Elevator Constructors, 5565 Sterrett Place, Clark Bldg., Suite 332, Columbia, Md. 21044.

FLOOR COVERING INSTALLERS

(D.O.T. 299.381 and 864.781)

Nature of the Work

Floor covering installers (also called *floor covering mechanics*) install and replace carpet or resilient floor covering materials such as tile, linoleum, and vinyl sheets. These workers install coverings over floors made of wood, concrete, or other materials. They generally specialize in either carpet or resilient floor covering installation, although some do both types.

Before putting down resilient covering, such as vinyl tile, installers first inspect the floor to be sure that it is firm, dry, smooth, and free of dust or dirt. Some floors have to be prepared for covering. For example, installers may sand a rough or painted floor and fill cracks and indentations. An extremely uneven floor may be resurfaced with wood or other materials.

On newly poured concrete floors or floors laid over earthwork, installers test for moisture content. If the moisture is too great, they may suggest postponing installation of floor covering or recommend a covering technique suited to the floor's condition.

Resilient-flooring installers measure and mark off the floor according to a plan. The plan may be architectural drawings that specify every detail of the covering design, or a simple, verbal description by the customer. When the plan is completed, installers, often assisted by apprentices or helpers, cut, fit, and glue the flooring into place. It must be carefully fit, particularly at door openings, along irregular wall surfaces, and around fixtures, such as columns or pipes. Installers must take special care also in cutting out and setting in decorative designs. After the flooring is in place, they may run a roller over it to insure good adhesion.

Carpet installers, like the installers of resilient coverings, first inspect the floor to determine its condition. Then they plan the layout after allowing for expected traffic patterns so that best appearance and long wear will be obtained.

For wall-to-wall carpet, installers lay underlayment—a 1/2 to 1 inch thick, foam rubber pad—that is cut slightly smaller than the entire floor. Next, they roll out, measure, mark, and cut the carpet, allowing for 3 to 4 inches of extra carpet on each side. This provides some leeway for mistakes. Workers then lay the carpet and stretch it to fit evenly against the floor and snugly against each wall and door threshold. With the carpet stretched, the excess around the perimeter is cut to fit the room precisely. To hold the carpet in place, workers either tack or tape each edge of the carpet to the floor.

For precut and seamed carpet, installers simply lay a foam rubber pad on the floor and roll the carpet over the slightly smaller pad. To hold the pad and carpet in place, installers may apply tape that has adhesive on both sides to the bottom edges of the carpet.

Places of Employment

An estimated 85,000 floor covering installers were employed in 1976. About four-fifths worked primarily with carpet, and the remainder with resilient flooring.

Most installers worked for flooring contractors. Many others worked for retailers of floor covering and home alteration and repair contractors. About 1 out of 4 floor covering installers was self-employed, a higher proportion than the average for all building trades.

Installers are employed throughout the Nation, but most are concentrated in urban areas that have high levels of construction activity.

Training, Other Qualifications, and Advancement

The vast majority of floor covering installers learn their trades informally on the job by working as helpers to experienced installers. Most others learn through formal apprenticeship programs, which include on-the-job training as well as related classroom instruction.

Informal training programs usually are sponsored by individual contractors and generally take about 1 1/2 years. Helpers begin with simple assignments. Helpers on resilient flooring jobs carry materials and tools, prepare floors for the tile, and help with its installation. Carpet helpers install tackless stripping and padding, and help stretch newly installed carpet. With experience, helpers in either trade take on more difficult assignments, such as measuring, cutting, and fitting the materials to be installed.

Some contractor-sponsored programs and apprenticeship programs provide comprehensive training that covers both carpet and resilient flooring work.

Applicants for helper or apprentice jobs should be at least 16 years old, mechanically inclined, and licensed to drive. A high school education is preferred, though not necessary. Courses in general mathematics and shop may provide a helpful background.

Floor covering installers may advance to supervisors or installation managers for large floor laying firms. Some installers become salespersons or estimators. Installers also may go into business for themselves.

Employment Outlook

Employment of floor covering installers is expected to increase about as fast as the average for all occupations through the mid-1980's. In addition to job openings resulting from employment growth, many openings will arise as experienced installers retire, die, or leave the occupation for other reasons.

Employment of floor covering installers is expected to increase mainly because of the expected expansion in construction and the more widespread use of resilient floor coverings and carpeting. In many new buildings, plywood will continue to replace hardwood floors, thus making wall-to-wall carpet or resilient floors a necessity. Carpet and resilient flooring also will continue to be used extensively in renovation work. Moreover, versatile materials and colorful patterns will contribute to the growing demand for floor coverings.

Most job opportunities will be for carpet installers and workers who can install both carpet and resilient flooring. Fewer opportunities will arise for workers who can install only resilient flooring because this is a relatively small field.

Earnings and Working Conditions

Information from a limited number of firms indicates that experienced floor covering installers earned between $6.25 and $9 per hour in 1976. Starting wage rates for apprentices and other trainees usually are about half of the experienced worker's rate.

Most installers are paid by the hour. In some shops, part of the pay may be in bonuses. In others, installers receive a monthly salary or are paid according to the amount of work they do.

Installers generally work regular daytime hours. Particular circumstances, however, such as installing a floor in a store or office, may require work during evenings or weekends.

Unlike many construction workers, floor covering installers usually do not lose time due to weather conditions. During the winter, most work is done in heated buildings. The jobs are not hazardous, but installers may get injuries from lifting heavy materials or from working in a kneeling position for long periods. Most injuries can be avoided if proper work procedures are followed.

Many floor covering installers belong to unions, including the United Brotherhood of Carpenters and Joiners of America, and the International Brotherhood of Painters and Allied Trades.

Sources of Additional Information

For details about apprenticeships or work opportunities, contact local flooring contractors or retailers; locals of the unions previously mentioned; or the nearest office of the State apprenticeship agency or the State employment service.

For general information about the work of floor covering installers, contact:

Carpet and Rug Institute, P.O. Box 2048, Dalton, Ga. 30720.

Resilient Floor Covering Institute, 1030 15th St. NW., Suite 350, Washington, D.C. 20005.

GLAZIERS

(D.O.T. 865.781)

Nature of the Work

Construction glaziers cut and install all types of building glass. For some jobs, the glass is precut and ready to install. For other jobs, glass must be cut before being installed.

To prepare the glass for cutting, glaziers measure and mark the glass to fit the window opening, then rest the glass either on edge or flat against a carpeted table. To help the cutting tool move smoothly across the glass, workers sometimes brush on a thin layer of oil along the line of the intended cut.

Glaziers cut glass with a special tool that has a very hard metal wheel about 1/6 inch in diameter. Using a "straightedge" as a guide, the glazier presses the cutter's wheel firmly to the glass, guiding and rolling it carefully over the surface. This creates a cut on and just below the surface. Immediately after cutting, the glazier presses on the small end, thereby causing the glass to break cleanly along the cut.

Glaziers may need the help of a crane when installing a large, heavy piece of glass. In all cases, however, since there is a risk of shattering the glass, glaziers use their hands to guide the glass carefully to the opening and to position the glass precisely in its frame.

Glaziers secure glass in an opening with materials such as putty, rubber gaskets, metal clips, and metal or wood molding. When using putty, which is similar to very soft taffy, workers first spread it neatly against and around the edges of the molding on the inside of the opening. Next, they install the glass. With it pressed against the putty on the inside molding, workers then screw or nail outside molding that loosely holds the glass in place. To hold it firmly, they pack the space between the molding and the glass with putty, then trim any excess putty with a putty knife.

Glaziers sometimes use a rubber gasket—a very heavy molded rubber hose with a split running its length—to secure glass. They first glue the gasket around the perimeter within the opening, then set the glass into the split side of the gasket, causing it to clamp to the edges of the glass and hold it firmly in place.

When metal clips and molding are used to secure glass, glaziers first secure the molding, then force springlike metal clips between the glass and the molding. The clips exert pressure on the molding and the glass, thereby keeping it firmly in place.

Glaziers also install glass doors, mirrors, and steel sash.

In addition to handtools such as glasscutters and putty knives, glaziers use power tools, such as cutters and grinders.

Places of Employment

About 10,000 persons worked as construction glaziers in 1976. Most worked for glazing contractors engaged in new construction, alteration, and repair. Others worked for government agencies or businesses that do their own construction work.

Glaziers work throughout the country, but jobs are concentrated in metropolitan areas. Glaziers occasionally may travel to work for a day or two in small outlying towns where few people, if any, are equipped and qualified to install glass in commercial buildings such as stores.

Training, Other Qualifications, and Advancement

The majority of construction glaziers learn the trade through a 4-year apprenticeship program. Others learn the trade informally, on the job, by assisting experienced workers.

Apprenticeship programs, usually sponsored by local union-management committees, consist of on-the-job training as well as 144 hours of classroom instruction each year. Some apprenticeship programs also require a comprehensive home study course.

On the job, apprentices learn to use the tools and equipment of the trade; handle, measure, cut, and install glass; cut and fit moldings; and install and balance glass doors. In the classroom, they are taught mathematics, blueprint reading, general construction techniques, safety practices, and first-aid.

Those who learn this trade informally usually start by carrying glass and cleaning up debris in large glass shops. They often have the opportunity to practice their cutting techniques on discarded glass. After a year or so, they may have an opportunity to cut glass for a job. Eventually, helpers assist experienced workers on a simple installation job. Learning the trade this way may take considerably longer than through apprenticeship.

Applicants for apprenticeships or helper positions should be in good physical condition and licensed to drive. Persons applying for helper positions will find that employers prefer high school or vocational school graduates. Applicants for apprenticeships must be at least 18 years old and have a high school diploma or its equivalent. Courses in general mathematics, blueprint reading or mechanical drawing, general construction, and shop provide a helpful background.

Glaziers who have leadership ability may advance to supervisory jobs. Some glaziers become contractors.

Employment Outlook

Employment of construction glaziers is expected to increase faster than the average for all occupations through the mid-1980's. Besides the jobs resulting from employment growth, many openings will arise as experienced glaziers retire, die, or leave the occupation for other reasons. The number of openings may fluctuate from year to year, however, because employment in this trade is sensitive to changes in construction activity.

Over the long run, population and business growth will create a rising demand for new residential and commercial buildings, such as apartments, offices, and stores. Since glass will continue to be popular in building design, the demand for glaziers to install and replace glass also will grow.

Employment opportunities should be greatest in metropolitan areas, where most glazing contractors are located.

Earnings and Working Conditions

In 1976, union construction glaziers in metropolitan areas had estimated average wages of $9.25 an hour, or about twice the average hourly wage for production or nonsupervisory workers in private industries, except farming. Apprentice wage rates usually start at 50 percent of the rate paid to experienced glaziers and increase periodically. Yearly earnings of glaziers and apprentices, however, generally are slightly lower than hourly rates would indicate because the annual number of hours they work can be adversely affected by poor weather and fluctuations in construction activity.

Glaziers may be injured by glass edges or cutting tools, falls from scaffolds, or from lifting glass. To reduce injuries, employers and unions emphasize safety training.

Many glaziers employed in construction are members of the International Brotherhood of Painters and Allied Trades.

Sources of Additional Information

For more information about glazier apprenticeships or work opportunities, contact local glazing or general contractors; a local of the International Brotherhood of Painters and Allied Trades; a local joint union-management apprenticeship agency; or the nearest office of the State employment service or State apprenticeship agency.

For general information about the work of glaziers, contact:

International Brotherhood of Painters and Allied Trades, 1750 New York Ave. NW., Washington, D.C. 20006.

INSULATION WORKERS

(D.O.T. 863.381, .781, and .884)

Nature of the Work

Properly insulated homes and buildings reduce fuel costs by preventing excessive loss of cool air on warm days and hot air on cold days. Meat storage rooms, steam pipes, and boilers are other examples where the wasteful transfer of heat to or from the space inside can be minimized by insulation. Selecting the proper material and method of installation is the responsibility of insulation workers.

Insulation workers—sometimes called applicators—may paste, wire, tape, or spray insulation to an appropriate surface. When covering a steam pipe, for example, insulation workers may cut a tube of insulation to the necessary length, stretch it open along a cut which runs the length of the tube, and then slip it over the pipe. To secure the insulation they wrap and fasten wire bands around it, tape it, or wrap a cover of tar paper, cloth, or canvas over it and then sew or staple the cover in place. Care is required to cover joints completely.

When covering a wall or other flat surface, workers may use a hose to spray foam insulation onto a wire mesh. The wire mesh provides a rough surface to which the foam can cling and adds strength to the fin-

ished wall. If desired, workers apply a final coat for a finished appearance.

In some places, such as attics which do not require either wire mesh for adhesion or a final coat for appearance, applicators use a compressor to "blow-in" the insulation. "Blowing-in" insulation is a simple task. The worker fills the machine with shredded fiberglass insulation, allows the compressor to force the insulation through a hose, and controls the direction and flow of the insulation until the required amount is installed.

Insulation workers use common handtools—trowels, brushes, scissors, sewing equipment, and stapling guns. Powersaws, as well as handtools, are used to cut and fit insulating materials.

Compressors for "blowing-in" or for "spraying-on" insulation also may be used. In using these tools, applicators may have to bend or squat while working on ladders or on scaffolds in dimly lit and sometimes very dusty areas.

Places of Employment

About 30,000 insulation workers were employed in 1976. Most worked for insulation contractors. Others were employed to alter and maintain insulated pipework in chemical factories, petroleum refineries, power plants, and similar structures which have extensive steam installations for power, heating, and cooling. Some large firms which have cold-storage facilities also employ these workers for maintenance and repair.

Training, Other Qualifications, and Advancement

Almost all insulation workers learn their trade through either informal on-the-job training or a formal 4-year "improvership" program; both of these programs stress conservation and safety. A trainee in an informal on-the-job program, usually provided by and paid for by an insulation contractor, is assigned to an experienced insulation worker for instruction and supervision. A trainee begins with simple tasks, such as "blowing-in" insulation, supplying insulation material to experienced workers, or holding the material while they fasten it in place. In about 6 to 8 months, assignments become more complex, and within a year a trainee usually learns to measure, cut, fit, and install various types of insulation. With experience, the trainee receives less supervision, more responsibility, and higher pay.

Trainees who receive informal instruction usually learn to specialize in only three or four types of installation. In contrast, trainees in 4-year "improvership" programs—much like the apprenticeship programs of other trades—receive in-depth instruction in almost all phases of insulation work. The in-depth instruction is provided by and paid for by a joint committee of local insulation contractors and the local union of insulation applicators. The committee determines the need for "improverships," screens and tests applicants, and ensures the availability of proper training programs. Programs consist of on-the-job training as well as classroom instruction, and trainees must pass practical and written tests to demonstrate a knowledge of the trade.

For entry jobs, insulation contractors prefer high school graduates who are in good physical condition and licensed to drive. High school courses in blueprint reading, shop math, and general construction provide a helpful background.

Applicants seeking 4-year "improvership" positions must have a high school diploma or its equivalent, and be at least 18 years old. Application can be made through local contractors, unions, or a joint committee.

Skilled insulation workers may advance to supervisor, shop superintendent, or insulation contract estimator, or may open an insulation contracting business.

Employment Outlook

Employment of insulation workers is expected to grow much faster than the average for all occupations through the mid-1980's. In addition to jobs from employment growth, several hundred openings will arise annually from the need to replace workers who transfer to other occupations, retire, or die.

More workers will be needed to install energy-saving insulation in new homes and businesses. Insulation for boilers and pipes in new factories and power plants also will stimulate employment growth. Moreover, old buildings that need extra insulation to save fuel will add to employment requirements.

Employment opportunities will be best in metropolitan areas, where most insulation contractors are located. In small towns much of the insulation work is done by persons in other trades, such as heating and air-conditioning installers, carpenters, and drywall installers, rather than by insulation workers.

Earnings and Working Conditions

Union insulation workers in metropolitan areas had estimated average wages of $9.75 an hour in 1976, slightly higher than the average for all union building trades workers. Apprentice wage rates start about half the rate paid to experienced workers and increase periodically.

According to limited information, experienced nonunion insulation workers earn from $200 to $300 per week. Nonunion trainees earn from $120 to $140 per week.

Insulation workers spend most of the workday on their feet, either standing, bending, stooping, or squatting. Sometimes they work from ladders or in tight spaces. Removing old insulation before installing new materials is often dusty and dirty. Tearing out asbestos—at one time the most common form of insulation but rarely used today—can be very dangerous to the workers' health unless they follow proper safeguards.

A large proportion of the workers in this trade are members of the International Association of Heat and Frost Insulators and Asbestos Workers.

Sources of Additional Information

For information about insulation workers' improvership programs or other work opportunities in this trade, contact a local insulation contractor; a local of the union mentioned above; or the nearest office of the State employment service or State apprenticeship agency.

IRONWORKERS

(D.O.T. 801.281, .381, .781, .884; 809.381, .781, .884; and 869.883)

Nature of the Work

Ironworkers erect steel framework and other metal parts in buildings, bridges, and other structures. They also rig heavy construction machinery (prepare it for moving) and deliver the machinery to new sites. In addition, ironworkers make alterations, such as installing steel stairs or adding window guards to buildings, and do repair work, such as replacing metal bridge parts.

Ironworkers comprise four related trades—structural ironworkers, riggers and machine movers, ornamental ironworkers, and reinforcing ironworkers. Many ironworkers are skilled in two of these trades or more.

Structural ironworkers (D.O.T. 809.381) erect, align, and fasten the steel framework of bridges, buildings, and other structures such as storage tanks. They also install floor decking and the doors and frames of bank vaults. Ironworkers follow blueprint specifications in erecting steel framework. They direct crane operators to hoist each steel part into proper position. Workers often push, pull, or pry beams and girders for last-second positioning before temporarily bolting them in place.

To permanently connect a steel member, ironworkers measure for correct alignment, using plumb bobs, levels, and measuring tapes. They remove temporary bolts if necessary, then jockey the steel beam or girder into position, using winches, hoists, and jacks. When the member is correctly aligned, workers bolt, rivet, or weld it to others for final fastening.

Riggers and machine movers (D.O.T. 869.883) set up and rig the hoisting equipment used to erect and dismantle structural steel frames. These skilled workers also move heavy construction machinery and equipment. They study the size, shape, and weight of the object to be moved, choose lines and cables to support its weight, and select points of attachment that will provide a safe and secure hold on the load. Next, they hook or bolt one or more cables to both the hoisting equipment and the item to be moved. Workers then direct the load into position by giving hand signals and other directions to the hoisting machine operator. In many instances, riggers build platforms or containers on the job to move unusually shaped materials and machines. This work requires a knowledge of hoisting equipment and lifting devices.

Ornamental ironworkers (D.O.T. 809.381) install metal stairways, catwalks, floor gratings, ladders, and window frames. They also install lampposts, fences, and decorative ironwork. In addition, they work with prefabricated aluminum, brass, and bronze items. Examples are recently developed ornamental building facades that are bolted or welded to a building.

Since other workers cut and shape most of the ornamental metal away from the construction site, ornamental ironworkers spend most of their time fitting, aligning, and assembling. On the job, workers make sure ornamental pieces fit correctly and hold firmly. Workers hacksaw oversized pieces to size and sometimes must drill holes. For secure connections, they rivet or weld the metals.

Reinforcing ironworkers (D.O.T. 801.884) set steel rods or bars in concrete forms to reinforce the concrete. They place the steel bars on suitable supports in the concrete form, then tie the bars together by wrapping and twisting wire around them. Workers follow supervisory instructions or blueprint specifications to make sure the reinforcing rods are positioned properly. Some concrete is reinforced with a coarse mesh made of welded wire. When using mesh, ironworkers measure the surface to be covered, cut and bend the mesh to the desired shape, and place it over the area to be reinforced. While a concrete crew pours the slab, ironworkers use hooked rods to position the wire mesh in the freshly poured mixture.

Places of Employment

About 71,000 structural and ornamental ironworkers were employed in 1976. Thousands of additional workers were employed as riggers, machine movers, and reinforcing ironworkers.

Most of these workers are employed by general contractors on large building projects, steel erection contractors, or ornamental iron contractors. Many are employed by large steel companies or their subsidiaries engaged in the construction of bridges, dams, and large buildings. Some work for government agencies, public utilities, or large industrial firms that do their own construction work. Very few are self-employed.

Ironworkers work in all parts of the country, but they are concentrated in metropolitan areas.

Training, Other Qualifications, and Advancement

Most training authorities recommend the completion of an apprenticeship as the best way to learn these trades. Some people, however, learn these trades informally by working as helpers to experienced ironworkers.

Apprenticeship programs, many of which are sponsored by local union-contractor agreements, usually consist of 3 years of on-the-job training and a minimum of 144 hours a year of classroom instruction in subjects such as drafting, blueprint reading, and mathematics applicable to layout work. Apprentices learn ornamental assembling, reinforcing, rigging, structural erecting, and welding.

Those who learn the trade informally usually start by moving materials—hauling rods and disposing of debris. Within a short period they can set reinforcing rods. Eventually, they do ornamental or structural work.

Applicants for apprenticeship or helper positions generally must be at least 18 years old and have a high school or vocational school education; courses in general mathematics and mechanical drawing provide a helpful background.

Since materials used in ironworking trades are heavy and bulky, above-average physical strength is

necessary. Agility and a good sense of balance also are required in order to work at great heights and on narrow footings.

Experienced ironworkers can advance to supervisory positions. A small number go into the ironworking business.

Employment Outlook

Employment of ironworkers is expected to increase much faster than the average for all occupations through the mid-1980's. Growth in construction activity will increase the demand for these workers. Besides jobs resulting from employment growth, many openings will result from the need to replace experienced ironworkers who transfer to other fields of work, retire, or die. The number of job openings may fluctuate from year to year, however, because construction activity is sensitive to changes in the economy.

Employment in all ironworking occupations is expected to increase over the long run. The growing use of structural steel in buildings will create a need for more structural ironworkers. Work opportunities for ornamental ironworkers will result from the growing popularity of ornamental panels for large buildings, and of metal frames to hold large glass installations. More riggers and machine movers will be needed to handle the increasing amount of heavy construction machinery. The growing demand for prestressed concrete will create additional job opportunities for reinforcing ironworkers.

Job openings for ironworkers usually are more abundant during the early spring when the weather warms up and the level of construction activity increases.

Earnings and Working Conditions

Union structural and reinforcing ironworkers in metropolitan areas earned estimated average wages of $10 an hour in 1976, or about twice the average wage of nonsupervisory and production workers in private industry, except farming. Apprentices start at 60 percent of the hourly rate paid to experienced workers. They receive increases as they gain experience. Annual earnings for these workers, however, are generally lower than hourly wages would indicate because the annual number of hours they work can be adversely affected by poor weather and fluctuations in construction activity.

Ironworkers often work at great heights, sometimes walking on mere 1 foot wide girders 20 floors or more above the ground. Although many of these workers risk injury from falls, safety devices such as nets, safety belts, and scaffolding have helped prevent accidents.

Ironwork can involve considerable travel because demand may be insufficient to keep local crews continually employed.

Many workers in these trades are members of the International Association of Bridge, Structural and Ornamental Iron Workers.

Sources of Additional Information

For more information on apprenticeships or other work opportunities, contact local general contractors; a local of the union mentioned above; a local joint union-management apprenticeship committee; or the nearest office of the State employment service or apprenticeship agency.

For general information about ironworkers, contact:

Associated General Contractors of America, Inc., 1957 E St. NW., Washington, D.C. 20006.

LATHERS

(D.O.T. 842.781)

Nature of the Work

What makes cement cling to a ceiling? Lath does. If properly installed, lath creates a firm support to which wet cement, plaster, or stucco will hold fast to form ceilings and walls. The one who installs lath is called a lather.

Until the last century, lath was made exclusively of wood. Since then, metal and gypsum have replaced wood because of their versatility, strength, and fire proofing properties. Metal lath comes in different forms, but it is usually wire mesh. Gypsum lath comes in 1/2 inch thick sheets, ranging from 1 1/4 feet by 4 feet to 4 feet by 8 feet.

Each type of lath holds cement, plaster, or stucco in a particular way. For example, wet plaster penetrates openings in the lath and is held in place mechanically. When applied to gypsum lath, however, chemicals in the wet plaster react with other chemicals on the lath's surface, bonding the materials together.

Lathers use various methods of installation depending on the purpose of the job, the kind of building, and the type of lath specified. On walls and ceilings, lathers usually clip, nail, screw, staple, or wire-tie the lath directly to the building's framework. On cinder block or masonry walls, it is necessary to build a light metal or wood frame, called furring, onto the building's structure. Then they attach the lath to the furring. While installing lath, workers cut openings in it for electrical outlets and water pipes.

Lathers install a special wire mesh reinforcement on inside angles and corners or walls to prevent cracking. On outside or exposed corners, they attach a corner support that provides protection and strength.

Sometimes lathers install two layers of lath. For example, when stucco (a mixture of portland cement and sand) is to be applied over a wood framework, workers may install two layers of wire mesh, separated by a layer of felt, to serve as a base for the stucco.

In ornamental work or curved surface work, workers build a frame approximating the desired shape, and then attach the lath to the frame.

Lathers also install suspended ceilings. They wire-tie metal bands to rods or wires attached to the structure above. Installers run the metal bands horizontally across the room, crisscrossing them to form rectangular spaces. These spaces can serve to hold either ceiling panels or lath to which plaster is applied.

To do their work, lathers use drills, hammers, hacksaws, shears, wirecutters, hatchets, stapling machines, and power-actuated fastening devices.

Places of Employment

Most lathers—who numbered about 20,000 in 1976—work for lathing and plastering contractors on new residential, commercial, or industrial construction. They also work on modernization and alteration jobs. A relatively small number of lathers are employed outside the construction industry; for example, some make the lath backing for plaster display materials or scenery.

Training, Other Qualifications, and Advancement

Most training authorities recommend apprenticeship as the best way to learn lathing. However, many lathers, particularly in small communities, have acquired their skills informally by working as helpers, observing or being taught by experienced lathers.

Apprenticeship programs usually last a minimum of 2 years, and are usually sponsored by various local joint labor-management committees. All programs include on-the-job training; some also include classroom instruction. On the job, under the guidance of an experienced worker, apprentices learn to use the tools and materials of the trade. Initially, they work on simple tasks, such as nailing gypsum lath to wall partitions. After gaining experience, they advance to more complex jobs, such as installing wire mesh on curved surfaces. Classroom instruction includes applied mathematics, blueprint reading, sketching, estimating, basic welding, and safety.

Informal on-the-job training provides only the essential knowledge needed by trainees. They start with easy jobs such as carrying materials or holding lath in place while experienced workers secure it. Trainees soon learn to clip, nail, staple, and wire-tie the lath—first, to walls and later, to floors and ceilings.

Generally, applicants for apprentice or helper should be at least 16 years old, in good physical condition, and licensed to drive. Apprenticeship applicants are usually required to have a high school or vocational school education, or the equivalent. Courses in general mathematics and mechanical drawing can provide a helpful background. Aptitude tests often are given to determine manual dexterity and mechanical ability.

Some experienced lathers may become supervisors. Others may be able to start their own lath contracting business.

Employment Outlook

Employment of lathers is expected to grow about as fast as the average for all occupations through the mid-1980's. In addition to growth, additional jobs will result from the need to replace workers who retire, die, or leave the occupation for other reasons. Because the number of lathers is small, however, there will be relatively few job openings annually.

Growth in population and business activity are expected to stimulate the construction of new, and the renovation of old, buildings. As a result, more lathers will be needed to construct some of the more expensive new buildings, to renovate older buildings, and to fill the demand for lath and plaster on curved surfaces where drywall is not a practical substitute.

Earnings and Working Conditions

In 1976, union lathers in metropolitan areas had estimated average wages of $9.80 an hour. This is about twice the average wage of nonsupervisory and production workers in private industry, except farming. Apprentices start at about 50 percent of the wage rate paid to experienced lathers and receive more as they gain experience. However, yearly earnings for lathers and apprentices generally are lower than hourly rates would indicate because the annual number of hours that they work can be adversely affected by poor weather and fluctuations in construction activity.

Although lathers' work is not strenuous, it does require standing, squatting, or working overhead for long periods. Workers can be injured by falls from scaffolds or by cuts from various working materials or tools.

A large proportion of lathers are members of The Wood, Wire and Metal Lathers International Union.

Sources of Additional Information

For information about lathers' apprenticeships or other work opportunities in the trade, contact a local lathing or plastering contractor; a local of the Wood, Wire and Metal Lathers International Union; a local joint labor-management apprenticeship committee; or the nearest office of the State employment service or apprenticeship agency.

For general information about the work of lathers, contact:

International Association of Wall and Ceiling Contractors, Gypsum Drywall Contractors International, 1711 Connecticut Ave. NW., Washington, D.C. 20009.

National Lathing Industries Joint Apprenticeship Program, 815 16th St. NW., Washington, D.C. 20006.

OPERATING ENGINEERS (CONSTRUCTION MACHINERY OPERATORS)

(D.O.T. 850.782 through .884, 851.883, 852.883, 853.782 and .883, and 859.782 and .883)

Nature of the Work

Lifting a quarter-ton pane of glass by crane and positioning it into an 8-foot by 10-foot window opening 10 stories above the ground requires considerable skill. At the crane's controls is an operating engineer. Operating engineers also work the controls of bulldozers, trench excavators, paving machines, and many other types of construction machinery. Some workers know how to operate several kinds of machines; others, only a few. Because the skills and training required vary, operating engineers usually are classified by ei-

ther the type or the capacity of machines they operate.

Heavy machines are usually complex and difficult to operate. A large crane, for example, requires a high degree of skill. Operators must accurately judge distances and heights and push or pull a number of buttons, levers, and pedals in proper sequence while picking up and delivering materials. These controls rotate the crane, raise and lower its boom and loadline, or open and close attachments such as steel-toothed buckets for lifting dirt or clamps for lifting materials. At times, operators may not see either the pickup or delivery point and must follow the hand or flag signals of another worker.

Medium-sized equipment, on the other hand, usually requires less skill to operate. Bulldozer operators, for example, generally handle fewer controls than crane operators, and since the "dozer" operator works at ground level, estimating distances is less of a problem.

Operating a bulldozer is somewhat like driving a car and can be a relatively simple task. The huge "blade" attached to the front can be raised or lowered by pushing a button or by pushing or pulling a lever. To clear land, a bulldozer operator simply lowers the blade to the ground, shifts to forward gear and presses a pedal for power, causing the blade to scrape and level the ground. The operator will back up and repeat the process until the land is cleared.

Of the three weight classifications, light equipment such as an air compressor is the easiest to operate and, therefore, requires the least skill.

Before starting an air compressor (a diesel engine that takes in air and forces it through a narrow hose), the operator checks for tight hose connections and may manually pump air through the compressor to check for leaks. The operator also makes sure the compressor has fuel and water. The operator then starts the air compressor and allows it to build sufficient pressure to run special "air" tools. While the compressor is running, the operator periodically checks fuel, water, and pressure levels. At the end of the work day, the operator turns the compressor off and "bleeds-off" pressure in the air hose by opening an air pressure release valve. This allows for easy engine starting the next time it is to be used.

Operating engineer helpers, sometimes called "oilers," make sure the machines have gas and oil and are properly lubricated. Helpers also make minor repairs and adjustments. Experienced operators who are working alone also perform these tasks. Major repairs, however, usually are made by heavy-equipment mechanics.

Places of Employment

Approximately 600,000 operating engineers were employed in 1976. An estimated 290,000 operated excavating, grading, and road machinery; about 130,000 worked as bulldozer operators; and nearly 165,000 operated other construction machinery, including cranes, derricks, hoists, air compressors, trench-pipe layers, and dredges.

Most operating engineers work for contractors in highway, dam, airport, and other large-scale construction projects. Others work for utility companies, manufacturers, and other business firms that do their own construction work, as well as State and local highway and public works departments. Some operating engineers are employed in factories and mines to operate cranes, hoists, and other power-driven machinery. Less than one-tenth of all operating engineers are self-employed, a smaller proportion than in most building trades.

Operating engineers are employed in every section of the country, both in large cities and in small towns. Some work on highways and dams being built in remote locations.

Training, Other Qualifications, and Advancement

Although in years past, some operating engineers have learned their skills on the job without formal instruction, employers today prefer individuals with some formal training. Most training authorities recommend completion of a 3-year formal apprenticeship as the best way to become an operating engineer. Since apprentices learn to operate a variety of machines, they have better job op-

portunities. Less extensive training is available through special heavy-equipment training schools.

The apprenticeship program, usually sponsored through a union-management committee but also available in the Armed Forces, consists of at least 3 years of on-the-job training, as well as 144 hours a year of related classroom instruction.

Under the supervision of experienced operating engineers, apprentices work as oilers or as helpers. Initial tasks include cleaning, greasing, repairing, and starting machines. Within a year, apprentices usually are given the opportunity to perform simple machine operations, such as light lifts with a crane. In time, they receive less supervision and more responsibility. In the classroom, apprentices receive instruction in engine operation and repair, cable splicing, hydraulics, welding, and safety and first aid.

A number of private schools offer instruction in the operation of certain types of construction equipment. Persons considering enrolling in any school, whether public or private, that offers training for an operating engineer career should contact construction employers in their area to determine the school's performance in producing suitably trained condidates.

For apprentice jobs, employers prefer to hire high school or vocational school graduates who are at least 18 years old. Courses in driver education and automobile mechanics provide a helpful background. Experience in operating tractors and other farm machinery also is helpful.

Operating engineers who have leadership ability may become supervisors, but opportunities are few. Some operating engineers start their own excavating and grading business.

Employment Outlook

Job opportunities for operating engineers should be fairly plentiful over the long run. Employment in this occupation is expected to grow faster than the average for all occupations through the mid-1980's. Population and business growth will lead to the construction of more factories, mass

transit systems, office buildings, powerplants, and other structures, thereby increasing the demand for operating engineers. More operating engineers also will be needed in other areas, such as maintenance on highways and materials movement in factories and mines.

Besides the job openings created by employment growth, many openings will arise as experienced operating engineers retire, die, or leave the occupation for other reasons. Jobs should be easiest to find during spring and summer since construction picks up as the weather becomes warmer. However, because construction activity is sensitive to ups and downs in the economy, the number of job openings may fluctuate from year to year.

Earnings and Working Conditions

Wage rates for operating engineers vary according to the machine operated. According to 1976 estimates of union wages in metropolitan areas, hourly rates for crane operators averaged $9.90; for bulldozer operators, $9.55; and for air compressor operators, $8.65. These rates are about twice as much as the average for all nonsupervisory and production workers in private industry, except farming. Annual earnings, however, generally are lower than hourly wage rates would indicate because the annual number of hours worked can be adversely affected by poor weather and fluctuations in construction activity. Hourly wage rates for apprentices start at about 70 percent of the full rate paid to experienced workers and increase periodically.

Operating engineers work outdoors; consequently, they usually work steadily during the warmer months and experience slow periods during the colder months. Time also may be lost due to rain or snow. Operating some machines, particularly bulldozers and some types of scrapers, is physically tiring because the constant movement of the machine shakes or jolts operators and may subject them to high noise levels.

Many operating engineers are members of the International Union of Operating Engineers.

For further information about apprenticeships or work opportunities in this occupation, contact a local of the International Union of Operating Engineers; a local joint apprenticeship committee; or the nearest office of the State apprenticeship agency. In addition, the local office of the State employment service may provide information about apprenticeship and other programs that provide training opportunities.

For general information about the work of operating engineers, contact:

Associated General Contractors of America, Inc., 1957 E St. NW., Washington, D.C. 20006.

International Union of Operating Engineers 1125 17th St. NW., Washington, D.C. 20036.

PAINTERS AND PAPERHANGERS

(D.O.T. 840.381, .781 and .844, and 841.781)

Nature of the Work

Painting and paperhanging are separate, skilled trades although some people do both types of work. Painters apply paint varnish, and other finishes to decorate and protect building surfaces. Paperhangers cover walls and ceilings of rooms with decorative wallpaper, fabric, vinyl, or similar materials.

Painters sand or scrape away old paint from the surface to be painted so that paint will adhere properly. If the paint is difficult to remove, they loosen it with special materials or equipment before sanding. They also remove grease, fill nail holes and cracks, sandpaper rough spots, and brush off dust. When painting new surfaces, they cover them with a primer or sealer to make a suitable surface for the finish coat.

Painters must be skilled in handling brushes and other painting tools so that they can apply paint thoroughly, uniformly, and rapidly to any type of surface such as wood, concrete, metal, masonry, plastic, or drywall. They must be able to mix paints and match colors, using a knowledge of paint composition and color harmony. They also must know the characteristics of common types of paints and finishes from the standpoints of durability, suitability, and ease of handling and application.

Painters often use rollers or spray guns instead of brushes. Rollers are used on even surfaces such as walls and ceilings. Spray guns are used on surfaces that are difficult to paint with a brush, such as cinder block and metal fencing. Both rollers and spray guns permit faster painting.

Painters also erect scaffolding, including "swing stages" (scaffolds suspended by ropes or cables attached to roof hooks) and "bosun chairs" (a device somewhat like a child's swing), which they use when working on tall buildings and similar structures.

Generally, painters only paint. Paperhangers, however, both paint and hang wallpaper. As a result, paperhangers require more training and additional skills.

The first step in paperhanging is to prepare the surface to be covered. Paperhangers apply "sizing," a material that seals the surface and enables the paper to stick better. In redecorating, they may have to remove old paper by wetting it with water-soaked sponges or—if there are many layers—by steaming. Frequently, it is necessary for paperhangers to patch holes with plaster.

After carefully positioning the patterns to match at the ceiling and baseboard, paperhangers measure the area to be covered and cut a length of wallpaper from the roll. They then apply paste to the strip of paper, place it on the wall, and smooth it by hand or with a brush. They cut and fit edges at the ceiling and base, and smooth seams between strips with a roller or other special tool. They inspect the paper for air bubbles and other imperfections in the work. Air bubbles are removed by smoothing the paper strip toward the outer edges. When working with wall coverings other than paper, such as fabric or vinyl, paperhangers follow the same general procedure.

Places of Employment

About 410,000 painters and 15,000 paperhangers were employed in 1976. Many worked for contractors engaged in new construction, repair, alteration, or modernization work. Hotels, office buildings, shipyards, manufacturing firms, schools, and other organizations that own or manage extensive property holdings also employed maintenance painters.

A high proportion of workers in these trades are in business for themselves. About one-fourth of the painters and more than half of the paperhangers are self-employed. In comparison, only one-tenth of all building trades workers are self-employed.

Training, Other Qualifications, and Advancement

Opportunities to learn painting and paperhanging range from formal apprenticeship to informal, on-the-job instruction.

Most training authorities recommend the completion of a formal apprenticeship as the best way to become a painter or paperhanger. However, apprenticeship opportunities are very limited, and new workers generally begin as helpers to experienced painters. Very few informal training programs exist for paperhanger trainees because there are very few paperhangers and most work alone. As a result, a larger percentage of paperhangers than painters are trained through apprenticeship.

The apprenticeship for painters and paperhangers generally consists of 3 years of on-the-job training, in addition to 144 hours of related classroom instruction each year. Apprentices receive instruction in subjects such as color harmony; use of tools; surface preparation; cost estimating; paint mixing and matching; and safety. They also learn the relationship between painting and paperhanging and the work performed by the other building trades.

On-the-job instruction, unlike the apprenticeship, has neither a set period of training nor related classroom instruction. Under the direction of experienced painters, trainees carry supplies, erect scaffolds, and do other simple tasks while they learn about the different kinds of paint and painting equipment. Within a short time, trainees learn to prepare metal, wood, and other surfaces for painting; to mix paints; and to paint with a brush, roller, and sprayer. Near the end of their training, they learn decorating concepts, color coordination, and cost-estimating techniques.

Applicants for apprentice or helper jobs generally must be at least 16 years old and in good physical condition. A high school or vocational school education is preferred, although not essential. Courses in chemistry and general shop are useful. Applicants should have manual dexterity and a good color sense. They cannot be allergic to fumes from paint or other materials used in these trades.

Painters and paperhangers may advance to jobs as cost estimators for painting and decorating contractors. Some may become superintendents on large contract painting jobs, or they may establish their own painting and decorating businesses.

Employment Outlook

Employment of painters is expected to grow about as fast as the average for all occupations through the mid-1980's. Replacement needs will create more job openings than growth. Many new workers will be hired to replace experienced painters who retire, die, or leave their jobs for other reasons. The number of job openings, however, may vary greatly from year to year as well as within any given year because the demand for painters is sensitive to fluctuations in construction activity caused by economic and seasonal conditions.

Over the long run, population and business growth will create a rising demand for new houses and buildings and more workers will be needed to paint these structures. Additional workers also will be hired to repaint existing structures.

Employment of paperhangers is expected to increase much faster than the average for all occupations through the mid-1980's. The demand for these workers should be stimulated by the rising popularity of wallpaper and more durable wall coverings such as vinyl. Since this is a relatively small trade, however, job openings for paperhangers will be far less numerous than those for painters.

Earnings and Working Conditions

Based on a survey of metropolitan areas, union hourly rates for painters and paperhangers averaged about $9.25 in 1976. In comparison, the average rate for experienced union workers in all union building trades was $9.47 an hour while production workers in manufacturing as a whole averaged $4.87 an hour. Annual incomes for some painters, particularly those on outside jobs, may not be as high as hourly rates would indicate because some worktime is lost due to bad weather and occasional unemployment between jobs.

Hourly wage rates for apprentices usually start at 50 percent of the rate paid to experienced workers and increase periodically until the full rate of pay is reached at the completion of apprenticeship.

Painters and paperhangers must stand for long periods. Their jobs also require a considerable amount of climbing and bending. A painter must have strong arms because much of the work is done with arms raised overhead. Painters and paperhangers risk injury from slips or falls off ladders and scaffolds. However, the injury rate for employees of painting, paperhanging, and decorating contractors in the construction industry has been significantly lower than the average for contract construction as a whole.

A large proportion of painters and paperhangers are members of the International Brotherhood of Painters and Allied Trades. A few are members of other unions.

Sources of Additional Information

For details about painting and paperhanging apprenticeships or other work opportunities in these trades, contact local painting and decorating contractors; a local of the International Brotherhood of Painters and Allied Trades; a local joint union-management apprenticeship committee; or the nearest office of the State apprenticeship agency or State employment service.

For general information about the work of painters and paperhangers, contact:

International Brotherhood of Painters and Allied Trades, 1750 New York Ave. NW., Washington, D.C. 20006.

Painting and Decorating Contractors Association of America, 7223 Lee Hwy., Falls Church, Va. 22046.

National Joint Painting, Decorating, and Drywall Finishing Apprenticeship and Training Committee, 1709 New York Ave. NW., Suite 110, Washington, D.C. 20006.

PLASTERERS

(D.O.T. 842.381 and .781)

Nature of the Work

Plasterers finish interior walls and ceilings with plaster coatings that form fire-resistant and relatively soundproof surfaces; they apply durable cement plasters or stucco to exterior surfaces. Plasterers also cast ornamental designs in plaster.

To interior surfaces such as cinder block or gypsum lath, plasterers apply two coats of plaster. The first or "brown" coat is a heavy, brown mixture; the second or "finish" coat a thin, pasty plaster. However, when the foundation consists of metal lath (a supportive wire mesh), plasterers apply a preparatory coat to the lath.

When applying a preparatory or "scratch" coat, plasterers either spray or use a trowel (a flat, 4 inch by 10 inch, metal plate with a handle) and wavelike motions to spread a thick, gritty plaster into and over the metal lath. Before the plaster on the lath dries, workers scratch its already uneven surface with a rakelike tool, producing ridges so the "brown" coat will cling tightly.

For the first or "brown" coat—whether applied to a scratch coat, cinder block or gypsum lath—workers prepare a thick, but smooth plaster. Workers either spray or trowel this mixture onto the surface, pushing plaster into cracks and holes, and then smoothing the plaster to an even surface for finishing.

For the finish coat, plasterers prepare a thin plaster of very fine granules. They usually hand trowel this mixture very quickly onto the "brown" coat to produce a very thin, very smooth finish for a ceiling or wall.

Plasterers create decorative surfaces as well. For example, while the final coat is still moist, they press firmly against the surface with a brush and use a circular hand motion to create decorative swirls.

For exterior work, plasterers apply a scratch coat to wire lath in the same way that they plaster interior surfaces. To the exterior scratch coat, workers usually apply a gritty mixture of white cement and sand—called stucco—to produce a durable final coat. As an alternative, they plaster an extra heavy mixture over the scratch coat, then embed marble or gravel chips about halfway into the mixture, thus achieving a uniform, pebble like surface.

Plasterers sometimes do complex decorative and ornamental work. For example, they may mold intricate designs for the walls and ceilings of public buildings. To make these designs, plasterers mix a special plaster, pour it into a mold, and allow time for drying. When these are dry, workers remove the molded plaster and paste it to the desired surface. Plasterers who do this work must follow blueprints and other specifications furnished by architects.

Plasterers use many special tools. They hold the plaster mixture on a hawk (a light metal plate with a handle) and apply the wet mixture with a trowel. Smoothing and finishing are done with straightedges, beveledges, rods, floats, and other handtools. They also may use spray machines to apply plaster on both base and finish coats.

Places of Employment

Plasterers—who numbered about 24,000 in 1976—worked mostly on new construction and alteration work, particularly where special architectural and lighting effects were part of the job. Some plasterers repaired older buildings.

About 1 out of every 5 plasterers was self-employed.

Training, Other Qualifications, and Advancement

Most training authorities recommend completion of an apprenticeship as the best way to learn plastering. However, many people learn the trade by working as helpers or laborers, observing and being taught by experienced plasterers.

Apprenticeship programs, sponsored by local joint committees of contractors and unions, generally consist of 3 or 4 years of on-the-job training, in addition to at least 144 hours of annual classroom instruction in drafting, blueprint reading, and mathematics for layout work. Training is extensive. In class, apprentices start with a history of the trades and the industry. They also learn about the uses of plaster, costs, and many other concepts. On the job, they learn about lath bases, plaster mixes, methods of plastering, blueprint reading, and safety. Trainees follow the directions of and receive assistance from experienced plasterers.

Those who learn the trade informally as helpers gain only the basics—mixing and applying plasters. They usually start by carrying materials, setting up scaffolds, and mixing plaster. In a short time, they learn—through trial and error—to apply the scratch and brown coats. Learning to apply the finish coat takes considerably longer.

Applicants for apprentice or helper jobs generally must be at least 17 years old, in good physical condition, and have manual dexterity. Applicants who have a high school or vocational school education are preferred. Courses in general mathematics, mechanical drawing, and shop provide a useful background.

Plasterers may advance to supervisor, superintendent, or estimator for plastering contractors, or may become self-employed.

Employment Outlook

Little change is expected in the employment of plasterers through the mid-1980's. Nevertheless, a relatively small number of job openings will result from the need to replace experienced workers who retire, die, or transfer to other occupations.

The use of drywall materials in place of plaster has reduced the demand for plasterers in recent years. Nevertheless, plasterers still are needed for renovating older buildings that have plaster walls. Plaster is also used in some of the more expensive new buildings and on curved surfaces where drywall materials are not practical.

Earnings and Working Conditions

Union wage rates for plasterers in metropolitan areas averaged $9.48 an hour in 1976. This is about twice the average wage of nonsupervisory and production workers in private industry, except farming. Apprentice wage rates start at about half the rate paid to experienced plasterers and increase periodically. However, yearly earnings for plasterers and apprentices are generally lower than hourly rates would indicate because the annual number of hours that they work can be adversely affected by poor weather and fluctuations in construction activity.

Plastering requires considerable standing, stooping, and lifting. Plasterers work outdoors when applying stucco but most jobs are indoors.

A large proportion of plasterers are members of unions. They are represented by either the Operative Plasterers' and Cement Masons' International Association of the United States and Canada, or the Bricklayers, Masons and Plasterers' International Union of America.

Sources of Additional Information

For information about apprenticeships or other work opportunities, contact local plastering contractors; locals of the unions previously mentioned; a local joint union-management apprenticeship committee; or the nearest office of the State apprenticeship agency or the State employment service.

For general information about the work of plasterers, contact:

Bricklayers, Masons and Plasterers' International Union of America, 815 15th St. NW., Washington, D.C. 20005.

International Association of Wall and Ceiling Contractors/Gypsum Drywall Contractors International, 1711 Connecticut Ave., NW., Washington, D.C. 20009.

Operative Plasterers' and Cement Masons' International Association of the United States and Canada, 1125 17th St. NW., Washington, D.C. 20036.

PLUMBERS AND PIPEFITTERS

(D.O.T. 862.381)

Nature of the Work

Plumbers and pipefitters install pipe systems that carry water, steam, air, or other liquids or gases. They also alter and repair existing pipe systems and install plumbing fixtures, appliances, and heating and refrigeration units.

Although plumbing and pipefitting are sometimes considered a single trade, workers can specialize in either craft. Plumbers install water, gas, and waste disposal systems in homes, schools, factories, and other buildings. Pipefitters, on the other hand, install both high- and low-pressure pipes that carry hot water, steam, and other liquids and gases for use in industrial processes. For example, pipefitters install the complex pipe systems in oil refineries and chemical processing plants.

In each of these trades, installation techniques are similar because they all involve pipes, faucets, and valves, and problems encountered in one trade are similar to those in another.

Most pipes are copper, cast iron, or some other metal; others may be plastic, glass, or other non-metallic material. While some iron pipes come ready to install, other metal or plastic pipes may have to be "fitted" for the job. To fit pipes, workers may have to measure, bend, cut, and thread pipes, then bolt, braze, glue, screw, solder, or weld them together.

For exacting cuts, workers use a pipecutter. This tool has a long handle and two very sharp, 1- to 2-inch, steel-cutting wheels. Workers separate the wheels' edges, set the pipe between them, then tighten the wheels against the pipe. Tightening causes the sharp edges of the wheels to cut just into the pipe's surface on opposite sides. Using the handle for leverage, workers rotate the tool, causing the steel wheels to cut a groove in an exact line around the pipe. To cut entirely through the pipe, workers repeatedly tighten the wheels and rotate the tool around the pipe.

To prepare pipes that will be screwed together, workers sometimes must thread pipes. Threads are the grooves that spiral around the ends of pipes either on the outside or the inside.

Workers thread pipes with a pipethreader, a tool similar to the pipecutter. The pipethreader has one or more steel cutting dies (like rows of teeth) pitched at an angle. Workers fasten this tool to the end of a pipe. As they rotate the threader around the pipe, the dies' pitched angle and sharp edges cause the threader to move along as it shaves a groove around the pipe.

Workers also may bend pipes to fit around obstructions. To bend a pipe, workers fasten it securely within a bending device at or near the point of the intended bend, then apply pressure to one end of the pipe.

When the pipes and other pieces are ready, workers install and connect them according to the instructions on blueprints. They may have to drill holes in ceilings, floors, and walls, or hang steel supports from ceilings to position the pipes properly.

After setting the pipes in place, workers connect them. They insert the end of a pipe into the slightly larger end of a valve or properly shaped connector. Workers then may use wrenches to screw threaded pipes tightly together, or may glue, solder, or weld connections to prevent leaks. To connect large pipes, such as those in buildings or industrial plants, workers bolt together the raised collars on the ends of pipes and valves.

Some plumbers and pipefitters specialize in gas, steam, or sprinkler fitting. Gasfitters install and maintain the fittings and extensions that connect gasline mains with the lines leading to homes. Steamfitters assemble and install steam or hot water systems for commercial and industrial uses. Sprinkler fitters install and maintain the piping for fire extinguishing systems.

Plumbers and pipefitters use wrenches, reamers, drills, braces and bits, hammers, chisels, saws, and other handtools. Power machines often are used to cut, bend, and thread pipes. Hand-operated hydraulic pipe benders also are used. In addition, plumbers and pipefitters use gas or acetylene torches and welding, soldering, and brazing equipment.

Places of Employment

Most plumbers and pipefitters—who numbered about 385,000 in 1976—work for plumbing and pipefitting contractors engaged in new construction activity, and work mainly at the construction site. A substantial proportion of plumbers are self-employed or work for plumbing contractors doing repair, alteration, or modernization work. Some plumbers install and maintain pipe systems for government agencies and public utilities, and some work on the construction of ships and aircraft. Others do maintenance work in industrial and commercial buildings. Pipefitters, in particular, are employed as maintenance personnel in the petroleum, chemical, and food-processing industries where manufacturing operations include the processing of liquids and gases through pipes.

Training, Other Qualifications, and Advancement

Apprenticeship is the best way for plumbers or pipefitters to learn all aspects of these trades. A large number of people, however, learn plumbing and pipefitting by working for several years as helpers to experienced plumbers and pipefitters, and observing and receiving instruction from them.

Most apprenticeship programs for plumbers and pipefitters are sponsored through union-management agreements and usually consist of 5 years of on-the-job training, in addition to at least 216 hours annually of related classroom instruction. Subjects include drafting and blueprint reading, mathematics applicable to layout work, applied physics and chemistry, and local building codes and regulations.

On the job, helpers and apprentices begin with simple tasks such as carrying materials and cleaning up debris. In a short time they learn to measure and cut pipe, and later to bend, thread, and connect it. The most difficult form of connecting pipe is welding. This is taught toward the end of training. In the final phase of training, helpers and apprentices may learn to estimate costs.

Applicants for apprentice or helper jobs generally are required to be at least 16 years old and in good physical condition. A high school or vocational school education generally is recommended. Courses in chemistry, general mathematics, mechanical drawing, physics, and shop are helpful. Applicants may be given tests to determine whether they have the mechanical aptitude required in these trades. To obtain a plumber's or pipefitter's license, which some communities require, individuals must pass a special examination to demonstrate knowledge of the trade and of the local plumbing codes.

Some plumbers and pipefitters may become supervisors for plumbing and pipefitting contractors. Many go into business for themselves. As they expand their activities, they may employ other workers and become contractors. In most localities, contractors are required to obtain a master plumber's license.

Employment Outlook

Employment of plumbers and pipefitters is expected to grow faster than the average for all occupations through the mid-1980's. Thousands of job openings are expected because of employment growth and the need to replace plumbers and pipefitters who retire, die, or stop working for other reasons.

Employment is expected to grow mainly as a result of the anticipated increase in construction activity. Furthermore, plumbing will become more important in many types of construction. For example, a larger proportion of homes will have air-conditioning equipment, solar heating devices, and appliances such as washing machines and kitchen waste-disposal equipment. Chemical and petroleum refineries and coal gasification and nuclear powerplants, which use pipe extensively in their processing activities, are expected to expand, thus creating additional jobs for plumbers and pipefitters. Maintenance, repair, and modernization of existing plumbing or piping systems also will create employment opportunities.

Employment growth is expected to be fairly steady in the years ahead since plumbing and pipefitting are less sensitive to ups and downs in construction activity than are most other building trades.

Earnings and Working Conditions

According to a survey of metropolitan areas, union wage rates for plumbers and for pipefitters in 1976 averaged $10.40 an hour, or about twice the average wage for nonsupervisory and production workers in private industry, except farming. Apprentice wage rates start at 40 to 50 percent of the rate paid to experienced plumbers or pipefitters and increase as they gain experience. Annual earnings of workers in these fields are among the highest in the building trades because plumbing and pipefitting are affected less by bad weather and fluctuations in construction activity than are most other building trades.

Plumbing and pipefitting work is active and sometimes strenuous. These workers frequently must stand for long periods and occasionally work in cramped or uncomfortable positions. They risk the danger of falls from ladders, cuts from sharp tools, and burns from hot pipes. The injury rate for employees of plumbing, heating, and air-conditioning contractors in the construction industry has been about the same as the average for contract construction as a whole, but higher than the average for manufacturing.

Many plumbers and pipefitters are members of the United Association of Journeymen and Apprentices of the Plumbing and Pipe Fitting Industry of the United States and Canada. Some plumbers and pipefitters who are contractors are members of the National Association of Plumbing-Heating-Cooling Contractors.

Sources of Additional Information

For information about apprenticeships or work opportunities in these trades, contact local plumbing, heating, and air-conditioning contractors; a local of the union mentioned above; a local joint union-management apprenticehip committee; or the nearest office of the State employment service or State apprenticeship agency.

For general information about the work of plumbers, pipefitters, and sprinkler fitters, contact:

National Association of Plumbing-Heating-Cooling Contractors, 1016 20th St. NW., Washington, D.C. 20036.

National Automatic Sprinkler and Fire Control Association, P.O. Box 719, Mt. Kisco, N.Y. 10549.

United Association of Journeymen and Apprentices of the Plumbing and Pipe Fitting Industry of the United States and Canada, 901 Massachusetts Ave. NW., Washington, D.C. 20001.

ROOFERS

(D.O.T. 804.281, 843.844, and 866.381)

Nature of the Work

A leaky roof can cause damage to ceilings, walls, and furnishings. To keep out water, roofers apply materials such as asphalt, felt, shingles, slate, and tile to the roofs of buildings. These workers also waterproof walls and floors.

Roofers work with various kinds of roofing. To apply composition roofing, such as tar-and-gravel, roofers first measure, cut, and place strips of tarred felt over the entire surface. Next, they pour hot tar from a bucket and mop the tar over the felt and seams to seal them and make the surface watertight. They repeat the first two steps to build up the thickness of the tar. For the last coat, they use a broom like device to spread a hot mixture of thick tar over the surface. Finally, they add gravel, which sticks firmly to the tar.

When applying asphalt shingles, another type of composition roofing, roofers first lay, cut, and tack three-foot strips of roofing felt lengthwise over the entire roof. Then, starting from the bottom edge, they overlap and nail succeeding rows of asphalt shingles. Workers measure and cut the felt and shingles to fit around corners, pipes, and chimneys. Wherever two roof surfaces intersect, roofers cement or nail flashing (strips of felt or metal) over the joints to make them watertight.

Roofers also use metal, tile, and slate. They build metal roofs by soldering together metal sheets and nailing them over the wood sheathing. To install tile and slate roofs, they place a covering of felt over the wood sheathing, punch holes in the slate or tile, and nail it to the sheathing. Each row of slate or tile overlaps the preceding row. Finally, roofers cover exposed nailheads with cement to prevent rust and water leakage. They use handtools such as hammers, roofing knives, mops, and calking guns.

Some roofers also waterproof and dampproof masonry and concrete walls and floors. To prepare surfaces for waterproofing, they hammer and chisel away rough spots or remove them with a rubbing brick before brushing on a coat of liquid waterproofing compound. They also may paint or spray surfaces with a waterproofing material or nail waterproofing fabric to surfaces. When dampproofing, they usually spray a coating of tar or asphalt on interior or exterior surfaces.

Places of Employment

About 90,000 roofers were employed in 1976. Most worked for roofing contractors on construction or repair jobs. Some worked for businesses and government agencies that do their own construction and repair work. A few roofers were self-employed.

Training, Other Qualifications, and Advancement

A 3-year apprenticeship program—usually sponsored by a local union-management committee—generally provides the most thorough training for this trade. However, the majority of roofers acquire their skills informally by working as helpers for experienced roofers.

Helpers learn the trade on the job. They start by carrying equipment and material and by erecting scaffolds. Within 2 or 3 months they are taught to measure, cut, and fit roofing materials such as felt. Soon, they are able to lay asphalt shingles. After a year or so, they learn to lay and fit tile, and eventually slate. Whether or not helpers learn to dampproof or waterproof depends upon the employer.

The apprenticeship program generally consists of a minimum of 1,400 hours of on-the-job training annually, in addition to 144 hours of classroom instruction in subjects such as blueprint reading, mathematics, and safety. On-the-job training for apprentices is similar to that for helpers, except that the apprenticeship program is broader and more structured. For example, apprentices work on specific areas of roofing for specified periods. They also learn to dampproof and waterproof.

For those interested in becoming roofers, a high school education or its equivalent is helpful, as are courses in mechancial drawing, and basic mathematics. Good physical condition and a good sense of balance also are important assets. Applicants for apprenticeship programs must be at least 18 years old.

Roofers may advance to supervisor or to superintendent for a roofing contractor. Also, they may enter business for themselves and hire other roofers.

Employment Outlook

Employment of roofers is expected to increase faster than the average for all occupations through the mid-1980's. More roofers will be needed due to the longrun increase in construction activity. New construction and repairs on existing roofs will provide most of the work opportunities. Dampproofing and waterproofing, however, will provide an increasing proportion of roofers' work. Besides the job openings resulting from employment growth, some openings will arise from the need to replace experienced roofers who retire, die, or stop working for other reasons. Because construction activity fluctuates, however, job openings may be plentiful in some years, scarce in others. Jobs should be easiest to find during spring and summer since roofing work picks up as the weather becomes warmer.

Earnings and Working Conditions

In 1976, union roofers in metropolitan areas had estimated average wages of $9.30 an hour, or about twice the average hourly rate paid to nonsupervisory or production workers in private industry, except farming. Yearly earnings for roofers and apprentices, however, generally are lower than hourly rates would indicate because the annual number of hours they work can be adversely affected by poor weather and fluctuations in construction activity.

Apprentices usually start at 65 percent of the skilled roofer's pay rate and receive increases periodically.

Roofers' work is sometimes strenuous. It involves a lot of standing, as well as climbing, bending, and squatting. Roofers risk injuries from slips or falls from scaffolds or roofs, and may have to be outdoors in all types of weather, particularly when making repairs. The work may be especially hot during the summer months.

Many roofers are members of the United Slate, Tile and Composition Roofers, Damp and Waterproof Workers Association.

Sources of Additional Information

For information about roofing apprenticeships or work opportunities in this trade, contact local roofing contractors; a local of the union previously mentioned; a local joint union-management apprenticeship committee; or the nearest office of the State employment service or State apprenticeship agency.

For information about the work of roofers, contact:

National Roofing Contractors Association; 1515 N. Harlem Ave., Oak Park, Ill. 60302.

SHEET-METAL WORKERS

(D.O.T. 804.281 and .884)

Nature of the Work

Sheet-metal workers fabricate and install sheet-metal ducts for air-conditioning, heating, and ventilating systems; flat metal for kitchen walls and counters; and stamped metal for roofing and siding. Some workers specialize in either shopwork or on-site installation; others do both.

Sheet-metal workers fabricate much of the metal at the shop. Working from blueprint specifications, they measure, cut, bend, shape, and fasten most of the pieces that will be used on the job. Tapes are used for measuring; hand shears, hack saws, and power saws for cutting; and specially designed, heavy steel presses for cutting, bending, and shaping. Once the metal is measured and cut, workers then bolt, cement, rivet, solder, or weld the seams and joints together to form ducts, pipes, tubes, and other items.

At the construction site, sheet-metal workers usually just assemble and install pieces fabricated at the shop. Sometimes, however, workers make parts by hand at the worksite, using hammers, shears, and drills.

Workers install ducts, pipes, and tubes by joining them end to end and hanging them with metal braces secured to a ceiling or a wall. To hold the pieces together, workers sometimes bolt, glue, or solder the connections.

Molded and pressed sheet-metals, such as roofing and siding, usually are measured and cut on the job. After securing the first panel in place, workers interlock and fasten the grooved edge of the next panel into the grooved edge of the first. They nail the free edge of the panel to the structure. This two-step process is repeated for each additional panel. Finally, at joints, along corners, and around windows and doors, workers fasten machine-made molding for a neat, finished effect.

Places of Employment

Sheet-metal workers in the construction industry—who numbered about 65,000 in 1976—are employed mainly by contractors who specialize in heating, refrigeration, and air-conditioning equipment, and by general contractors engaged in residential, industrial, and commercial building. Additional sheet-metal workers are employed by government agencies or businesses that do their own construction and alteration work. Very few are self-employed.

Sheet-metal workers are employed throughout the country, but jobs are concentrated in metropolitan areas.

Training, Other Qualifications, and Advancement

Many sheet-metal workers have acquired their skills by working as helpers, observing and being taught by experienced workers. The majority, however, have learned through apprenticeship, which provides the most thorough training.

The apprenticeship program usually consists of 4 years of on-the-job training, in addition to related classroom instruction. On the job, apprentices learn to use the tools, machines, equipment, and materials of the trade. In the first 2 years, they learn to measure, cut, bend, fabricate, and install sheet-metal. They begin with duct work and gradually advance to fabricating decorative pieces. Toward the end of their training, they learn to use materials such as plastics and acoustical tile, which may be substituted for metal on some jobs. Classroom instruction covers subjects such as drafting, blueprint reading, mathematics, and first-aid. Safety is stressed throughout the program. In addition, apprentices learn the relationship between sheet-metal work and other construction work.

Workers who pick up the trade informally usually begin by carrying metal and cleaning up debris in a metal shop. While there, they learn about materials and their costs as well as tools and their uses. Then, as employers permit, helpers learn to set switches and operate levers on machines that bend or cut metal. In time, helpers leave the shop and go out on the job to learn installation.

Applicants for jobs as apprentices or helpers should be in good physical condition and have mechanical aptitude. Apprentices should have a high school or vocational school education or equivalent education. Courses in mathematics, mechanical drawing, and shop provide a helpful background for learning the trade.

Sheet-metal workers in construction may advance to supervisory jobs or may go into the contracting business.

Employment Outlook

Employment of sheet-metal workers in construction is expected to increase about as fast as the average for all occupations through the mid-1980's. In addition to jobs from employment growth, many openings will arise as experienced workers retire, die, or leave work for other reasons.

As population and business grow, more sheet-metal workers will be needed to install air-conditioning and heating duct work and other sheet-metal products in new houses, stores, offices, and other buildings. The demand for air-conditioning systems in older buildings also will boost employment growth.

Athough employment is expected to increase over the long run; job openings may fluctuate from year to year due to ups and downs in construction activity. When construction activity is depressed, jobs for sheet-metal workers may be available in other industries.

Earnings and Working Conditions

Union sheet-metal workers in metropolitan areas had estimated average wages of $10.10 an hour in 1976. This is about twice the average for production and nonsupervisory workers in private industry, except farming. Sheet-metal apprentices generally start at 45 percent of the rate paid to experienced workers and receive periodic pay raises.

Many sheet-metal workers spend considerable time at the construction site, working either indoors or outdoors. Others work primarily in shops doing fabricating and layout work.

When installing gutters and skylights, they work high above ground. When installing ventilation and air-conditioning systems, they may work in awkward and cramped positions. Sheet-metal workers risk cuts and burns from materials and tools. The injury rate for workers in this trade is higher than the average for all construction workers.

A large proportion of sheet-metal workers are members of the Sheet Metal Workers' International Association.

Sources of Additional Information

For more information about apprenticeships or other work opportunities, contact local sheet-metal contractors or heating, refrigeration, or air-conditioning contractors; a local of the union mentioned above; a local joint union-management apprenticeship committee; or the nearest office of the State employment service or apprenticeship agency.

For general information about sheet-metal workers, contact:

Sheet Metal and Air Conditioning Contractors' National Association, Inc., 8224 Old Courthouse Rd., Tyson's Corner, Vienna, Va. 22180.

TILESETTERS

(D.O.T. 861.781)

Nature of the Work

In ancient Egypt and Rome, tile was used for the design and construction of mosaics—an art form using small, decorative ceramic squares. Today, in a fashion similar to that of the ancient artists, tilesetters apply tile to floors, walls, and ceilings.

To set tile, which ranges in size from 1/2 inch to 6 inches square, workers in this trade use either cement or mastic (a very sticky paste). When using cement, tilesetters first must tack a support of screenlike mesh to the floor, wall, or ceiling. They mix a coarse cement, spread it onto the screen with a trowel, and, with a rakelike device, scratch the surface of the wet cement. After the cement has dried workers trowel on a richer coat of cement, working it back and forth in sweeping motions until it is smooth and even.

When using mastic to set tile, tilesetters need a flat, solid surface such as drywall or concrete. Workers spread the mastic with a tooth-edged metal trowel to create tiny ridges in the mastic. When the tile is set onto the ridges, it creates a suction that helps hold the tile.

Since tile is of various çolors, shapes, and sizes, workers sometimes prearrange the tiles on a dry floor according to a specified design. This allows workers to examine the pattern and make any necessary changes.

Whether or not the tiles are prearranged, tilesetters place each tile onto the cement or mastic. Some tiles are cut with either a machine saw or a special cutting tool so they can fit into corners and around pipes, tubs, and wash basins. Once the tile is placed, tilesetters gently tap the surface of the tiles with a small block of wood so that all the tiles rest evenly and flatly.

When the cement or the mastic has "set" behind the tile, tilesetters use a rubber trowel to cover the tile and the joints with grout—a very fine cement mixture. They then scrape the surface with a rubber-edged device called a squeegee. This action safely removes grout from the face of the tiles, forces it into the joints, and removes any excess. Before the grout dries, workers wash the surface with water.

Places of Employment

Tilesetters—who numbered about 36,000 in 1976—are employed mainly in nonresidential construction projects, such as schools, hospitals, and public and commercial buildings. A significant proportion of tilesetters—about one out of five—are self-employed.

Tilesetters are employed throughout the country but are found largely in the more populated urban areas.

Training, Other Qualifications, and Advancement

Most training authorities recommend the completion of a 3-year apprenticeship program as the best way to learn tilesetting. A substantial proportion of tilesetters, however, acquire their skills informally by working as helpers and being taught by experienced workers.

The apprenticeship program generally consists of on-the-job training and related classroom instruction in subjects such as blueprint reading, layout work, and basic mathematics.

Apprentices begin by learning the names of tools and how to use them. Within a short time they are taught to mix and apply cement, then to apply mastic. Later, they learn to cut tile and install it.

Those who learn informally generally receive less thorough training. They start by carrying supplies, cleaning work areas, and washing off the finished tile. Depending on the employer, a helper may learn to spread cement or mastic. Eventually, a helper is taught to cut and set tile.

When hiring apprentices or helpers, employers usually prefer high school or vocational school graduates who have had courses in general mathematics, mechanical drawing, and shop. Good physical condition, manual dexterity, and a good sense of color harmony also are important assets.

Skilled tilesetters may become supervisors or start their own contracting businesses.

Employment Outlook

Employment of tilesetters is expected to increase about as fast as the average for all occupations through the mid-1980's. While employment growth will provide some new job opportunities, most will result from the need to replace tilesetters who retire, die, or leave the occupation for other reasons. Because tilesetters is a small occupation, however, there will be relatively few job openings annually.

Population and business growth is expected to cause an increase in the construction of houses and other buildings, thus increasing the demand for tilesetters. The trend toward two tile bathrooms or more in houses and apartments also will spur employment in this trade.

Earnings and Working Conditions

According to 1976 estimates of union wages in metropolitan areas, hourly rates for tilesetters averaged $9.35, or about twice the hourly rate paid to nonsupervisory and production workers in private industry, except farming. Hourly wage rates for apprentices start at about 50 to 60 percent of the rate paid to union workers and increase periodically.

Since tilesetters work mostly indoors, the annual number of hours they work generally is higher than some of the other contruction crafts. This difference may be reflected in added annual earnings.

The principal unions organizing these workers are the International Union of Bricklayers and Allied Craftsmen; and the International Association of Marble, Slate and Stone Polishers, Rubbers and Sawyers, Tile and Marble Setters' Helpers and Marble Mosaic and Terrazzo Workers' Helpers.

Sources of Additional Information

For details about apprenticeship or other work opportunities in this trade, contact local tile setting contractors; locals of the unions previously mentioned; or the nearest office of the State employment service or State apprenticeship agency.

For general information about the work of tilesetters, contact:

International Union of Bricklayers and Allied Craftsmen, International Masonry Apprenticeship Trust, 815 15th St. NW., Washington, D.C. 20005.

Tile Contractors' Association of America, Inc., 112 North Alfred St., Alexandria, Va. 22314.

OCCUPATIONS IN TRANSPORTATION ACTIVITIES

RAILROAD OCCUPATIONS

People, food, and industrial materials all move along the 200,000 miles of railroad lines that crisscross the Nation. In 1976, the railroads provided jobs for about 531,000 people. Railroad jobs are found in all States except Hawaii, and in communities of all sizes.

Large numbers of railroad workers are employed at terminal points where the railroads maintain control offices, freight yards, and maintenance and repair shops. Chicago, the hub of the Nation's railroad system, has more railroad workers than any other area, but many also are employed in or near New York, Los Angeles, Philadelphia, Minneapolis, Pittsburgh, and Detroit.

Railroad workers can be divided into four main groups: Operating employees; station and office workers; equipment maintenance workers; and property maintenance workers.

Operating employees make up almost one-third of all railroad work-ers. This group includes locomotive engineers, conductors, and brake operators. Whether on the road or at terminals and railroad yards, they work together as traincrews. Some other employees in this group are hostlers, who prepare locomotives for the traincrews, and switchtenders, who throw track switches within railroad yards.

One-fourth of all railroad workers are *station and office employees*, who direct train movements and handle the railroads' business affairs. Professionals such as managers, accountants, statisticians, and systems analysts do administrative and planning work, while clerks handle business transactions, keep records, and prepare statistics. Agents manage the business affairs of the railroad stations. Telegraphers and telephoners pass on instructions to traincrews and help agents with clerical work.

More than one-fifth of all railroad employees are *equipment maintenance workers*, who service and re-pair locomotives and cars. This group includes car repairers, machinists, electrical workers, sheet-metal workers, boilermakers, and blacksmiths.

Property maintenance workers, who make up about one-sixth of all railroad employees, build and repair tracks, tunnels, signal equipment, and other railroad property. Track-workers repair tracks and roadbeds. Bridge and building workers construct and repair bridges, tunnels, and other structures along the right-of-way. Signal workers install and service the railroads' vast network of signals, including highway-crossing protection devices.

Discussions of the work, training, outlook, and earnings for some major occupations in railroads are presented in the statements that follow. Information on employment also is available in the statement on occupations in the railroad industry elsewhere in the *Handbook*. Details about specific jobs may be obtained from local railroad offices. General information on the industry is available from:

Association of American Railroads, American Railroads Building, 1920 L St. NW., Washington, D.C. 20036.

BRAKE OPERATORS

(D.O.T. 910.364 and .884)

Nature of the Work

Brake operators play a pivotal role in making locomotives and cars into trains. Working with engineers and under the direction of conductors, they do the physical work involved in adding and removing cars at railroad stations and assembling and disassembling trains in railroad yards.

All passenger and most freight traincrews include two road brake operators—one in the locomotive with the engineer and another in the caboose with the conductor. A few small freight trains need only one in the locomotive. Before departure, road brake operators inspect the train to make sure that all couplers

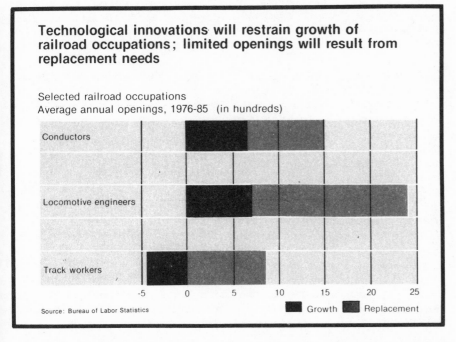

Technological innovations will restrain growth of railroad occupations; limited openings will result from replacement needs

Selected railroad occupations
Average annual openings, 1976-85 (in hundreds)

	-5	0	5	10	15	20	25
Conductors							
Locomotive engineers							
Track workers							

Source: Bureau of Labor Statistics ■ Growth ■ Replacement

and airhoses are fastened, that hand-brakes on all the cars are released, and that the airbrakes are functioning correctly. While underway they regularly look for smoke, sparks, and other signs of sticking brakes, over-heated axle bearings, and other faulty equipment. They may make minor repairs to airhoses and cou-plers. In case of unexpected stops, brake operators set out signals to protect both ends of the train.

When freight trains approach an industrial site, the brake operator in the locomotive jumps off the moving train and runs ahead to switch the train to the proper track. The brake operators uncouple cars that are to be delivered and couple those that are to be picked up.

On passenger trains, brake opera-tors regulate car lighting and temper-ature, and help the conductor collect tickets and assist passengers.

Yard brake operators (also known as yard couplers or helpers) help as-semble and disassemble trains in rail-road yards, according to instructions from yard conductors. They use hand signals or two-way radios to signal engineers where to move cars. Rail-road cars generally are not pushed very far by the engine, but instead are allowed to roll to their destina-tion in the yard. Brake operators un-couple the cars and throw track switches to route them to certain tracks if they are to be unloaded, or to an outgoing train if their final des-tination is further down the line. They may ride a car, operating the handbrake to regulate its speed.

Training, Other Qualifications, and Advancement

On most railroads, beginning brake operators make several trips with conductors and experienced op-erators to become familiar with the job. Their names are then put on the "extra board" and they are given as-signments to substitute for workers who are absent for vacations, illness, or other reasons. On some railroads, however, new brake operators first are given several days of training, in-cluding instruction on signaling, cou-pling and uncoupling cars, throwing

switches, and boarding moving equipment. Following this training period, these brake operators accom-pany experienced crews for several trips before being placed on the "ex-tra board." It usually takes several years before brake operators acquire enough seniority to get regular as-signments.

Employers prefer applicants who are high school graduates or the equivalent. Good eyesight and hear-ing are essential. Mechanical apti-tude is helpful. Physical stamina is necessary to board moving trains, throw switches, and operate hand-brakes. Most employers require that applicants pass physical examina-tions.

With sufficient seniority, brake op-erators may become conductors. These jobs are always filled by pro-moting experienced brake operators who have qualified by passing written and oral tests on signals, brake sys-tems, timetables, operating rules, and other subjects. Some companies re-quire that these tests be passed with-in the first few years of the brake operator's employment. Since pro-motions on almost all railroads are controlled by seniority rules, brake operators usually wait at least 10 years before becoming conductors. Advancement is limited by the num-ber of conductor jobs, and there are many more brake operators than conductors. A few brake operators in freight service move to passenger service, usually considered more de-sirable because it is less strenuous.

Employment Outlook

Employment of brake operators—who numbered nearly 65,000 in 1976—is not expected to change through the mid-1980's. Employ-ment is expected to increase in the short run, however, as an improving economy leads to more freight traf-fic. Although many of the available openings will be taken by experi-enced brake operators now on fur-lough, some jobs will be available for new workers. Openings also will de-velop as experienced brake operators retire, die, advance to jobs as con-ductors, or transfer to other work. Even though total employment of

brake operators is not expected to change in the long run, the number of those in road service will increase since more trains will be needed to haul the additional freight volume created by growth in population and industry. Employment gains will be moderated, however, by innovations that make it possible to move freight more efficiently. For example, trains will be able to carry more freight as the railroads continue to replace older freight cars with larger, better designed ones.

The number of yard brake opera-tors is expected to decrease, primar-ily due to the installation of automat-ic classification systems in more yards. In an automatic classification yard, cars are braked and routed by electronic controls. Fewer brake op-erators are needed in these yards, mainly to connect airhoses, uncouple cars, and retrieve misrouted ones. Yard employment also will be affect-ed by the new freight cars, which take as much time to route as older ones but carry more freight.

Earnings and Working Conditions

In 1976, brake operators had aver-age monthly earnings of $1,206 in yard service, $1,523 in freight ser-vice, and $1,637 in passenger ser-vice. These earnings were about twice as much as the average for all nonsupervisory workers in private in-dustry, except farming.

Yard brake operators usually work a scheduled 40-hour week and re-ceive premium pay for overtime. Road brake operators are paid ac-cording to miles traveled or hours worked, whichever is greater. Brake operators often work nights, week-ends, and holidays.

Most freight trains are unsched-uled so few road brake operators have scheduled assignments. Instead, their names are placed on a list and when their turn comes they are as-signed the next train, usually on short notice and often at odd hours. Since freight and passenger brake opera-tors often work on trains that operate between terminals that are hundreds of miles apart, they may spend sever-al nights a week away from home. Brake operators assigned to extra board work have less steady work, more irregular hours, and lower earnings than those with regular jobs.

Most brake operators are members of the United Transportation Union.

SIGNAL DEPARTMENT WORKERS

(D.O.T. 822.281 and .884)

Nature of the Work

Railroad signal workers install, repair, and maintain the train control, communication, and signaling systems that direct train movement and assure safety. These include gate crossings and signal lights, as well as systems that operate signals and throw switches by remote control. The work usually consists of either general maintenance of the signal systems or installation and major repair.

Signal installers work in crews, usually consisting of at least five workers. They install new equipment and make major repairs. They do mostly construction work that includes digging holes and ditches, hoisting poles, and mixing and pouring concrete to make foundations. They also assemble the control and communications devices, make the electrical connections, and perform the extensive testing that is required to assure that new signal systems work properly.

Individual *signal maintainers* are assigned a section of track and are responsible for keeping gate crossings, signals, and other control devices within their section in good operating condition. They periodically inspect and repair or replace wires, lights, and switches. They may have to climb poles to reach signals and sometimes work near high voltage wires. Signal maintainers and installers must have a thorough knowledge of electricity and electronics.

Training, Other Qualifications, and Advancement

New employees usually are as-

signed as helpers to installation crews. After a 60- to 90-day probationary period, helpers are eligible to advance to assistants. Some railroads hire applicants directly as assistants. After 2 to 4 years, which may include classroom instruction, qualified assistants are promoted to signal installer or maintainer. Assistants usually advance to signal installer, though, since openings in the more desirable maintenance positions usually are filled by senior signal installers. These promotions and assignments are made on the basis of seniority, provided ability is sufficient.

When hiring helpers or assistants, railroads prefer applicants who are high school or vocational school graduates. Courses in blueprint reading, electricity, and electronics provide a helpful background. Applicants also should be capable of doing heavy work.

Both signal installers and maintainers may be promoted to signal inspector or technician. Technicians assist installers with complicated systems while inspectors check the work of both installers and maintainers. Some installers and maintainers become gang supervisors and a few advance to higher supervisory positions.

Employment Outlook

Employment of signal department workers—who numbered about 11,500 in 1976—is not expected to change significantly through the mid-1980's. Nevertheless, some job openings for new workers will arise as experienced workers retire, die, or transfer to other fields.

Signal workers will continue to be needed to repair the existing stock of equipment as well as install and maintain the new signal and train control systems that are planned for the future. Employment is not expected to grow, however, since many new signal systems, which have fewer moving parts, require less maintenance. Employment also will be affected as the railroads continue to close some sections of track that are unprofitable or are made unnecessary as the installation of improved

train control systems enables railroads to use less track.

Earnings and Working Conditions

In 1976, signal installers and maintainers averaged $6.77 an hour, about two-fifths more than the average for all nonsupervisory workers in private industry, except farming. Assistants averaged $5.85 an hour and helpers $5.74 an hour. Most signal workers have a 40-hour week and receive premium pay for overtime.

Since they work over large sections of track, installers usually live away from home during the workweek, frequently in camp cars provided by the company. Maintainers usually live at home and service signals over a limited stretch of track. However, they must make repairs regardless of weather conditions or time of day.

Most signal installers and maintainers are members of the Brotherhood of Railroad Signalmen.

TRACK WORKERS

(D.O.T. 182.168, 859.883, 869.887, and 910.782)

Nature of the Work

A major factor limiting train speed is the quality of the track. Many locomotives are capable of pulling hundreds of cars at speeds as fast as 75 miles an hour, but train speed must drop sharply on poorly maintained track to avoid accidents. Preventing track deterioration and the accompanying loss in railroad efficiency is the job of track workers, who service, repair, and replace railroad track and roadway.

Most track workers are members of large, heavily mechanized traveling crews which do scheduled preventive maintenance and major repair work over hundreds of miles of track. Many of these workers operate heavy machinery, such as bulldozers, cranes, and machines which they use to lay rail, replace ties, or clean ballast. Others use power tools to drive and pull spikes, cut rails, and tighten bolts. Handtools, such as picks and shovels, are used less frequently.

Section crews, which are smaller and less mechanized than the traveling ones, do less extensive repairs. They are assigned a smaller section of track to keep in condition between the major overhauls of the traveling crews. Section workers regularly inspect the track and roadway, and repair or replace malfunctioning switches, weak ties, cracked rails, washouts, and other defects.

Training, Other Qualifications, and Advancement

Most track workers learn their skills through on-the-job training that lasts about 2 years. Machine-operating jobs are assigned to qualified workers by seniority.

Railroads prefer applicants who can read, write, and do heavy work. Applicants may be required to pass physical examinations.

Some track workers who have the necessary seniority and other qualifications may advance to gang or section supervisor, then to positions such as track supervisor.

Employment Outlook

Employment of track workers—who numbered about 56,200 in 1976—is not expected to change through the mid-1980's. But employment is expected to increase in the short run as funds for track renovation become available through government action.

Railroads are expected to upgrade much of the right-of-way in an effort to increase efficiency, and the speed and extent of this renovation will determine the need for additional workers. Over the long run, however, increased productivity of track workers—as machines do more of the work—will moderate employment needs. In addition, railroads will continue to close some sections of track that are unprofitable or are made unnecessary as the installation of improved train control systems enables railroads to use less track. Despite this lack of growth, new track workers will be needed each year to replace experienced workers who retire, die, or transfer to other occupations. Most job openings will be in traveling crews.

Earnings and Working Conditions

In 1976, track workers averaged $5.89 an hour, slightly more than the average for all nonsupervisory workers in private industry, except farming. Equipment operators and helpers averaged $6.16 and crew supervisors averaged $6.54 an hour. A 40-hour workweek is standard, and premium rates are paid for overtime. Some track workers, especially those working on traveling crews on the northern railroads, are furloughed during the winter months.

Track workers on traveling crews may have to commute long distances to reach the worksite. Many, however, live in camp cars or trailers provided by the railroads. Workers on section crews sometimes have to perform emergency repairs at night during bad weather conditions. Track workers have strenuous and active jobs. The tools they use are fairly heavy and they often work in bent and stooped positions.

Most track workers are members of the Brotherhood of Maintenance of Way Employees.

DRIVING OCCUPATIONS

Nearly 2.5 million truck, bus, and taxi drivers moved passengers and goods over highways and city streets in 1976. Some drivers are behind the wheel practically all their working time. Others also spend part of their time loading and unloading goods, making pickups and deliveries, and collecting money. Route drivers do some selling as well as driving.

Employment of long-distance and local truckdrivers is expected to expand through the mid-1980's as more and more freight is moved by trucks. Employment of busdrivers also is expected to increase as intercity passenger travel continues to grow and as cities expand their transit systems. Employment in other driving occupations is not expected to change much, but many new employees will be hired to replace those who retire, die, or stop working for other reasons.

Driving jobs offer excellent opportunities for persons who are not planning to attend college. The pay for most drivers is relatively high, and working conditions are fairly good. Many persons also will enjoy the freedom from close supervision and the frequent contact with people that are characteristic of most driving jobs.

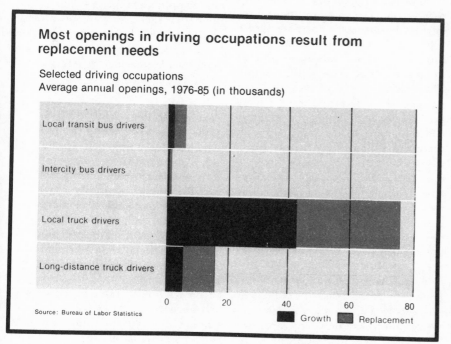

Most openings in driving occupations result from replacement needs

Selected driving occupations
Average annual openings, 1976-85 (in thousands)

Local transit bus drivers
Intercity bus drivers
Local truck drivers
Long-distance truck drivers

0   20   40   60   80

Growth   Replacement

Source: Bureau of Labor Statistics

INTERCITY BUSDRIVERS

(D.O.T. 913.363 and 913.463)

Nature of the Work

In many smaller towns and cities, buses provide the only public transportation to other communities. In large cities, they are an alternative to railroad and airline transportation and, in many cases, provide more frequent service.

When busdrivers report to the terminal or garage, they are assigned buses and pick up tickets, report blanks, and other items needed for their trips. They inspect their buses carefully to make sure the brakes, steering mechanism, windshield wipers, lights, and mirrors work properly. They also check the fuel, oil, water, and tires, and make certain that the buses are carrying safety equipment, such as fire extinguishers, first-aid kits, and emergency reflectors.

Drivers move the buses to loading platforms where they take on passengers. They collect fares—tickets usually—as passengers board the buses and may use the buses' public address system to announce the destination, route, time of arrival, and other information concerning the trips.

Drivers' routes vary. On local runs, drivers stop at many small towns only a few miles apart. On express runs, however, they may stop only at major cities after several hours of driving. Although drivers must always be alert in preventing accidents, they must be especially careful in fast-moving highway traffic. They must operate the bus at safe speeds while trying to keep schedules, and often must cope with adverse road conditions.

Before arriving at major terminals, they announce the stop and the scheduled departure time. At some small stations, drivers stop only if they see passengers waiting or if they have been told to pick up or deliver freight. Drivers also regulate lighting, heating, and air-conditioning equipment for the passengers' comfort. In an emergency, they are required to change flat tires.

Upon arriving at their final destinations, drivers may unload or supervise the unloading of baggage and freight. They prepare reports for their employers on mileage, time, and fares, as required by the U.S. Department of Transportation. They also report any repairs the buses need before being used again.

At times, drivers operate chartered buses. In these cases, they pick up a group of people, take them to the group's destination, and remain with them until they are ready to return. These trips frequently require drivers to remain away from home one night or more.

Places of Employment

Over 25,000 intercity busdrivers were employed by about 950 bus companies in 1976. Some work out of terminals located in some of the small communities served by buses, but most work out of major terminals in large cities.

Training, Other Qualifications, and Advancement

Intercity busdrivers must meet qualifications established by the U.S. Department of Transportation. Drivers must be at least 21 years old and be able to read, write, and speak English well enough to communicate with passengers and to complete reports. They also must have good hearing, at least 20/40 vision in each eye with or without glasses, and normal use of their arms and legs. In addition, they must take comprehensive written examinations which test their knowledge of Department of Transportation and State motor vehicle regulations, as well as a driving test in the type of bus they will operate. Most States require that drivers have a chauffeur's license, which is a commercial driving permit.

Many intercity bus companies have considerably higher requirements. Most prefer applicants who are at least 25 years of age; some

prefer applicants who have bus or truckdriving experience. One large company requires applicants to have 20/20 vision with or without glasses.

Since they represent their companies in dealing with passengers, busdrivers must be courteous and tactful. An even temperament and emotional stability are important qualifications, because driving buses in heavy, fast-moving traffic and dealing with passengers can be a strain.

Most intercity bus companies conduct training programs for new drivers. These programs, which usually last from 2 to 8 weeks, include both classroom and driving instruction. In the classroom, trainees learn about rules of the company and the U.S. Department of Transportation, about State and municipal driving regulations, and about safe driving practices. They also learn how to determine ticket prices and how to keep records. In addition, new employees learn to deal courteously with passengers.

Trainees spend considerable time learning and practicing driving skills. Courses are set up and trainees practice turns, zig-zag maneuvers, backing up, and driving into narrow lanes. A good deal of practice is necessary before trainees can adapt their automobile driving skills to these larger vehicles. Trainees ride with regular drivers to observe safe driving practices and other aspects of the job. They also make trial runs, without passengers, to improve their driving skills. After completing the training, which includes final driving and written examinations, new drivers begin a "break in" period. During this period, they make regularly scheduled trips with passengers, accompanied by an experienced driver. The experienced driver gives helpful tips, answers questions, and determines that the new driver is performing satisfactorily.

New drivers start out on the "extra board," which is a list of drivers who are given temporary assignments. While on this list, they may substitute for regular drivers who are ill or on vacation, or they may drive chartered buses. Extra drivers may have to wait several years before they have

enough seniority to get a regular assignment.

Opportunities for promotion generally are limited, particularly in small companies. For most drivers, advancement consists of receiving better driving assignments in the form of higher earnings or a more leisurely route. Experienced drivers may be promoted to jobs as dispatchers, supervisors, or terminal managers.

Employment Outlook

Employment of intercity busdrivers is expected to increase about as fast as the average for all occupations through the mid-1980's. Additional openings will become available each year because of the need to replace experienced drivers who retire, die, or transfer to other occupations. Since many qualified persons are attracted to this relatively high paying job, applicants can expect stiff competition for the openings that arise. Applicants in excellent physical condition who have good driving records stand the best chance of being hired.

A growing population is expected to lead to a moderate increase in bus travel. However, should government energy policies make gasoline for automobiles very expensive or difficult to obtain, many persons may ride buses rather than drive their own cars, thus increasing the demand for intercity busdrivers.

Earnings and Working Conditions

Drivers employed by large intercity bus companies had estimated annual average earnings of $16,100 in 1976, about three-quarters more than the average for all nonsupervisory workers in private industry, except farming. The wages of intercity busdrivers typically are computed on a mileage basis, but short runs may be on an hourly rate. Most regular drivers are guaranteed a minimum number of miles or hours per pay period. For work on other than regular assignments they receive additional pay, customarily at premium rates.

Since intercity buses operate at all hours of the day and every day of the year, drivers may work nights and weekends. Extra drivers may be on call at all hours and may be required to report for work on very short notice. Drivers on some long routes have to remain away from home overnight. Driving schedules may range from 6 to 10 hours a day and from 3-1/2 to 6 days a week. However, U.S. Department of Transportation regulations specify that intercity drivers shall not drive more than 10 hours without having at least 8 hours off, and shall not drive at all after being on duty for 15 hours.

Driving an intercity bus usually is not physically difficult, but it is tiring and requires steady nerves. The busdriver is given a great deal of independence on the job, and is solely responsible for the safety of the passengers and bus. Many drivers like working without direct supervision and take pride in assuming these responsibilities. Some also enjoy the opportunity to travel and to meet the public.

Most intercity busdrivers belong to the Amalgamated Transit Union. The Brotherhood of Railroad Trainmen, and the International Brotherhood of Teamsters, Chauffeurs, Warehousemen and Helpers of America (Ind.) also have organized these workers in some areas of the country.

Sources of Additonal Information

For further information on job opportunities in this field, contact intercity bus companies or the local office of the State employment service.

LOCAL TRANSIT BUSDRIVERS

(D.O.T. 913.363 and 913.463)

Nature of the Work

Local transit busdrivers relieve millions of Americans of the bother of fighting city traffic every day.

These drivers follow definite time schedules and routes over city and suburban streets, to provide passengers with an alternative to automobile driving and even ownership.

The workday for local busdrivers begins when they report to the terminal or garage to which they are assigned. Large cities have several garages while a small city may have only one. At the garage, drivers are given transfer and refund forms. Some are assigned buses and drive them to the start of their run. Others go to designated intersections and relieve drivers who are going off duty. Drivers inspect the inside and outside of the buses and check the tires, brakes, windshield wipers, and lights before starting their runs. Those who work for small bus companies also may check the water, oil, and fuel.

On most runs, drivers pick up and discharge passengers at locations marked with a bus stop sign. As passengers board the bus, drivers make sure the correct cash fare, token, or ticket is placed in the fare box. They also collect or issue transfers. Drivers often answer questions about schedules, routes, and transfer points, and sometimes call out the name of the street at each bus stop.

A busdriver's day is run by the clock, as they must pay special attention to their complicated schedules. Although drivers may run late in heavier than average traffic, they avoid letting light traffic put them ahead of schedule so that they do not miss passengers.

Busdrivers especially must be alert to the traffic around them. Since sudden stops or swerves will jar standing passengers, drivers try to anticipate traffic developments, not react to them.

At the end of the day, busdrivers turn in trip sheets which usually include a record of fares received, trips made, and any significant delays in schedule. They also turn in a report on the mechanical condition of the bus that day. In case of an accident, drivers must make out a report describing exactly what happened before and after the event and obtain the names, addresses, and phone numbers of persons on the bus.

At times, drivers operate chartered buses—buses arranged for in advance by an organization or group. In these cases, they pick up a group of people, take them to their destination, and remain with them until they are ready to return.

Places of Employment

About 81,000 local busdrivers were employed in 1976. About four-fifths worked for publicly owned transit systems. Most of the remainder worked for privately owned transit lines; a small number worked for sightseeing companies. Most busdrivers work in large cities.

Training, Other Qualifications, and Advancement

Applicants for busdriver positions should be at least 21 years old, be of average height and weight, be in good health, and have good eyesight—with or without glasses. Most employers require applicants to pass a physical examination and a written test that determines if they are capable of following the often complex schedules busdrivers use. Although educational requirements are not high, many employers prefer applicants who have a high school education or its equivalent. A relaxed personality is important since drivers face many minor aggravations each day due to traffic congestion, bad weather, and the many different personalities they must deal with.

A motor vehicle operator's license is a basic requirement. A good driving record is essential because the busdriver is responsible for passenger safety. Most States require busdrivers to have a chauffeur's license, which is a commercial driving permit.

Most local transit companies conduct training courses that may last several weeks and include both classroom and "behind-the-wheel" driving instruction. In the classroom, trainees learn company rules, safety regulations, and safe driving practices. They also learn how to keep records and how to deal tactfully and courteously with passengers. Actual driving instruction may begin with several hours of instruction on a training course, but trainees quickly advance to practice on city streets. Because a busdriver is seated above other traffic, defensive driving—seeing and avoiding possible traffic dangers ahead of time—has much potential and is stressed. Trainees are assigned to a particular garage, and must memorize and drive each of the runs based at this garage before graduating. They also take several trips with passengers while supervised by an experienced driver. At the end of the course, trainees may have to pass a written examination and a driving examination.

Most drivers have regularly scheduled runs. New drivers, however, often are placed on an "extra" list to substitute for regular drivers who are ill or on vacation. New drivers also may be assigned to make extra trips during morning and evening rush hours. They remain on the extra list until they have enough seniority to get a regular run. This may take several months or more than a year.

The different runs are assigned on the basis of length of service, or seniority. Therefore, as drivers develop seniority they can choose runs they prefer, such as those that lead to overtime, or that have little traffic.

Opportunities for promotions generally are limited, although experienced drivers may advance to jobs such as instructor, supervisor or dispatcher. Supervisors patrol the bus routes and check whether drivers are on schedule. If a schedule becomes impossible to meet due to heavy traffic, a blocked street, or some other problem, the supervisor may reroute buses. Dispatchers work in the transit system's main office and organize the day to day bus operation by coordinating all activity. They assign buses to drivers, determine that drivers are available for all runs, call extra list drivers to substitute if experienced drivers will be out, and keep a record of the drivers and buses that were assigned to each run. A few drivers advance to management positions. Promotion in publicly owned bus systems is usually by competitive civil service examination.

Employment Outlook

Employment of local busdrivers is expected to increase about as fast as the average for all occupations through the mid-1980's. In addition, many job openings will result from the need to replace drivers who transfer to other occupations, retire, or die.

The increased use of privately owned automobiles in cities and the population shift to the suburbs—where most people drive their own cars—has caused a decline in bus passengers and driver employment. However, in urban areas, the automobile now is recognized as the main source of air pollution and traffic congestion. As part of the effort to reduce the number of cars used by commuters, many cities are trying to improve local bus service. Some now have commuter buses with reserved seats. In addition, express lanes reserved for buses on city streets, more convenient routes, and more comfortable buses reflect the impact of Federal, State, and local government interest in providing better bus service. Improved bus service will require more drivers.

Earnings and Working Conditions

According to a survey of union contracts in 67 large cities, local busdrivers averaged $6.53 an hour in 1976, about one-third more than the average for all nonsupervisory workers in private industry, except farming. Hourly wages were highest in the larger cities. Wage scales for beginning drivers were generally 10 to 20 cents an hour less.

The workweek for regular drivers usually consists of any 5 days during the week; Saturdays and Sundays are counted as regular workdays. Some drivers have to work evenings and after midnight. To accommodate the demands of commuter travel, many local busdrivers have to work "split shifts." For example, a driver may work from 6 a.m. to 10 a.m., go home, and then return to work from 3 p.m. to 7 p.m. Drivers may receive extra pay for split shifts.

Driving a bus is not physically strenuous, but busdrivers may suffer nervous strain from maneuvering a large vehicle through heavy traffic while dealing with passengers. However, local busdrivers enjoy steady year-round employment, and work without close supervision.

Most local busdrivers are members of the Amalgamated Transit Union. Drivers in New York City and several other large cities belong to the Transport Workers Union of America. The United Transportation Union and the International Brotherhood of Teamsters, Chauffeurs, Warehousemen and Helpers of America also have organized some local busdrivers.

Sources of Additional Information

For further information on employment opportunities, contact a local transit system or the local office of the State employment service.

LOCAL TRUCKDRIVERS

(D.O.T. 900.883, 902.883, 903.883, 906.883, and 909.883)

Nature of the Work

Although goods from near and far may begin their trip to customers by trucks, trains, ships, or planes, final deliveries almost always are made by truck. Local truckdrivers move goods from terminals and warehouses to factories, stores, and homes in the area. They are skilled drivers who can maneuver trucks into tight parking spaces, through narrow alleys, and up to loading platforms.

When local truckdrivers arrive at the terminal or warehouse, they receive assignments from the dispatcher to make deliveries, pickups, or both. They also get delivery forms and check the condition of their trucks. Before the drivers arrive for work, material handlers generally have loaded the trucks and arranged the items in order of delivery to minimize handling of merchandise.

At the customer's place of business, drivers generally load or unload the merchandise. If there are heavy loads such as machinery, or if there are many deliveries to make during the day, drivers may have helpers. Drivers of moving vans usually have crews of helpers to assist in loading and unloading household or office furniture.

Drivers get customers to sign receipts for the goods, and may receive money for the material delivered. At the end of the day, they turn in receipts, money, and records of the deliveries made. They also report whatever repairs the trucks need before being used again.

The work of these drivers varies, depending on the product they transport. Produce truckers, on the one hand, pick up a loaded truck in the early morning and spend the rest of the day delivering the product to many different grocery stores. The day for a driver of a lumber truck, on the other hand, consists of several round trips between the lumber yard and one construction site or more.

Places of Employment

About 1.6 million people worked as local truckdrivers in 1976, mostly in and around large cities. Some drivers are needed in almost all communities, however.

Most local drivers work for businesses which deliver their own products and goods—such as department stores, foodstores, and lumber yards. Many others are employed by trucking companies. Some work for Federal, State and local government agencies.

A large number of local truckdrivers are owner-operators. Drivers who own one or two trucks account for a sizable proportion of the local for-hire trucking industry.

Training, Other Qualifications, and Advancement

Qualifications for local truckdrivers vary considerably, depending upon the type of truck and the nature of the employer's business. In most States, however, applicants must have a chauffeur's license, which is a commercial driving permit. Information on how to get this license can be obtained from State motor vehicle departments. Applicants may have to pass a general physical examination, a written examination on driving regulations, and a driving test. They should have good hearing and at least 20/40 vision, with or without glasses, be able to lift heavy objects, and be in good health.

Employers prefer applicants with some previous experience driving a truck. A person may obtain such experience by working as a truckdriver's helper. Employers also give consideration to driving experience gained in the Armed Forces. Many drivers start out as dock workers, loading and unloading freight. They get a general idea of the trucking operation and their work may give them the opportunity to move trucks around the yard. When a need for a truckdriver develops, a capable dock worker may be promoted.

Since drivers often deal directly with the company's customers, the ability to get along well with people is important. Employers also look for responsible, self-motivated individuals, since drivers work with little supervision. Many employers will not hire applicants who have bad driving records.

Training given to new drivers usually is informal, and may consist only of a few hours instruction from an experienced driver, sometimes on the new employee's own time. New drivers also may ride with and observe experienced drivers before being assigned their own runs. Additional training may be given if they are to drive a special type of truck. Some companies give 1 to 2 days of

classroom instruction which covers general duties, the efficient operation and loading of a truck, company policies, and the preparation of delivery forms and company records.

Although most new employees are assigned immediately to regular driving jobs, some start as extra drivers and do the work of regular drivers who are ill or on vacation. They receive a regular assignment when an opening occurs.

Local truckdrivers may advance to dispatcher, manager, or to traffic work—for example, planning delivery schedules. However, relatively few of these jobs are available. For the most part, a local truckdriver may advance to driving heavy or special types of trucks or by transferring to long-distance truckdriving. Local drivers working for companies that also employ long-distance drivers have the best chances of advancing to these positions. Experienced drivers who have business ability can become owner-operators when they have enough money to purchase a truck.

Employment Outlook

Employment of local truckdrivers is expected to increase faster than the average for all occupations through the mid-1980's. In addition to the job openings from growth, thousands of openings will result from the need to replace experienced drivers who transfer to other occupations, retire, or die. Job openings may vary from year to year, however, since the number of drivers needed fluctuates with general business conditions. Applicants with good driving records have the best chance of being hired.

The rise in total business activity anticipated in the years ahead will increase the amount of freight to be distributed. Since trucks carry virtually all local freight, employment of drivers will grow.

Earnings and Working Conditions

On the average, union wage scales

were $7.22 an hour for local truckdrivers and $6.59 an hour for helpers in 1976, according to a survey in 70 large cities. This is about 1 1/2 times as much as the average for all nonsupervisory workers in private industry, except farming.

As a rule, local truckdrivers are paid by the hour and receive extra pay for working overtime, usually after 40 hours. Some drivers are guaranteed minimum daily or weekly earnings. Local truckdrivers frequently work 48 hours or more a week. Night or early morning work is sometimes necessary, particularly for drivers handling foodstuffs for chain grocery stores, produce markets, or bakeries. Most drivers deliver over regular routes, although some may be assigned different routes each day.

Truckdriving has become less physically demanding because most trucks now have more comfortable seating, better ventilation, and improved cab designs, but when drivers make many deliveries during a day, their work can be exhausting. Moreover, driving in heavy traffic can cause nervous strain. Local truckdrivers, however, do have certain work advantages. Employment is steady and, unlike long-distance drivers, they usually work during the day and return home in the evening.

Many local truckdrivers are members of the International Brotherhood of Teamsters, Chauffeurs, Warehousemen and Helpers of America (Ind.). Some local truckdrivers employed by companies outside the trucking industry are members of unions that represent the plantworkers of their employers.

Sources of Additional Information

Information on truck driver training schools and on career opportunities in the trucking industry may be obtained from:

American Trucking Associations, Inc., 1616 P St. NW., Washington, D.C. 20036.

For details on truck driver employment opportunities, contact local trucking companies or the local office of the State employment service.

MECHANICS AND REPAIRERS

In the technologically advanced society we live in today, mechanical equipment of one type or another touches almost all aspects of our lives. Transportation equipment such as cars, trucks, buses, and airplanes carries both goods and people anywhere in the world. Telephones and other communication equipment enable messages to be conveyed quickly and efficiently. Household appliances and machinery such as air-conditioners make our lives easier and more comfortable. The approximately 3 million people who worked as mechanics and repairers in 1976 performed the vital function of keeping these and other types of machinery running and in good working order.

Of the mechanics and repairers employed in 1976, more than one-third worked on motor vehicles in occupations such as automobile mechanic, truck or bus mechanic, and automobile body repairer. Some other large occupations—each employing more than 100,000 workers—were appliance repairer, industrial machinery repairer, airplane mechanic, and television and radio service technician. Employment in some occupations, including vending machine mechanic, electric sign repairer, and locksmith, was relatively small.

In addition to the nearly 3 million mechanics and repairers employed in 1976, almost 700,000 people worked in three related occupations: Maintenance electrician, telephone craftworker, and watch repairer. Altogether these 3.7 million maintenance and repair workers represented about 1 out of every 3 skilled workers.

Almost one-fourth of the mechanics and repairers worked in manufacturing industries—the majority in plants that produce durable goods such as steel, automobiles, and aircraft. About one-fifth worked in retail trade—mainly in firms that sell and service automobiles, household appliances, farm implements, and other mechanical equipment. Another one-fifth worked in shops that service such equipment. Most of the re-

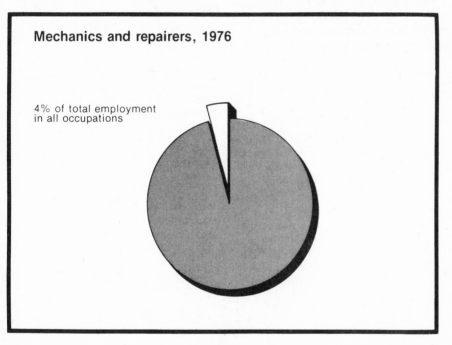

Mechanics and repairers, 1976

4% of total employment in all occupations

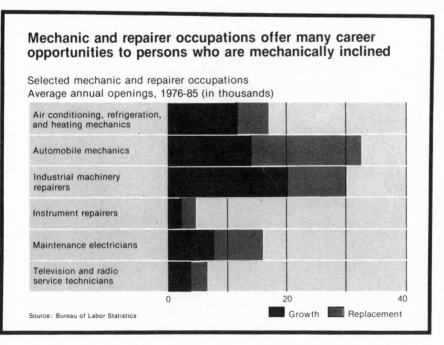

Mechanic and repairer occupations offer many career opportunities to persons who are mechanically inclined

Selected mechanic and repairer occupations
Average annual openings, 1976-85 (in thousands)

Air conditioning, refrigeration, and heating mechanics

Automobile mechanics

Industrial machinery repairers

Instrument repairers

Maintenance electricians

Television and radio service technicians

0   20   40

Source: Bureau of Labor Statistics

■ Growth   ■ Replacement

maining mechanics and repairers worked for transportation, construction, and public utilities industries, and all levels of government.

Mechanics and repairers work in every section of the country, but most employment opportunities are in populous and industrialized areas.

Training, Other Qualifications, and Advancement

Many mechanics and repairers learn their skills on the job or through apprenticeship training. Some acquire basic training or increase their skills in vocational and technical schools; others take correspondence courses. Training and experience in the Armed Forces also may help people prepare for some of these occupations, including television and radio service technician, airplane mechanic, and telephone craftworker.

Most employers consider a 3- to 4-year apprenticeship, supplemented each year by at least 144 hours of related classroom instruction in courses such as mathematics, physics, and basic economics, as the best way to learn skilled maintenance and repair work. Formal apprenticeship agreements are registered with a State apprenticeship agency or the U.S. Department of Labor's Bureau of Apprenticeship and Training.

Employers look for applicants who have mechanical aptitude and like to work with their hands. Many employers prefer people whose hobbies or interests include automobile repair, model building, or radio and television repair. A high school education often is required, and employers generally prefer applicants who have had courses in mathematics, chemistry, physics, blueprint reading, and machine shop.

Physical requirements for work in this field vary greatly among occupations. For example, telephone lineworkers should be strong and agile to climb poles, lift heavy equipment, and work in awkward positions. Instrument and watch repairers need patience, finger dexterity, and good vision.

Many maintenance and repair workers advance to supervisory jobs; others to sales or technician jobs. Some open their own businesses.

Employment Outlook

Employment in maintenance and repair occupations as a whole is expected to increase about as fast as the average for all occupations through the mid-1980's. In addition to jobs created by employment growth, many thousands of openings will arise in this relatively large occupational category as experienced workers retire, die, or transfer to other fields.

Many factors are expected to contribute to the growing need for mechanics and repairers, including increased demand for household appliances, automobiles, and other items, and repair of complex machinery in industry.

TELEPHONE CRAFT OCCUPATIONS

More than 1 out of every 3 employees in the telephone industry is a craft worker who installs, repairs, and maintains phones, cables, and related equipment. This chapter discusses the four groups of telephone craft occupations: Central office craft occupations, central office equipment installers, line installers and cable splicers, and telephone installers and repairers.

CENTRAL OFFICE CRAFT OCCUPATIONS

Nature of the Work

Telephone companies employed about 135,000 craft workers in 1976 to maintain and repair the complex equipment in their central offices. Most worked as frame wirers, central office repairers, and trouble locators.

In small telephone companies, central office craft workers must perform a variety of jobs, but most specialize in one of these three areas.

Frame wirers (D.O.T. 822.884) connect and disconnect wires that run from telephone lines and cables to equipment in central offices. This equipment consists of a frame having many terminal lugs mounted on it, each of which is assigned a specific telephone number. It also contains one pair of wires for each customer's telephone that is connected to that central office. To connect a new telephone, the frame wirer solders the customer's pair of wires to a set of terminal lugs. To disconnect a telephone, a frame wirer melts off the solder and removes the wires from the terminal. Frame wirers occasionally change a customer's phone number. This is done by reconnecting the customer's pair of wires to a different set of terminal lugs.

Central office repairers (D.O.T. 822.281) maintain the switching equipment that automatically connects lines when customers dial numbers. Electromechanical switching systems contain moving parts that must be cleaned and oiled periodically. Also, electronic switching circuits must be checked occasionally for breakages.

When customers report trouble with their telephones, *trouble locators* (D.O.T. 822.381) work at special switchboards to find the source of the problem. To do this, they communicate with telephone installers and repairers as they attempt to make connections from a portable telephone through the customer's service line to the central office. The trouble shooter locates the problem by having the telephone repairer connect the portable phone at various places on the customer's line until a connection can be made through to the central office. If the problem is found to be at the central office, the trouble locator repeats this procedure with a central office repairer. In addition, trouble locators must also test new equipment when it is installed to make sure installations are made correctly. They also work with other employees, such as central office repairers and cable splicers, who help find the cause of trouble and make repairs.

Training, Other Qualifications, and Advancement

Telephone companies give classroom instruction and on-the-job training to new central office craft employees. In addition, telecommunications equipment manufacturers often train central office craft workers in the use, maintenance, and repair of equipment that they sell to telephone companies. Some vocational schools, particularly those in rural areas served by small independent telephone companies, also offer training to persons interested in becoming central office craft workers. A few people may learn these crafts through apprenticeship programs designed by State employment agencies in conjunction with local telephone companies. Often classrooms are supplied with equipment similar to that which the trainee will be using on the job.

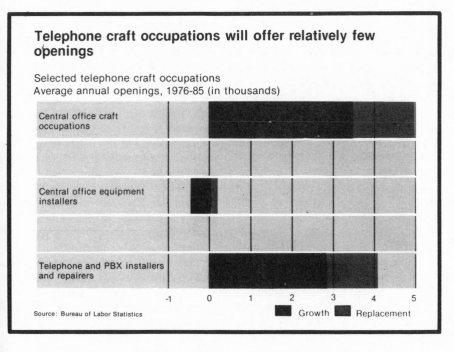

Telephone craft occupations will offer relatively few openings

Selected telephone craft occupations
Average annual openings, 1976-85 (in thousands)

Central office craft occupations

Central office equipment installers

Telephone and PBX installers and repairers

-1 0 1 2 3 4 5

Growth   Replacement

Source: Bureau of Labor Statistics

Trainee jobs generally are filled by employees already with the company, such as telephone operators or line installers. Occasionally workers are hired from outside. Usually, trainees are assigned to the starting job of frame wirer, and take basic courses in telephone communications. They gain practical experience by observing and helping experienced frame wirers under the direction of supervisors. With additional training and experience, a frame wirer can advance to central office repairer or trouble locator. Usually it takes at least 5 years for an inexperienced worker to advance to the top pay rate in either of these two jobs.

Since electrical wires are usually color coded, persons who are considering careers in central office crafts should not be color blind. They also should be able to work closely with others, because teamwork often is essential in solving complex problems. A basic knowledge of electricity and electronics and telephone training in the Armed Forces are helpful.

Telephone companies give central office craft employees continued training throughout their careers to keep them abreast of the latest developments. As new types of equipment and tools and new maintenance methods are introduced, employees are sent to schools to learn about them.

Central office craft workers who have managerial ability can advance to supervisory positions.

Employment Outlook

Employment in central office craft occupations is expected to increase about as fast as the average for all occupations through the mid-1980's. Many new central offices will be built to meet the expected increase in demand for telephone services. Older, outdated central offices will be remodeled to include improved electronic switching systems (ESS). As population grows and becomes more mobile, a greater demand for telephone installations and removals will result in employment growth for frame wirers, trouble locators, and central office repairers. Additional employment growth for trouble locators and central office repairers will result from the use of increasingly complex equipment which requires more maintenance. Also, newer and more complex central office equipment will require more testing when installed, thus increasing the demand for trouble locators.

In addition to employment growth, many job openings will arise from the need to replace experienced workers who retire, die, or transfer to other occupations. Retirements and deaths alone may result in several thousand openings each year. Although most job openings are filled by the advancement of operators and other workers already employed by telephone companies, some trainee positions as frame wirers should be available for new employees. Most job openings will be in metropolitan areas.

Earnings and Working Conditions

In late 1976, average hourly rates were $7.24 for trouble locators and $6.95 for central office repairers. By comparison, nonsupervisory workers in all private industries, except farming, averaged $4.87 an hour.

Earnings increase considerably with length of service. Under the terms of a major union contract in effect in late 1976, frame wirers started at $4.68 an hour and could work up to a maximum of $7.03 an hour after 4 years. Central office repairers and trouble locators could earn a maximum of $8.34 an hour after 5 years.

Employees in central offices work in clean and well-lighted surroundings. Since the telephone industry gives continuous service to its customers, central offices operate 24 hours a day, 7 days a week. Some central office craft workers, therefore, have work schedules that include shift work and some weekends and holiday work for which they receive extra pay. Central office craft workers are covered by the same provisions governing overtime pay, vacations, holidays, and other benefits that apply to telephone workers generally.

LINE INSTALLERS AND CABLE SPLICERS

Nature of the Work

The vast network of wires and cables that connect telephone central offices to each other and to customers' telephones and switchboards is constructed and maintained by line installers and cable splicers and their helpers. Telephone companies employed almost 55,000 of these workers in 1976 including about 33,000 cable splicers, 15,000 line installers, and 7,000 helpers, laborers, and other workers.

To construct new telephone lines, line installers (D.O.T. 822.381) place wires and cables that lead from the central office to customers' premises. They use power-driven equipment to dig holes and set in telephone poles which support cables. Line installers climb the poles to attach the cables, usually leaving the ends free for cable splicers to connect later. In cities where telephone lines are below the streets, installers place cables in underground conduits. On construction jobs, installers work in crews of two persons or more. A supervisor directs the work of several crews.

When wires or cables break or a pole is knocked down, line installers often are called upon to make emergency repairs. These repairs are most common in parts of the country that have hurricanes, tornadoes, and heavy snowfalls. The line crew supervisor keeps in radio contact with the central office, which directs the crew to problem locations on the lines. Some installers periodically inspect sections of lines in rural areas and make minor repairs.

After line installers place cables on poles or in underground conduits, *cable splicers* (D.O.T. 829.381) generally complete the line connections. Splicers work on poles, on aerial ladders and platforms, in manholes, or in basements of large buildings. They connect individual wires within the cable and rearrange wires when lines have to be changed. At each splice, they either wrap insulation around the wires and seal the joint with a lead sleeve or cover the splice with some other type of closure. Usually, they fill the cable sheathing with compressed air to keep out moisture.

Splicers also install terminal boxes that connect customers' telephones to outside cables. An innovation in telephone connecting, these terminal boxes are often placed in the basements of apartment buildings or other buildings containing multiple telephone customers. When a telephone installer wishes to connect or disconnect a customer's telephone, it can be done quickly at the terminal box.

Splicers also maintain and repair cables. The preventive maintenance work that they do is extremely important, because a single defect in a cable may cause a serious interruption in service. Many trouble spots are located through air pressure or electric tests.

Training, Other Qualifications, and Advancement

Telephone companies hire inexperienced workers to train for jobs as line installers or cable splicers. Knowledge of the basic principles of electricity and training in installing telephone systems with the Armed Forces are helpful. Physical examinations usually are given to prospective employees, since some line and cable work is strenuous, requiring workers to climb poles and lift heavy cables and equipment. The ability to distinguish colors is necessary because wires usually are coded by color.

Telephone companies have training programs for line installers and cable splicers that include classroom instruction as well as on-the-job training. Classrooms are equipped with actual telephone apparatus, such as poles, cable supporting clamps, and other fixtures to simulate working conditions as closely as possible. Trainees learn to climb poles and are taught safe working practices to avoid falls and contact with power wires. After a short period of classroom training, some trainees are assigned to a crew to work with experienced line installers and cable splicers under the supervision of a line supervisor.

In addition to the training provided by the telephone companies, some manufacturers of cable installation equipment also train line installers and cable splicers in the use of equipment that the manufacturers sell to telephone companies. Often a telephone company will send its line and cable workers to the manufacturer's training school. At other times manufacturers send their instructors to the job site.

Some small independent telephone companies, particularly those in rural areas, do not have adequate facilities to train their employees. Therefore, they may rely on local vocational and technical schools to provide classroom training to craft employees. A few apprenticeships also are available for line and cable workers. In these cases, employees receive classroom training in courses such as mathematics and electronic theory sponsored by outside agencies, for example State employment agencies, while they receive on-the-job training. Apprenticeships generally last 4 years.

Line installers and cable splicers continue to receive training throughout their careers, to qualify for more difficult assignments and to keep up with technological changes. Due to the strenuous nature of the job, most line installers and cable splicers find it necessary to transfer to other occupations as they advance in age. Those having the necessary qualifications find many additional advancement opportunities in the telephone industry. For example, a line installer, may be transferred to telephone installer and later to telephone repairer or other higher rated job.

Employment Outlook

Employment of cable splicers is expected to show little or no change through the mid-1980's. Technological developments such as the telephone splicing van which uses the truck engine to heat and ventilate manholes and drive power tools and equipment will improve the efficiency of splicers, thus limiting the need for additional workers. Nevertheless, many job openings will arise due to the need to replace experienced splicers who retire, die, or transfer to other occupations.

Little or no change is expected in the number of line installers because the increasing use of mechanical improvements such as plows that can dig a trench, lay cable, and cover it in a single operation have eliminated much of the heavier physical work of the line crews and have caused reductions in crew size. Also, satellites are expected to carry an increasing volume of telephone traffic, thus slightly reducing the emphasis on cable installation. On the other hand, as urban and suburban areas expand outward, some employment opportunities for line installers and cable splicers may be created by the desire to place unsightly cables underground in localities where cables presently are hung from poles. In addition, some job openings will occur as experienced line installers retire, die, or transfer to other occupations.

Due to the many miles of cable which must be installed and maintained in rural areas, job openings for line installers and cable splicers may be easier to find in small cities than in metropolitan areas.

Earnings and Working Conditions

In late 1975, wage rates of cable splicers averaged $6.86 an hour, line installers averaged $6.49, and cable splicers' helpers, $5.46. By comparison, nonsupervisory workers in all private industries, except farming, averaged $4.87 an hour.

Pay rates for cable splicers and line installers depend to a considerable extent upon length of service and geographic location. For example, under the terms of a major union contract in effect in late 1976, new workers in line construction jobs in the highest pay-scale cities began at $4.71 an hour and could reach a maximum of $8.34 after 5 years of service. The maximum hourly rate for cable splicers also was $8.34. Line installers and cable splicers are covered by the same contract provisions governing overtime pay, vacations, holidays, and other benefits that apply to telephone workers generally.

Line installers and cable splicers work outdoors. They must do considerable climbing, and often work in stooped and cramped positions. Safety standards, developed over the years by telephone companies with the cooperation of labor unions, have greatly reduced the hazards of these occupations. When severe weather damages telephone lines, line installers and cable splicers may be called upon to work long and irregular hours to restore service.

TELEPHONE AND PBX INSTALLERS AND REPAIRERS

Nature of the Work

About 1 in every 3 telephone craft workers is a telephone installer or repairer. About 110,000 were employed in 1976. They install and service telephones and switchboard systems such as PBX and CENTREX on customers' property and make repairs on the equipment when trouble develops. These workers generally travel to customers' homes and offices in trucks equipped with telephone tools and supplies. When customers move or request new types of service, they relocate telephones or make changes on existing equipment. For example, they may install a switchboard in an office, or change a two-party line to a single-party line in a

residence. Installers also may fill a customer's request to add an extension in another room, or to replace an old telephone with a new model. Most installers and repairers specialize in one or two of the jobs described below; however, installers and repairers employed at small telephone companies may perform all of these jobs.

Telephone installers (D.O.T. 822.381) install and remove telephones in homes and business places. They connect telephones to outside service wires and sometimes must climb poles to make these connections. Occasionally, especially in apartment buildings, the service wires or terminals are in the basement of the building in which the installation or removal is being done. Telephone installers are sometimes called station installers.

PBX installers (D.O.T. 822.381) perform the same duties as telephone installers, but they specialize in more complex telephone system installations. They connect wires from terminals to switchboards and make tests to check their installations. Some PBX installers also set up equipment for mobile radiotelephones, data processing equipment, and telephone switchboard systems for radio and television broadcasts that involve receiving phone calls from the audience.

Telephone repairers (D.O.T. 822.281), with the assistance of trouble locators in the central office, locate trouble on customers' equipment. A repairer finds the source of the problem by connecting a portable telephone to the customer's telephone cord and then dialing the trouble locator in the central office. If the proper connection is made, the problem is in the customer's telephone. If a connection cannot be completed, the problem is in the service line between the phone and the central office, and the repairer repeats this procedure at various points along the service line until the problem is located. The repairer then makes the necessary repairs to restore service.

PBX repairers (D.O.T. 822.281), with the assistance of trouble locators, locate trouble on customers' PBX, CENTREX, or other complex

telephone systems and make the necessary repairs. They also maintain associated equipment such as batteries, relays, and power plants. Some PBX repairers maintain and repair equipment for radio and television broadcasts, mobile radiotelephones, and data processing equipment.

Training, Other Qualifications, and Advancement

Telephone companies give new service workers classroom instruction in subjects such as mathematics and electrical and electronic theory. Trainees supplement their classroom instruction with on-the-job training. Often additional training is conducted in classroom set-ups that simulate actual working conditions. For example, telephone installer trainees are instructed in classrooms equipped with telephone poles, lines and cables, terminal boxes, and other equipment. They practice installing telephones and connecting wires just as they would on the job. After a few weeks in the classroom, trainees are assigned to the field for on-the-job training by experienced workers, often supervisors.

Many small independent telephone companies, especially those located in rural areas, do not have the facilities, such as simulated classrooms, necessary to train their employees. Therefore, vocational and technical schools may provide training for installers and repairers employed by telephone companies in the area. A few installers and repairers may enter apprenticeship programs conducted jointly by State employment agencies and telephone companies. In these programs apprentices receive on-the-job training at the company where they are employed. At the same time, they receive classroom instruction from the State agencies. Generally apprenticeships last 4 years.

Because telephone wires usually are color-coded, applicants must have good eyesight—no color blindness. Physical examinations are sometimes required since the work may involve strenuous activity such as climbing poles. In addition, applicants may have to pass a test de igned to determine the applicant's aptitude for the job. Often trainees are chosen from current telephone company employees, such as operators or line installers.

Telephone service workers continue to receive training throughout their careers to qualify for more responsible assignments and to keep up with technical changes. Those who have managerial ability can advance to supervisory jobs.

Employment Outlook

Employment of telephone installers and repairers is expected to increase about as fast as the average for all occupations through the mid-1980's. Most job openings will result from employment growth, but many openings will arise from the need to replace workers who retire, die, or transfer to other occupations. These openings usually are filled by workers from other telephone jobs, such as operators, service representatives, line installers, or cable splicers, but some should be available to new employees.

Employment will increase due to the growing demand for telephones and PBX and CENTREX systems. Employment of installers will increase most rapidly in areas where the population is growing rapidly, thus creating a large demand for telephone installations. Also, areas that have a large influx or outflow of people, such as those with military bases or colleges nearby, will have a relatively large demand for telephone installations and removals.

On the other hand, technological improvements may limit the demand for installers and repairers. For example, terminal boxes allow a number of installations to be connected at one central location and make it unnecessary for installers to climb telephone poles.

Earnings and Working Conditions

In late 1975, the average hourly rate for PBX repairers was $7.01, and the average for telephone and PBX installers was $6.75. In comparison, nonsupervisory workers in all private industries, except farming, had average earnings of $4.87 an hour.

Earnings increase considerably with length of service. Under the terms of a major union contract in effect in late 1976, in one of the higher pay-scale cities, telephone installers and repairers earned a starting rate of $4.49 an hour, with periodic pay increases up to a maximum of $7.63 an hour after 5 years of service. Installers and repairers are covered by the same provisions governing overtime pay, vacations, holidays, and other benefits that apply to telephone workers generally.

Telephone installers and repairers work indoors and outdoors in all kinds of weather. They may work extra hours when breakdowns occur in lines or equipment.

CENTRAL OFFICE EQUIPMENT INSTALLERS

(D.O.T. 822.381)

Nature of the Work

Central office equipment installers set up the complex switching and dialing equipment used in central offices of telephone companies. They may install equipment in new central offices, add equipment in an expanding office, or replace outdated equipment.

On a job, installers follow blueprints, diagrams, and floor plans in order to position the equipment properly and wire it correctly. They often use hoists to lift heavy items into place and use handtools, such as screwdrivers or soldering guns, to connect equipment once it is in place. Recently developed equipment sometimes comes in preassembled components and often requires only simple plug-in connections.

After the new equipment has been put in place, installers connect the outgoing and incoming telephone trunklines, often consulting diagrams to ensure that connections are made correctly. Once this is completed, installers then test the system, using electrical testing equipment, such as electrical pulse repeaters and ohmmeters, to measure the strength and consistency of the current flow. If installers discover that the system is not functioning properly, they must check the equipment and all connections to determine the cause, and then correct it.

Places of Employment

About 20,000 installers were employed in 1976. Most worked for manufacturers of central office equipment. Others worked directly for telephone companies or for private contractors who specialize in large-scale installations.

Most central office equipment installers work in metropolitan areas, where large central offices are found. Hundreds of installers may be required to work on large jobs such as a long-distance toll center in a big city. Other installers are assigned areas that include several States, and therefore they must travel frequently to small towns within their area. Installing equipment in small communities often requires only 2 or 3 installers.

Training, Other Qualifications, and Advancement

Individuals considering careers as central office equipment installers should have good eyesight and, since electrical wires are generally color coded, should not be color blind. They should be able to work with others, for teamwork often is essential to solving a complex problem. Although manufacturers generally provide all the necessary training to perform this job, courses in blueprint reading and electronic theory are helpful to those interested in this career.

New employees attend classes the first few weeks to learn basic installation and then begin on-the-job training. Often trainees will be transported to the plant where the equipment is manufactured to receive their training.

Workers who have several years of experience may qualify as skilled installers. Training continues, however, even after they become skilled; additional courses are given from time to time to improve skills and to teach new techniques in installing telephone equipment. Also, technological innovations are constantly resulting in changes in equipment. When manufacturers develop new equipment, installers must be trained to install it.

Installers who have managerial ability can advance to supervisory positions.

Employment Outlook

Employment of central office equipment installers is expected to decline through the mid-1980's. However, a few hundred openings will arise each year to replace experienced installers who transfer to other work, retire, or die.

Thousands of new central offices will be constructed in the next decade. In addition, in older offices obsolete manual and dial switching equipment will be replaced with more efficient electronic switching systems (ESS). However, most new central office equipment will be manufactured in components that come partially assembled, thus greatly reducing the time needed for installation. The greater complexity of ESS's will require more testing of new equipment, but this will not offset the time savings resulting from the use of component parts.

Employment may fluctuate from year to year, however, because investment in central office equipment is subject to changes in business conditions and availability of funds. Thus, when business is prospering, installations and modifications of central offices may occur at an above-average pace. When the business outlook is depressed, there is less likelihood that new central offices will be built or that existing offices will be enlarged or modernized.

Earnings and Working Conditions

Under the terms of a major union contract in effect in late 1976, covering most central office equipment installers, starting rates for inexperienced installers ranged from $3.73 to $4.71 an hour. The contract provided for periodic increases, and employees could reach rates of $7.20 to $8.34 an hour after 5 years of experience. Travel and expense allowances also were provided.

The Communications Workers of America represents most central office equipment installers, including those with the Bell System. The International Brotherhood of Electrical Workers represents some installers employed by various telephone companies, by manufacturers supplying the independent segment of the telephone industry, and by large installation contractors.

OTHER MECHANICS AND REPAIRERS

AIR-CONDITIONING, REFRIGERATION, AND HEATING MECHANICS

(D.O.T. 637.281 and .381, 862.281 and .381, and 869.281)

Nature of the Work

Heating and air-conditioning equipment makes buildings comfortable for work, study, or play. Refrigeration equipment makes it possible to safely store food, drugs, and other items. The types of equipment that provide these conveniences are complex. Air-conditioning, refrigeration, and heating mechanics are the skilled workers who install, maintain, and repair them. These workers usually specialize in one area but often have the ability to work in several.

Air-conditioning and refrigeration mechanics (D.O.T. 637.281 and 381) install and repair equipment ranging in size from small window units to large central air-conditioning or refrigeration systems. When installing new equipment, they put the motors, compressors, evaporators, and other components in place, following blueprints and design specifications. They connect duct work, refrigerant lines, and other piping and then connect the equipment to an electrical power source. After completing the installation, they charge the system with refrigerant and check it for proper operation.

When air-conditioning and refrigeration equipment breaks down, mechanics diagnose the cause and make repairs. When looking for defects they inspect components such as relays and thermostats.

Furnace installers (D.O.T. 862.381 and 869.281), also called heating equipment installers, follow blueprints or other specifications to install oil, gas, and electric heating units. After setting the heating unit in place, they install fuel supply lines, air ducts, pumps, and other components. They then connect electrical wiring and controls, and check the unit for proper operation.

Oil burner mechanics (D.O.T. 862.281) keep oil-fueled heating systems in good operating condition. During the fall and winter, when the system is needed most, they service and adjust oil burners. If a burner is not operating properly, mechanics check the thermostat, burner nozzles, controls, and other parts to locate the problem. Mechanics carry replacement parts in their trucks to make repairs in the customer's home or place of business. However, if major repairs are necessary, they usually complete the repairs in the shop. During the summer when most systems are off, mechanics service heating units, replace oil and air filters, and vacuum-clean vents, ducts, and other parts of the heating system that accumulate soot and ash.

Gas burner mechanics (D.O.T. 637.281), also called gas appliance servicers, have duties similar to those of oil burner mechanics. They diagnose malfunctions in gas-fueled heating systems and make necessary repairs and adjustments. They also repair cooking stoves, clothes dryers, and hot water heaters. During the summer, mechanics employed by gas utility companies may inspect and repair gas meters.

Air-conditioning, refrigeration, and heating mechanics use a variety of tools, including hammers, wrenches, metal snips, electric drills, pipe cutters and benders, and acetylene torches. They also use voltmeters, electronic circuit testers, and other testing devices.

Cooling and heating systems sometimes are installed or repaired by other craft workers. For example, on a large air-conditioning installation job, especially where workers are covered by union contracts, duct work might be done by sheet-metal workers; electrical work by electricians; and installation of piping, condensers, and other components by pipefitters. Appliance servicers often install and repair window air-conditioners.

Places of Employment

Approximately 175,000 persons worked as air-conditioning, refrigeration, and heating mechanics in 1976. Cooling and heating dealers and contractors employed most air-conditioning and refrigeration mechanics and furnace installers. Fuel oil dealers employed most oil burner mechanics, and gas utility companies, most gas burner mechanics. Approximately 1 out of 7 mechanics was self-employed.

Air-conditioning and refrigeration mechanics and furnace installers work in all parts of the country. Generally, the geographic distribution of these workers is similar to that of our population. Oil burner mechanics are concentrated in States where oil is a major heating fuel. More than half work in Massachusetts, New Jersey, New York, Pennsylvania, Illinois, and Michigan. Similarly, gas burner mechanics are concentrated in States where gas is a major heating fuel. Almost half worked in Texas, California, Ohio, Michigan, and Illinois.

Training, Other Qualifications, and Advancement

Most air-conditioning, refrigeration, and heating mechanics start as helpers and acquire their skills by working for several years with experienced mechanics. The remainder learn through apprenticeship.

All new workers in these trades receive similar on-the-job training, lasting 4 to 5 years. They begin by doing simple tasks such as carrying materials, insulating refrigerant lines, or cleaning furnaces. Within a year, they learn to cut, braze, and solder pipe and tubing; within three, to install fittings and work with sheet metal. By the end of training, they are capable of checking circuits and installing burners and pumps.

In addition to on-the-job training, apprentices must have related classroom instruction in subjects such as math, blueprint reading, and basic construction and engineering concepts.

When hiring helpers or apprentices, employers prefer high school graduates with mechanical aptitude who have had courses in mathematics, physics, electronics, and blueprint reading. Good physical condition also is necessary because workers sometimes have to lift and move heavy equipment.

Many high schools and vocational schools offer basic mechanic courses, some of which are taught by members of local firms and organizations such as the Air-conditioning and Refrigeration Institute and the Petroleum Marketing Education Foundation. These courses may last from 2 to 3 years.

Employment Outlook

Employment of air-conditioning, refrigeration, and heating mechanics is expected to increase much faster than the average for all occupations through the mid-1980's. In addition to the job openings from employment growth, many openings will occur as experienced mechanics transfer to other fields of work, retire, or die.

Most openings will be for air-conditioning and refrigeration mechanics. An increase in household formation and rising personal incomes should result in a very rapid increase in the number of air-conditioned homes. Air-conditioning in schools, factories, and other buildings also is expected to increase. In addition, more refrigeration equipment will be needed in the production, storage, and marketing of food and other perishables.

Employment of furnace installers and gas burner mechanics is expected to follow the growth trends in the construction of homes and business-

es. Employment of oil burner mechanics should also grow as customers have their heating systems serviced more frequently in order to conserve oil.

Earnings and Working Conditions

Depending on the area of the country and the experience of the worker, hourly rates for skilled air-conditioning, refrigeration, and heating mechanics ranged from about $6 to $10 in 1976, according to limited information. In comparison, the average hourly rate for production and nonsupervisory workers in private industry, except farming, was $4.87. Mechanics who worked on both air-conditioning and heating equipment frequently had higher rates of pay than those who worked on only one type of equipment. Starting rates for helpers and apprentices are about 55 to 65 percent of those paid to experienced workers; with experience, rates increase.

Most mechanics work a 40-hour week. However, during seasonal peaks they often work overtime or irregular hours. Air-conditioning and refrigeration mechanics are busiest during spring and summer, and heating mechanics are busiest during fall and winter. Most employers try to provide a full workweek the year round, but they may temporarily reduce hours or lay off some mechanics when seasonal peaks end. However, employment in most shops that service both air-conditioning and heating equipment is fairly stable throughout the year.

Mechanics sometimes are required to work at great heights when installing new equipment. They also may work in awkward or cramped positions. Hazards in this trade include electrical shock, torch burns, and muscle strains and other injuries from handling heavy equipment.

Sources of Additional Information

For more information about employment and training opportunities, contact the local office of the State employment service or firms that em-

ploy air-conditioning, refrigeration and heating mechanics.

For pamphlets on career opportunities and training, write to:

Air-Conditioning and Refrigeration Institute, 1815 N. Fort Myer Dr., Arlington, Va. 22209. (The Institute prefers not to receive individual requests for large quantities of pamphlets.)

For information about training in oil heating systems, write to:

Petroleum Marketing Education Foundation, P. O. Box 11187, Columbia, S.C. 29211.

For career information about gas burner mechanics, write to:

American Gas Association, Inc., 1515 Wilson Blvd., Arlington, Va. 22209.

APPLIANCE REPAIRERS

(D.O.T. 637.281, 723.381, 723.844, and 827.281)

Nature of the Work

In the past, most household chores such as cooking and cleaning were performed by hand and often involved a great deal of time and physical effort. Today, a variety of labor-saving appliances make many household jobs much simpler to do. Microwave ovens cook in minutes meals that once took hours to prepare. Washers and dryers clean clothes with little physical effort. Indeed the number of household jobs machines can do is almost limitless. Even simple tasks such as cooking a hamburger or opening a can are done with appliances made specifically for those purposes. Servicing these machines is the job of the appliance repairer.

Appliance repairers usually specialize in servicing either portable appliances such as toasters and irons or major appliances such as refrigerators and ranges. In large repair shops, they may specialize in particular items such as clothes washers and dryers or refrigerators and freezers. Repairers generally do not install major appliances. This job usually is done by technicians who work for retail stores.

Portable appliances and major appliances that are rebuilt for resale are worked on in shops. Major appliances usually are repaired in customers' homes by appliance repairers who carry their tools and a number of commonly used parts with them in a truck.

To determine why an appliance is not working properly, appliance repairers may operate it to detect unusual noises, overheating, or excess vibration. Repairers also look for common sources of trouble such as faulty electrical connections. They may disassemble the appliance to examine the mechanical and electrical parts. To check electric systems, repairers follow wiring diagrams and use testing devices, such as ammeters, voltmeters, and ohmmeters.

After locating the trouble, the repairer makes the necessary repairs or replacements. The repair procedure varies with the type of appliance and repair involved. To fix a portable appliance such as a toaster, the repairer may replace a defective heating element. To fix a major appliance such as a washer, the repairer may replace worn bearings, transmission belts, or gears. To remove old parts and install new ones, repairers use common handtools, including screwdrivers, soldering irons, files, and pliers, and special tools designed for particular appliances. Repairers operate the appliance after completing a repair to check their work.

Repairers may answer customers' questions and complaints about appliances and frequently advise customers about the care and use of the appliance. For example, they may show the owners the proper loading of automatic washing machines or how to arrange dishes in dishwashers. Appliance repairers may give customers estimates on the cost of repairs and collect the payment for the repairs. They also may keep records of parts used and hours worked on each job.

Places of Employment

About 144,000 people were employed as appliance repairers in 1976. Most repairers work in independent appliance stores and repair shops. Others worked for service centers operated by appliance manufacturers, department stores, wholesalers, and gas and electric utility companies.

Appliance repairers are employed in almost every community, but are concentrated in the more highly populated States and metropolitan areas.

Training, Other Qualifications, and Advancement

Most appliance repairers start as helpers and acquire their skills through on-the-job training. The form of training varies among companies and usually depends on the type of appliance repaired by the company. In some shops that fix portable appliances, helpers work on a single type of appliance, such as vacuum cleaners, until they master its repair. Trainees then move on to work on a different type of appliance; this process continues until they can repair a variety of appliances. In other shops, helpers progress from simple jobs, such as replacing a switch, to more difficult jobs such as rewiring an appliance.

In companies that repair major appliances, beginners usually learn by helping experienced repairers during house calls. In other cases, they learn basic skills by working in the shop rebuilding used parts such as washing machine transmissions.

Many helpers receive supplemental instruction through training seminars that are conducted periodically by appliance manufacturers. These seminars usually last 1 or 2 weeks and deal with the repair of one type of appliance such as ovens. Up to 3 years of on-the-job training may be needed to become skilled in all aspects of repairing some of the more complex appliances.

Some large companies such as department store chains have formal training programs, which include home study courses and shop classes, where trainees work with demonstration appliances and other training equipment.

Experienced repairers continue to attend training classes periodically, and study service manuals to become familiar with new appliances and the proper ways to repair them.

Formal training in appliance repair and related subjects is available from some vocational schools, technical schools, and community colleges. However, graduates of these schools must gain on-the-job experience to become fully qualified repairers.

Persons who want to become appliance repairers generally must have a high school diploma. High school or vocational school courses in electricity are very helpful, because most repairs involve work with electrical equipment. Mechanical aptitude is also desirable. Appliance repairers who work in customers' homes must be able to get along with people.

Appliance repairers who work in large shops or service centers may be promoted to supervisor, assistant service manager, or service manager. A few may advance to managerial positions such as regional service manager or parts manager for appliance manufacturers. Preference is given to those who show ability to get along with coworkers and customers. Experienced repairers who have sufficient funds may open their own appliance stores or repair shops.

Employment Outlook

Employment of appliance repairers is expected to grow about as fast as the average for all occupations through the mid-1980's. In addition to the jobs created by growth of this occupation, many openings will arise each year from the need to replace experienced repairers who retire, die, or transfer to other occupations.

The number of appliances in use is expected to increase very rapidly as a result of increases in population and income, and the introduction of new and improved appliances. Maintaining this large number of appliances will increase the need for qualified appliance repairers.

People who enter the occupation should have steady work because the appliance repair business is not very sensitive to changes in economic conditions.

Earnings and Working Conditions

Hourly earnings of appliance repairers ranged from $4 to $7 in 1976, based on the limited data available. The starting rate for inexperienced trainees was about $3 an hour. The wide variations in wages reflect differences in the repairers' skill and experience, geographic location, and the type of equipment serviced.

Repair shops generally are quiet, well-lighted, and adequately ventilated. Working conditions outside the shop vary considerably. For example, repairers sometimes work in narrow spaces and uncomfortable positions amidst dirt and dust. Those who repair appliances in homes may spend several hours a day driving, although the use of 2-way radios has decreased this time.

Appliance repair work generally is safe, although accidents are possible while handling electrical parts or lifting and moving large appliances. Inexperienced workers are shown how to use tools safely and how to avoid electric shock.

Appliance repairers usually work with little or no direct supervision. This feature of the job appeals to many people.

Many appliance repairers belong to the International Brotherhood of Electrical Workers.

Sources of Additional Information

For further information about jobs in the appliance service field, contact local appliance repair shops, appliance dealers and utility companies, or the local office of the State employment service.

Information about training programs or work opportunities also is available from:

Association of Home Appliance Manufacturers, 20 N. Wacker Dr.. Chicago, Ill. 60606.

AUTOMOBILE BODY REPAIRERS

(D.O.T. 807.381)

Nature of the Work

Every day thousands of motor vehicles are damaged in traffic accidents. Although some are wrecked, most can be made to look and drive like new. Automobile body repairers are the workers who straighten bent frames, remove dents, and replace crumpled parts that are beyond repair. Usually, they can fix all types of vehicles, but most repairers work mainly on cars and small trucks. A few specialize in working on large trucks, buses, or tractor trailers.

When a damaged vehicle is brought into the shop, body repairers generally receive instructions from their supervisors, who have determined which parts are to be restored or replaced and how much time the job should take.

Automobile body repairers use special machines to align damaged frames and body sections. They chain or clamp the semi-portable alignment machine to the damaged metal and apply hydraulic pressure to straighten it.

Body repairers remove badly damaged sections of body panels with a pneumatic metalcutting gun or acetylene torch, and weld in new sections to replace them. Sometimes, dented sections can be repaired rather than replaced; the repairers push dents out with a hydraulic jack or hand prying bar, or knock them out with a handtool or pneumatic hammer. Small dents and creases can be smoothed out by holding a small anvil against one side of the damaged area while hammering the opposite side. Very small pits and dimples are removed with pick hammers and punches.

Some small dents cannot be worked out of the metal. Body repairers fix these dents by first filling them with plastic or solder. Then, when the filler hardens, they file or grind it to its original shape and sand it smooth for painting. In most shops, automobile painters do the painting. (These workers are discussed else-where in the *Handbook*.) Some smaller shops employ workers who do both body repairing and painting.

Body repair work has variety—each damaged vehicle presents a different problem. Therefore, in addition to having a broad knowledge of automobile construction and repair techniques, repairers must develop appropriate methods for each job. Most of these skilled people find their work challenging and take pride in being able to restore automobiles.

Body repairers usually work by themselves with only general directions from supervisors. In some shops, they may be assisted by helpers. In large shops, body repairers may specialize in one type of repair such as straightening bent frames or repairing doors or fenders.

Places of Employment

About 174,000 persons worked as automobile body repairers in 1976. Most worked for shops that specialized in body repairs and painting, and for automobile and truck dealers. Other employers included organizations that maintain their own motor vehicles, such as trucking companies and buslines. Motor vehicle manufacturers employed a small number of these workers.

Automobile body repairers work in every section of the country, with jobs in this occupation distributed in about the same way as population.

Training, Other Qualifications, and Advancement

Most automobile body repairers learn the trade on the job. They usually start as helpers and pick up skills from experienced workers. Helpers begin by assisting body repairers in tasks such as removing damaged parts and installing repaired parts. They gradually learn to remove small dents and make other minor repairs, and progress to more difficult tasks such as straightening frames. Generally, 3 to 4 years of on-the-job training are needed to become skilled in all aspects of body repair. Most training authorities recommend a 3- or 4-year formal ap renticeship program as the best way to learn the trade, but relatively few of these programs are available. Apprenticeship includes both on-the-job and classroom instruction. Apprentices spend most of their time earning on the job, but they also are expected to attend classes in related subjects such as mathematics, job safety procedures, and business management.

Persons who want to learn this trade should be in good physical condition and know how to use tools. Courses in automobile body repair offered by high schools, vocational schools, and private trade schools provide helpful experience, as do courses in automobile mechanics. Although completion of high school generally is not a requirement, many employers believe graduation indicates that the person has at least some of the qualities of a good worker, such as the ability to see a task through to its completion. The latter is especially important as employers spend a good deal of time and money on training.

Automobile body repairers must buy handtools, but employers usually furnish power tools. The usual pattern is for trainees to accumulate tools as they gain experience. Many workers have a few hundred dollars invested in tools.

An experienced automobile body repairer with supervisory ability may advance to shop supervisor. Many workers open their own body repair shops. In fact, about one of every eight automobile body repairers is self-employed.

Employment Outlook

Employment of automobile body repairers is expected to increase about as fast as the average for all occupations through the mid-1980's.

Employment is expected to increase as a result of the rising number of motor vehicles damaged in traffic. Accidents are expected to increase as the number of motor vehicles grows, even though improved highways, driver training courses, lower speed limits, and improved bumpers and safety features on new vehicles may slow the rate of increase.

prenticeship program as the best way to learn the trade, but relatively few openings are expected each year from the need to replace experienced repairers who retire or die. Also job openings will occur as some workers transfer to other occupations.

Most persons who enter the occupation may expect steady work since the automobile repair business is not very sensitive to changes in economic conditions.

Earnings and Working Conditions

Body repairers employed by automobile dealers in 36 large cities had estimated average hourly earnings of $8.20 in 1976, about one and three-fourths times the average for all non-supervisory workers in private industry, except farming. Skilled body repairers usually earn between two and three times as much as inexperienced helpers and trainees.

Many body repairers employed by automobile dealers and repair shops are paid a commission, usually about half of the labor cost charged to the customer. Under this method, earnings depend on the amount of work assigned to the repairer and how fast it is completed. Employers frequently guarantee their commissioned workers a minimum weekly salary. Helpers and trainees usually receive an hourly rate until they are skilled enough to work on commission. Body repairers who work for trucking companies, buslines, and other organizations that maintain their own vehicles usually receive an hourly wage. Most body repairers work 40 to 48 hours a week.

Automobile body shops are noisy because of the banging of hammers against metal and the whir of power tools. Most shops are well-ventilated, but often they are dusty and have the odor of paint. Body repairers often work in awkward or cramped positions, and much of their work is strenuous and dirty. Hazards include cuts from sharp metal edges, burns from torches and heated metal, and injuries from power tools.

Many automobile body repairers are members of unions, including the International Association of Machinists and Aerospace Workers; the In-

ternational Union, United Automobile, Aerospace and Agricultural Implement Workers of America; the Sheet Metal Workers' International Association; and the International Brotherhood of Teamsters, Chauffeurs, Warehousemen and Helpers of America (Ind.). Most body repairers who are union members work for large automobile dealers, trucking companies, and buslines.

Sources of Additional Information

More details about work opportunities may be obtained from local employers, such as automobile body repair shops and automobile dealers; locals of the unions previously mentioned; or the local office of the State employment service. The State employment service also may be a source of information about apprenticeship and other programs that provide training opportunities.

For general information about the work of automobile body repair workers, write to:

Automotive Service Industry Association, 230 North Michigan Ave., Chicago, Ill. 60601.

Automotive Service Councils Inc., 188 Industrial Dr., Suite 112, Elmhurst, Ill. 60126.

AUTOMOBILE MECHANICS

(D.O.T. 620.131 through .381, .782, and .885; 721.281 and 825.281)

Nature of the Work

Anyone whose car has broken down knows how important the automobile mechanic's job is. The ability to make a quick and accurate diagnosis is one of the mechanic's most valuable skills. It requires good reasoning ability as well as a thorough knowledge of automobiles. In fact, many mechanics consider diagnosing "hard to find" troubles one of their most challenging and satisfying duties.

When mechanical or electrical troubles occur, mechanics first get a description of the symptoms from the owner or, if they work in a dealership, the service advisor who wrote the repair order. If the cause of the trouble is hard to find, the mechanic may test drive the car or use testing equipment, such as motor analyzers, spark plug testers, or compression gauges, to locate the problem. Once the cause of the problem is found, mechanics make adjustments or repairs. If a part cannot be fixed, they replace it.

Most automobile mechanics perform a variety of repairs; others specialize. For example, *automatic transmission specialists* work on gear trains, couplings, hydraulic pumps, and other parts of automatic transmissions. Because these are complex mechanisms, their repair requires considerable experience and training, including a knowledge of hydraulics. *Tune-up mechanics* adjust the ignition timing and valves, and adjust or replace spark plugs, distributor points, and other parts to ensure efficient engine performance. They often use scientific test equipment to locate malfunctions in fuel and ignition systems.

Automobile air-conditioning specialists install air-conditioners and service components such as compressors and condensers. *Front-end mechanics* align and balance wheels and repair steering mechanisms and suspension systems. They frequently use special alignment equipment and wheel-balancing machines. *Brake mechanics* adjust brakes, replace brake linings, repair hydraulic cylinders, and make other repairs on brake systems. Some mechanics specialize in both brake and front-end work.

Automobile-radiator mechanics clean radiators with caustic solutions, locate and solder leaks, and install new radiator cores. They also may repair heaters and air-conditioners, and solder leaks in gasoline tanks. *Automobile-glass mechanics* replace broken windshield and window glass and repair window operating mechanisms. They install preformed glass to replace curved windows, and they use window patterns and glass-cutting tools to cut replacement glass from flat sheets. In some cases they may repair minor

damage, such as pits, rather than replace the window.

To prevent breakdowns, most car owners have their cars checked regularly and parts adjusted, repaired, or replaced before they go bad. This responsibility of the mechanic is vital to safe and trouble-free driving. When doing preventive maintenance, mechanics may follow a checklist to be sure they examine all important parts. The list may include distributor points, spark plugs, carburetor, wheel balance, and other potentially troublesome items.

Places of Employment

Over 700,000 persons worked as automobile mechanics in 1976. Most worked for automobile dealers, automobile repair shops, and gasoline service stations. Others were employed by Federal, State, and local governments, taxicab and automobile leasing companies, and other organizations that repair their own automobiles. Some mechanics also were employed by automobile manufacturers to make final adjustments and repairs at the end of the assembly line. A small number of mechanics worked for department stores that have automobile service facilities.

Most automobile mechanics work in shops that employ from one to five mechanics, but some of the largest shops employ more than 100. Generally, automobile dealer shops employ more mechanics than independent shops.

Automobile mechanics work in every section of the country. Geographically, employment is distributed about the same as population.

Training, Other Qualifications, and Advancement

Most automobile mechanics learn the trade on the job. Beginners usually start as helpers, lubrication workers, or gasoline station attendants, and gradually acquire skills by working with experienced mechanics. Although a beginner can make simple repairs after a few months' experience, it usually takes 3 to 4 years to become familiar with all types of repairs. An additional year or two is

necessary to learn a difficult specialty, such as automatic transmission repair. In contrast, radiator mechanics, glass mechanics, and brake specialists, who do not need an all-round knowledge of automobile repair, may learn their jobs in about 2 years.

Most training authorities recommend a 3- or 4-year formal apprenticeship program. These programs include both on-the-job training and classroom instruction. On-the-job training includes instruction in basic service procedures, such as engine tune-up, as well as instruction in special procedures such as overhauling transmissions. Classroom instruction includes courses in related theory such as mathematics and physics and other areas such as shop safety practices and customer relations.

For entry jobs, employers look for young persons with mechanical aptitude and a knowledge of automobiles. Generally, a driver's license is required as mechanics occasionally have to test drive or deliver cars. Working on cars in the Armed Forces or as a hobby is valuable experience. Completion of high school is an advantage in obtaining an entry job because to most employers it indicates that a young person has at least some of the traits of a good worker, such as perseverance and the ability to learn, and has potential for advancement. Courses in automobile repair offered by many high schools, vocational schools, and private trade schools also are helpful. In particular, courses in physical science and mathematics can help a person better understand how an automobile operates.

The usual practice is for mechanics to buy their handtools and beginners are expected to accumulate tools as they gain experience. Many experienced mechanics have several hundred dollars invested in tools. Employers furnish power tools, engine analyzers, and other test equipment.

Employers sometimes send experienced mechanics to factory training centers to learn to repair new models or to receive special training in subjects such as automatic transmission or air-conditioning repair. Manufacturers also send representatives to lo cal shops to conduct short training sessions. Promising beginners may be selected by automobile dealers to attend factory-sponsored mechanic training programs.

Experienced mechanics who have leadership ability may advance to shop supervisor or service manager. Mechanics who like to work with customers may become service advisors. Many mechanics open their own repair shops or gasoline service stations and about 1 out of 7 automobile mechanics is self-employed.

Employment Outlook

Job opportunities for automobile mechanics will be plentiful in the years ahead. Because this is a large occupation, replacement needs are high. Thus, in addition to openings that will be created by employment growth, thousands of job openings will arise each year due to the need to replace experienced mechanics who retire, die, or change jobs.

Employment of automobile mechanics is expected to increase about as fast as the average for all occupations through the mid-1980's. The number of mechanics is expected to increase because expansion of the driving age population and consumer purchasing power will increase the number of automobiles on the road. Employment also is expected to grow because a greater number of automobiles will be equipped with pollution control and safety devices, air-conditioning, and other features that increase maintenance requirements.

Most persons who enter the occupation may expect steady work because the automobile repair business is not much affected by changes in economic conditions.

Earnings and Working Conditions

Skilled automobile mechanics employed by automobile dealers in 36 cities had estimated average hourly earnings of $7.76 in 1976, about two-thirds more than the average for all nonsupervisory workers in private industry, except farming.

Many experienced mechanics employed by automobile dealers and independent repair shops receive a commission, usually about half the labor cost charged to the customer. Under this method, weekly earnings depend on the amount of work completed by the mechanic. Employers frequently guarantee commissioned mechanics a minimum weekly salary. Skilled mechanics usually earn between two and three times as much as inexperienced helpers and trainees.

Most mechanics work between 40 and 48 hours a week, but many work even longer hours during busy periods. Mechanics paid by the hour frequently receive overtime rates for hours over 40 a week.

Generally, mechanics work indoors. Modern automobile repair shops are well ventilated, lighted, and heated, but older shops may not have these advantages.

Mechanics frequently work with dirty and greasy parts, and in awkward positions. Many of the automobile parts and tools that they must lift are heavy. Minor cuts and bruises are common, but serious accidents can be avoided by keeping the shop clean and orderly and observing other safety practices.

Some mechanics are members of labor unions. Among the unions organizing these workers are the International Association of Machinists and Aerospace Workers; the International Union, United Automobile, Aerospace and Agricultural Implement Workers of America; the Sheet Metal Workers' International Association; and the International Brotherhood of Teamsters, Chauffeurs, Warehousemen and Helpers of America (Ind.).

Sources of Additional Information

For more details about work opportunities, contact local employers such as automobile dealers and repair shops; locals of the unions previously mentioned; or the local office of the State employment service. The State employment service also may have information about apprenticeship and other programs that provide training opportunities.

For general information about the work of automobile mechanics, write to:

Automotive Service Industry Association, 230 North Michigan Ave., Chicago, Ill. 60601.

Automotive Service Councils, Inc., 188 Industrial Dr., Suite 112, Elmhurst, Ill. 60126.

National Automobile Dealers Association, 2000 K St. NW., Washington, D.C. 20006.

BOAT-ENGINE MECHANICS

(D.O.T. 623.281 and 625.281)

Nature of the Work

Boat engines have many things in common with automobile engines, including unannounced breakdowns. A reliable engine is particularly essential in boating. Breakdowns far from shore can leave a boater stranded for hours—a frustrating and potentially dangerous predicament if the weather turns bad.

To minimize the possibility of breakdowns, engine manufacturers recommend periodic inspections of engines by qualified mechanics to have engines examined and repaired and worn or defective parts replaced. Also, at periodic intervals the mechanic may replace ignition points, adjust valves, and clean the carburetor. After completing these tasks, the engine will be run to check for other needed adjustments. Routine maintenance jobs normally make up most of the mechanic's workload.

When breakdowns occur, mechanics diagnose the cause and repair faulty parts. A quick and accurate diagnosis—one of the mechanic's most valuable skills—requires problem-solving ability as well as a thorough knowledge of the engine's operation. Some jobs require only the replacement of a single item, such as a fuel pump, and may be completed in less than an hour. In contrast, tearing down and reassembling an engine to replace worn valves, bearings, or piston rings may take a day or more.

Mechanics may specialize in either

outboard or inboard engines, although many repair both. Most small boats have portable gasoline-fueled outboard engines. Larger craft such as cabin cruisers and commercial fishing boats are powered by inboard engines (located inside the boat) and are similar to automobile engines. Some inboards burn diesel fuel rather than gasoline.

In large shops, mechanics usually work only on engines and other running gear. In small shops they also may patch and paint hulls and repair steering mechanisms, lights, and other boat equipment, such as refrigerators, two-way radios, and depth finders. In addition, they may repair enginecycles, mini-bikes, snowmobiles, lawnmowers, and other machines which have small gasoline engines that are similar to outboard engines.

Mechanics use common handtools such as screwdrivers and wrenches; power and machine tools, including drills and grinders; and hoists to lift engines and boats. Engine analyzers, compression gauges, and other testing devices help mechanics locate faulty parts. Mechanics refer to service manuals for assistance in assembling and repairing engines.

Places of Employment

Most of the 15,000 full-time boat-engine mechanics employed in 1976 worked in the shops of boat dealers and marinas. The next largest area of employment was in boat manufacturing plants where mechanics are employed to make final adjustments and repairs at the end of assembly lines. A small number of mechanics worked for boat rental firms. Marinas operated by Federal, State, and local governments also employed mechanics.

Dealer and marina shops typically employ one to three mechanics; few employ more than 10. Some small dealers and marinas do not employ mechanics; owners do the repair work or send it to larger shops.

Boat-engine mechanics work in every State, but employment is concentrated along coastal areas in Florida, Texas, New York, California, Louisiana, Washington, and New Jersey, and near the numerous lakes and riv-

ers in Michigan, Minnesota, Wisconsin, Illinois, Ohio, Indiana, and Missouri. Mechanics who specialize in outboard engines work in all areas. Those who specialize in inboard engines generally work near oceans, bays, and large lakes.

Training, Other Qualifications, and Advancement

Boat-engine mechanics learn the trade on the job. At first, trainees clean boats and engines and do other odd jobs. Then, under the guidance of experienced mechanics, trainees learn to do other routine mechanical tasks such as replacing ignition points and spark plugs. As trainees gain experience, they progress to more difficult tasks such as diagnosing the cause of breakdowns and overhauling engines. Generally, an inexperienced beginner needs 2 to 3 years on the job to become skilled in repairing both outboard and inboard gasoline engines. A capable mechanic can learn to repair diesels in an additional year or two.

Employers sometimes send trainees and mechanics to factory-sponsored courses for 1 to 2 weeks. Trainees learn the fundamentals of engine repair. Mechanics upgrade their skills and learn to repair new models.

In the past few years, several schools around the country have begun to offer formal training courses in marine engine repair and maintenance.

When hiring trainees, employers look for persons who have mechanical aptitude, are in good physical condition, and have an interest in boating. High school graduates are preferred, but many employers will hire people with less education. High school courses in small engine repair, automobile mechanics, machine shop, and science are helpful. Before graduating, a person may be able to get a summer job as a mechanic trainee.

Mechanics usually are required to furnish their own handtools. Beginners are expected to accumulate tools as they gain experience. Many experienced mechanics have several hundred dollars invested in tools. Employers provide power tools and

test equipment.

Mechanics with leadership ability can advance to supervisory positions such as shop supervisor or service manager. Some boat-engine mechanics transfer to jobs as automobile mechanics. Others may become sales representatives. Mechanics who have the necessary capital may open their own dealerships or marinas.

Employment Outlook

Employment of boat-engine mechanics is expected to grow about as fast the average for all occupations through the mid-1980's. In addition to new positions, a few hundred openings will arise each year as experienced mechanics retire, die, or transfer to other occupations.

Employment is expected to increase due to the growth in the number of boats. The number of boats is expected to increase at about the same rate as the economy as a whole. As population grows, and people have more time for recreation, boating, like other leisure activities, will probably expand.

Employment opportunities will be particularly favorable for mechanics who have a knowledge of electricity and electronics. Electrical appliances are becoming more common on boats, and many new boats have two-way radios and depth finders.

Earnings and Working Conditions

According to a nationwide survey of boat dealers and marinas, estimated hourly earnings of experienced mechanics ranged from about $3.50 to $9.75 in 1976. Experienced mechanics generally earned two to three times as much as trainees.

Most mechanics are paid an hourly rate or weekly salary. Others are paid a percentage—usually 50 percent—of the labor charge for each repair job. If mechanics are paid on a percentage basis, their weekly earnings depend on the amount of work they are assigned and on the length of time they take to complete it.

Boating activity increases sharply as the weather grows warmer. Consequently, many mechanics work more than 40 hours a week in spring and summer. During the peak seaon, some mechanics may work 7 days a week. However, in the winter, they may work less than 40 hours a week; a relatively small number are laid off. In Northern States, some of the winter slack is taken up by repair work on snowmobiles.

The work is not hazardous, but mechanics sometimes suffer cuts, bruises, and other minor injuries. Shop working conditions vary from clean and spacious to dingy and cramped. All shops are noisy when engines are being tested. Mechanics occasionally must work in awkward positions to adjust or replace parts. For many mechanics, however, these disadvantages are more than compensated for by the variety of assignments and the satisfaction that comes from solving problems. Moreover, mechanics may enjoy working near water recreation areas.

Sources of Additional Information

For details about training or work opportunities, contact local boat dealers and marinas or local State employment offices.

BUSINESS MACHINE REPAIRERS

(D.O.T. 633.281)

Nature of the Work

Business machine repairers maintain and repair the machines that are used to speed the paperwork in business and government. These include typewriters, adding and calculating machines, cash registers, dictating machines, postage meters, and duplicating and copying equipment.

Business machine repairers (often called field engineers or customer engineers) make regular vists for preventive maintenance to the offices and stores of customers in their assigned area. The frequency of these service calls depends upon the type of equipment being serviced. For example, an electric typewriter may require preventive maintenance only three or four times a year, while a more complex copier probably would require more frequent attention. During these calls, the engineer inspects the machine for unusual wear and replaces any worn or broken parts. Then the machine is cleaned, oiled, and adjusted to insure peak operating efficiency and to prevent future breakdowns. The engineer also may advise machine operators how to operate the equipment more efficiently and how to spot a problem in its early stages.

Despite frequent maintenance, business machines do occasionally malfunction. When a field engineer is notified by the supervisor of a breakdown, he or she will make a prompt service call to that customer. The engineer determines the cause of the malfunction by talking to the operator and examining the machine. Once the problem has been isolated, repairs can be made. Minor repairs generally can be made on the spot; for more serious repairs, however, the entire machine or a component of the machine will be taken to the repair shop where a specialist will, work on it.

Business machine repairers generally specialize in one type of machine. Those employed by manufacturing companies or dealers usually are familiar only with the brand produced or sold by their employer. Repairers who work for small independent repair shops must be able to work on equipment from several different manufacturers.

Repairers use common handtools, such as screwdrivers, pliers, and wrenches, as well as other tools especially designed to fit certain kinds of business machines. In addition, they use meters and other types of test equipment to check for malfunctions in electronic circuits.

Places of Employment

About 58,000 people worked as business machine repairers in 1976. About three-fourths of them worked mainly on typewriters, calculators and adding machines, and copiers and duplicators. Most of the rest serviced accounting-bookkeeping machines, cash registers, and postage and mailing equipment. A small number repaired dictating machines.

About 8 of 10 repairers worked for business machine manufacturers, dealers, and repair shops. The remainder worked for large organizations that had enough machines to justify full-time repairers.

Business machine repairers work throughout the country. Even relatively small communities usually have at least one or two repair shops. Most repairers, however, work in large cities.

Training, Other Qualifications, and Advancement

The amount of formal education required for entry jobs as business machine repairers varies widely among employers. Some employers hire applicants with a high school education, while many others require at least 1 year of technical training in basic electricity or electronics. Employers agree, however, that electronics training received in the Armed Forces is valuable.

Applicants for entry jobs may have to pass tests that measure mechanical aptitude, knowledge of electricity or electronics, manual dexterity, and general intelligence. Good eyesight, including color vision, is needed to inspect and work on small, delicate parts. Persons considering this type of work also should have good hearing in order to detect malfunctions revealed by sound.

Employers seek applicants who have a pleasant, cooperative manner.

Because most machine servicing is done in customers' offices, the ability to work without interrupting the office routine is very important. A neat appearance and ability to converse effectively are essential.

Some employers require that business machine repairers be bonded. Applicants for these jobs must be honest and trustworthy because they sometimes are exposed to large sums of money and other valuables in banks and offices. In addition, these workers must be able to work without direct supervision. They must be able to set up a maintenance schedule for their customers' equipment and arrange their own schedule so that they can meet service deadlines and also handle emergency repairs.

Trainees who work in a manufacturer's branch office or for a franchised dealer usually attend a school sponsored by the manufacturer. Training programs at company schools usually last several weeks to several months, depending on the type of machine the repairer will service. Trainees then receive from 1 to 3 years of practical experience and on-the-job training before they become fully qualified repairers. These workers generally learn to service only the company's line of equipment.

Training offered by independent repair shops usually is less formal. Trainees generally complete a self-study course coupled with on-the-job training under the supervision of an experienced repairer. Because small repair shops usually don't specialize in the more sophisticated types of equipment, their repairers are expected to be familiar with the more common machines produced by many manufacturers. For example, business machine repairers in small shops should be able to repair several different makes of typewriters, adding machines, and calculators.

Wherever they work, business machine repairers frequently attend training seminars sponsored by business equipment manufacturers for special instruction in new business machine developments. Also, business machine repairers are encouraged to broaden their technical knowledge during nonworking hours. Many companies pay the repairer's tuition for work-related courses in college and technical schools.

Business machine repairers may move into sales positions for greater earnings. Repairers who show management abilities also may advance to service manager or supervisor. Experienced repairers sometimes open their own repair shops; those who work in manufacturers' branch offices sometimes become independent dealers or buy sales franchises from the company.

Employment Outlook

Employment of business machine repairers is expected to grow faster than the average for all occupations through the mid-1980's. In addition to jobs from employment growth, many openings will arise as experienced repairers retire, die, or change occupations.

Employment opportunities for qualified beginners are good. Business and government will buy more machines to handle the growing volume of paperwork and more people will be trained to maintain and repair these machines. In recent years, many technical changes have occurred in business machines. Electronic calculating machines have replaced mechanical models, for example, and electronic cash registers are replacing mechanical registers. Because of the greater use of such equipment, opportunities will be particularly favorable for repairers who have training in electronics; within several years training in basic electronics may even become a prerequisite for business machine repair jobs.

Business machine repairers work year round and have steadier employment than many other skilled workers. Office machines must be maintained, even when business slackens, since records must be kept, correspondence carried on, and statistical reports prepared.

Earnings and Working Conditions

Information from a limited number of employers in 1976 indicated that trainees earned from $150 to $200 a week, depending on their level of training. For example, people who have previous electronics training in the Armed Forces or civilian technical schools generally receive somewhat higher beginning wages than high school graduates.

Experienced repairers generally earned from $200 to $280 a week. Earnings usually were highest for those who repaired electronic business machines and complex duplicating and copying equipment. Repairers who prepare themselves to work on more than one type of equipment can increase their earnings by about 20 percent. Specialists earned salaries ranging between $220 and $310 a week in 1976, according to the limited information available.

Servicing business machines is cleaner and less strenuous than the work in most other mechanical trades. Repairers generally wear business clothes and do most of their work in the customer's office. Injuries are uncommon.

Repairers generally use their own cars to travel to their customers' offices and are reimbursed on a mileage basis. Employers usually pay for all tools and other equipment.

Sources of Additional Information

For more details about job opportunities, contact local firms that sell and service business machines and the local office of the State employment service.

The State department of education in your State capital can furnish information about approved technical institutes, junior colleges, and other institutions offering postsecondary training in basic electronics. Additional information about these schools is available from:

U.S. Office of Education, Division of Vocational/Technical Education, Washington DC. 20202.

DIESEL MECHANICS

(D.O.T. 625.281)

Nature of the Work

Diesel engines are stronger and thus last longer than gasoline engines. In addition, they use fuel more efficiently than gasoline engines because the higher compression ratios found in diesel engines convert a higher percentage of the fuel into power. Because of their greater durability and efficiency, diesel engines are used to power most of the Nation's heavy vehicles and equipment.

Diesel mechanics repair and maintain diesel engines that power transportation equipment, such as heavy trucks, buses, boats, and locomotives; and construction equipment such as bulldozers and cranes. They also service diesel farm tractors and a variety of other diesel-powered equipment, such as compressors and pumps used in oil well drilling and in irrigation.

Before making repairs, diesel mechanics may use devices such as dynamometers to inspect and test engine components to determine why an engine is not operating properly. After locating the trouble, they repair or replace defective parts and make adjustments. Preventive maintenance—avoiding trouble before it starts—is another major responsibility. For example, they may periodically inspect, test, and adjust engine parts such as fan belts and fuel filters.

Many mechanics make all types of diesel engine repairs. Others specialize, in rebuilding engines, for example, or in repairing fuel injection systems, turbochargers, cylinder heads, or starting systems. Some also repair large natural gas engines used to power generators and other industrial equipment. In addition to maintaining and repairing engines, diesel mechanics may work on other parts of diesel-powered equipment, such as brakes and transmissions.

Most workers who maintain and repair diesel engines are not called diesel mechanics. Instead, their job titles usually indicate the type of diesel equipment they repair. For example, workers who maintain and repair diesel trucks or buses are called truck or bus mechanics and those who work on diesel farm tractors are called farm equipment mechanics. Many of these occupations are discussed elsewhere in the *Handbook*. (See statements on truck mechanics, bus mechanics, automobile mechanics, and farm equipment mechanics.)

Diesel mechanics use pliers, wrenches, screwdrivers, and other common handtools as well as special tools, such as valve refacers and piston pin-fitting machines. In addition, they may use complex testing equipment, such as a dynamometer to measure engine power, and special fuel injection testing equipment. Mechanics also may use machine tools to make replacement parts. They use powered hoists and other equipment for lifting and moving heavy parts.

Places of Employment

About 100,000 persons worked as diesel mechanics in 1976. Many worked for distributors and dealers that sell diesel engines, farm and construction equipment, and trucks.

Others were employed by buslines, construction firms, and government agencies such as State highway departments. Some mechanics worked for diesel engine manufacturers and independent repair shops that specialize in diesels.

Because diesel engines are used throughout the country, diesel mechanics are employed in almost every town and city. However, those who work for trucking companies and buslines are employed mainly in large cities.

Training, Other Qualifications, and Advancement

Diesel mechanics learn their skills in several different ways. Many begin by repairing gasoline-powered automobiles, trucks, and buses. They usually start as helpers to experienced gasoline engine mechanics, becoming skilled in all types of repairs in 3 or 4 years. If the garage or business they work for uses or repairs diesel equipment, they receive several months of additional training in servicing this equipment. While learning to fix engines on the job, many find it helpful to take courses in diesel equipment maintenance offered by vocational, trade, and correspondence schools.

A few mechanics learn their trade through formal apprenticeship programs. These programs, which generally last 4 years, give trainees a combination of classroom training and practical experience. The classroom instruction usually covers blueprint reading, hydraulics, welding, and other subjects related to diesel repair.

Still another method of entry is through full-time attendance at trade or technical schools that offer training in diesel engine maintenance and repair. These programs generally last from several months to 2 years and provide classroom instruction and often practical experience. Graduates, however, usually need additional on-the-job training before they are capable of handling all types of diesel repair.

Experienced mechanics employed by companies that sell diesel-powered equipment sometimes are sent to special training classes conducted

by engine manufacturers. In these classes, mechanics learn to maintain and repair the latest engines, using the most modern equipment. In addition, they may receive training in specialties such as engine rebuilding.

Employers prefer trainees and apprenticeship applicants who have a high school or vocational school education and mechanical ability. Shop courses in blueprint reading, automobile repair, and machine shop work are helpful, as are courses in science and mathematics. Because the work often requires lifting heavy parts, persons interested in becoming diesel mechanics should be in good physical condition.

Many diesel mechanics have to buy their own handtools and beginners are expected to accumulate tools as they gain experience. Experienced mechanics usually have several hundred dollars invested in their tools.

Mechanics who work for organizations that operate or repair large numbers of diesel engines, such as buslines or diesel equipment distributors, may advance to a supervisory position, such as shop supervisor or service manager.

Employment Outlook

Employment of diesel mechanics is expected to increase faster than the average for all occupations through the mid-1980's. In addition to the jobs arising from employment growth, many openings will result from the need to replace experienced mechanics who transfer to other occupations, retire, or die.

Increased employment of mechanics is expected mainly because most industries that use diesel engines are expected to expand their activities in the years ahead. In addition, diesel engines will continue to replace gasoline engines in trucks, buses, and other equipment because properly tuned diesels use less fuel and produce less pollution.

Most new job openings in this field will be filled by mechanics who have experience in repairing gasoline engines. Companies that replace gasoline engine equipment with diesel-powered equipment usually retrain their experienced mechanics. Persons who have school training in diesel repair, but no practical experience, may be able to find jobs only as trainees.

Earnings and Working Conditions

According to a 1975-76 wage survey covering 36 metropolitan areas, mechanics employed by trucking companies, buslines, and other firms that maintain their own vehicles earned an average hourly wage of $6.67, more than one-third above the average for all nonsupervisory workers in private industry, except farming.

Diesel mechanics usually work 40 to 48 hours a week. Many work at night or on weekends, particularly if they work on buses, engines used in powerplants, or other diesel equipment used in serving the public. Some are subject to call for emergencies at any time. Mechanics generally receive a higher rate of pay when they work overtime, evenings, or weekends.

Most larger repair shops are pleasant places in which to work, but some small shops have poor lighting, heating, and ventilation. Diesel mechanics sometimes make repairs outdoors where breakdowns occur. If proper safety precautions are not taken, there is danger of injury when repairing heavy parts supported on jacks or hoists. In most jobs, mechanics handle greasy tools and engine parts. When making repairs, they sometimes must stand or lie in awkward positions.

Many diesel mechanics belong to labor unions, such as the International Association of Machinists and Aerospace Workers; the Amalgamated Transit Union; the Sheet Metal Workers' International Association; the International Union, United Automobile, Aerospace and Agricultural Implement Workers of America; and the International Brotherhood of Electrical Workers.

Sources of Additional Information

Information about work opportunities in this trade may be available from the local office of the State employment service. Other sources of information are firms that use or service diesel-powered equipment, such as truck and buslines, truck dealers, and construction and farm equipment dealers. Additional information on careers is available from:

International Association of Machinists and Aerospace Workers, 1300 Connecticut Ave. NW., Washington, D.C. 20036.

ELECTRIC SIGN REPAIRERS

(D.O.T. 824.281)

Nature of the Work

A common form of advertising for many businesses and products is the electric sign. Electric sign repairers maintain and repair neon and illuminated plastic signs so their owners can receive the most benefits from them.

When a sign requires service, repairers drive to its location, carrying their tools and a number of replacement parts in a truck. Repairers' trucks are equipped with ladders and boom cranes so they can work on tall signs or those placed high above the ground. Common sources of sign trouble such as burned-out bulbs are easy to fix. However, in some cases, the problem may not be obvious and repairers may need to use electronic test equipment to determine the cause of a breakdown. Although simple repairs such as replacing bulbs or transformers are done at the site, major repairs of faulty parts such as neon tubing, are made in sign shops.

Repairers also do preventive maintenance and periodic inspection of signs to locate and correct defects before breakdowns occur. They check signs and remove debris such as birds' nests and accumulated water. Repairers also tighten or weld parts that have been loosened by winds and repaint beams, columns, and other framework. They may repaint portions of neon tubing to make the sign more readable. Motors, gears, bearings, and other parts of revolving signs may be checked, adjusted, and lubricated.

During periods with few service calls, repairers who work for sign manufacturing companies may help to assemble signs. Some repairers also install signs.

Repairers use common handtools and power tools, such as screwdrivers, pliers, saws, and electric drills. They also use ammeters, voltmeters, and other testing devices to locate malfunctioning electric parts. When replacing burned out parts such as a lamp or a flasher in illuminated plastic signs, repairers may refer to wiring diagrams and charts.

Repairers usually must fill out reports noting the date, place, and nature of service calls. They also may estimate the cost of service calls and sell maintenance contracts to sign owners.

Places of Employment

About 10,000 persons worked as electric sign repairers in 1976, primarily in small shops that manufacture, install, and service electric signs. Some worked for independent sign repair shops.

Electric sign repairers work throughout the country. However, employment is concentrated in large cities and in populous States, where large numbers of electric signs are used.

Training, Other Qualifications, and Advancement

Most electric sign repairers are hired as trainees and learn the trade informally on the job. Trainees perform the various phases of signmaking in the shop to obtain a general knowledge of tasks—such as cutting and assembling metal and plastic signs, mounting neon tubing, wiring signs, and installing electrical parts. After they have a thorough knowledge of the construction of signs, trainees accompany experienced repairers on service calls to learn to do repairs and maintenance. At least 4 years of on-the-job training and experience are required to become a fully qualified repairer.

Some people learn the trade through sign repairer or electrician apprenticeship programs that are conducted by some union locals and sign manufacturing shops. The apprenticeships usually last 4 years, emphasize on-the-job training, and include classroom instruction in subjects such as electrical theory and blueprint reading. Apprentices generally must be at least 18 years old with a high school diploma. Attempts are being made by unions and the National Electric Sign Association to increase the number of apprenticeship programs, so the availability of this type of training should increase in the future.

Employers prefer to hire high school or vocational school graduates, although many repairers have less education. Courses in mathematics, science, electronics, and blueprint reading are helpful to young people who are interested in learning this trade.

Repairers need good color vision because electric wires are frequently identified by color. They also need manual dexterity to handle tools, and physical strength to lift transformers and other heavy equipment. Because much of their work is done on ladders or from the baskets of boom trucks, repairers cannot be afraid of heights.

All electric sign repairers must be familiar with the National Electric Codes. Many cities require repairers to be licensed. Licenses can be obtained by passing an examination in local electrical codes, and electrical theory and its application.

Highly skilled repairers may become supervisors. Because of their experience in servicing signs and dealing with customers, repairers sometimes become sign sales representatives. Repairers with sufficient funds can open their own sign manufacturing or repair shops.

Employment Outlook

Employment of electric sign repairers is expected to increase as fast as the average for all occupations through the mid-1980's. A rapid increase in the number of signs in use will spur demand for these workers. More signs will be needed as new businesses open and old ones expand and modernize their facilities. Signs already in use also will continue to require service because well maintained signs are good for business and also because many State and local governments require owners to keep their signs attractive. In addition to jobs from employment growth, some openings will arise as experienced workers retire, die, or leave the occupation for other reasons.

Earnings and Working Conditions

The earnings of electric sign repairers compare favorably with those of other skilled workers. It is estimated that the hourly wage rate of experienced repairers was about $7.80 in 1976, based on a survey of union wages and fringe benefits throughout the country. Apprentice rates usually range from $3.90 to $6.25 an hour.

Most electric sign repairers work an 8-hour day, 5 days a week, and receive premium pay for overtime. They also may receive extra pay for working at heights in excess of 30 feet.

Because most signs are out-of-doors, repairers are exposed to all kinds of weather. They sometimes make emergency repairs at night, on weekends, and on holidays. In some large cities, repairers patrol areas at night to locate and fix improperly operating signs. Hazards include electrical shock, burns, and falls from high places. Training programs emphasizing safety, and equipment, such as saskets on boom trucks, which allow easy access to signs, have reduced frequency of accidents. Repairers 4ay spend much time traveling to the site of a service call.

Many electric sign repairers belong to one the following unions: the International Brotherhood 6f Electrical Workers, the Sheet Metal Workers International Association, and the International Brotherhood of Painters and Allied Trades.

Sources of Additional Information

For further information on work opportunities, contact local sign manufacturing shops, the local office of the State employment service, or locals of the unions previously mentioned.

General information on job opportunities, wages, and the nature of the work is available from:

National Electric Sign Association, 2625 Butterfield Rd., Oak Brook, Ill. 60521.

FARM EQUIPMENT MECHANICS

(D.O.T. 624.281 and .381)

Nature of the Work

Years ago farmers planted, cultivated, and harvested their crops using only handtools and simple animal-drawn equipment. Few repairs were required and if a stray rock or stump broke a plow blade, the metal pieces could be hammered back together by the local blacksmith. Even when tractors began to replace animals as the prime source of power, their simplicity made it possible for most farmers to do their own repair work.

But in the last quarter century farm equipment has grown enormously in size and variety. Many farms have both diesel and gasoline tractors, some equipped with 300-horsepower engines. Other machinery, such as harvesting combines, hay balers, corn pickers, crop dryers, and elevators, also is common. In today's world of mechanized agriculture, few if any types of farming can be done economically without specialized machines.

As farm machinery grew more complex, it became important for the sellers of farm equipment to be able to service and repair the machines they sold. Almost every dealer employs farm equipment mechanics to do this work and to maintain and repair the smaller lawn and garden tractors dealers sell to surburban homeowners.

In addition, some mechanics assemble new implements and machinery for farm equipment dealers and wholesalers, and occasionally they must repair dented or torn sheet metal on the bodies of tractors or other machinery.

Mechanics spend much of their time repairing and adjusting malfunctioning diesel- and gas-powered tractors that have been brought to the shop. During planting or harvesting seasons, however, the mechanic may travel to the farm to make emergency repairs so that crops can be harvested before they spoil.

Mechanics also perform preventive maintenance. Periodically, they test, adjust, and clean parts and tune engines. In large shops, mechanics may specialize in certain types of work, such as engine overhaul or clutch and transmission repair. Others specialize in repairing the air-conditioning units often included in the cabs of modern tractors and combines, or in repairing certain types of equipment such as hay balers. Some mechanics also repair plumbing, electrical, irrigation, and other equipment on farms.

Mechanics use many simple handtools including wrenches, pliers, hammers, and micrometers. They also may use more complex testing equipment, such as a dynamometer to measure engine performance, or a compression tester to find worn piston rings or leaking cylinder valves. They may use welding equipment or power tools to repair broken parts.

Places of Employment

Most of the estimated 66,000 farm equipment mechanics employed in 1976 worked in service departments of farm equipment dealers. Others worked in independent repair shops, in shops on large farms, and in service departments of farm equipment wholesalers and manufacturers. Most farm equipment repair shops employ fewer than five mechanics, although a few dealerships employ more than 10. A small proportion of farm equipment mechanics are self-employed.

Because some type of farming is done in nearly every area of the United States, farm equipment mechanics are employed throughout the country. As employment is concentrated in small cities and towns, this may be an attractive career choice for people who do not wish to live the fast-paced life of an urban environ-

ment. However, many mechanics work in the rural fringes of metropolitan areas, so farm equipment mechanics who prefer city life need not live in rural areas.

Training, Other Qualifications, and Advancement

Most farm equipment mechanics are hired as helpers and learn the trade on the job by assisting qualified mechanics. The length of training varies with the helper's aptitude and prior experience. At least 2 years of on-the-job training usually are necessary before a mechanic can do most types of repair work, and additional training and experience are required for highly specialized repair and overhaul jobs.

Many farm equipment mechanics enter this occupation from a related occupation. For instance, they may gain experience as farmers and farm laborers, or as heavy equipment mechanics, auto mechanics, or air-conditioning mechanics. People who enter from related occupations also start as helpers, but they may not require as long a period of on-the-job training.

More and more mechanics who enter the trade have had vocational training in rural high schools, in junior and technical colleges, or in the Armed Forces. With the development of more complex farm implements, technical training in electronics has become more important.

A few farm equipment mechanics learn the trade by completing an apprenticeship program, which lasts from 3 to 4 years and includes on-the-job as well as classroom training in all phases of farm equipment repair and maintenance. Applicants for these programs usually are chosen from shop helpers.

Some farm equipment mechanics and trainees receive refresher training in short-term programs conducted by farm equipment manufacturers. These programs usually last several days. A company service representative explains the design and function of equipment and teaches maintenance and repair on new models of farm equipment. In addition,

some dealers may give employee time off to attend local vocation schools that teach special weeklon classes in subjects such as air-conditioning repair or hydraulics.

Employers prefer applicants wh have an aptitude for mechanic work. A farm background is an ad vantage since growing up on a farr usually provides experience in basi farm equipment repairs. Employer also prefer high school graduates, bu some will hire applicants who hav less education. In general, employer stress previous experience or trainin in diesel and gasoline engines, th maintenance and repair of hydrau lics, and welding—subjects that ma be learned in many high schools an vocational schools. Some employer also may require mechanics to b skilled at blueprint reading, because mechanics may have to refer to dia grams of machinery when makin complex repairs to electrical and oth er systems.

Persons considering careers in thi field should have the manual dexter ity needed to handle tools and equip ment. Occasionally, strength is re quired to lift, move, or hold in place heavy parts. Difficult repair jobs ma require problem-solving abilities, so experienced mechanics should be able to work independently with minimum supervision.

Farm equipment mechanics may advance to shop supervisor or manager of a farm equipment dealership. Some mechanics open their own repair shops. A few farm equipment mechanics earn 2-year associate degrees in agricultural mechanics and advance to service representatives for farm equipment manufacturers.

Employment Outlook

Employment of farm equipment mechanics is expected to increase about as fast as the average for all occupations through the mid-1980's. In addition to jobs from employment growth, several hundred job opportunities will arise each year as experienced mechanics retire, die, or transfer to other occupations. Opportunities will be best for applicants who have lived or worked on farms and know how to operate farm machinery and make minor repairs.

The development of more technically advanced farm equipment, some of which will require greater maintenance, will increase the demand for mechanics. For instance, many newer tractors have much larger engines, and feature advanced transmissions of up to 24 speeds. More complex electrical systems also are used to operate the great variety of gauges and warning devices now used to alert the operator to problems such as brake wear, low oil pressure in the transmission, or insufficient coolant in the radiator. Advances such as these and air-conditioned cabs, which have improved the comfort of the operator, have made it more difficult for farmers to do their own repairs. Thus farmers will have to rely more on skilled mechanics in the future.

In addition to the larger and more complex farm machinery, sales of smaller lawn and garden equipment have increased vastly over the past decade and are expected to continue to do so. Most of the large manufacturers of farm equipment now produce a line of these smaller tractors and sell them through their established dealerships. More mechanics will be needed to service this additional equipment.

Earnings and Working Conditions

Average hourly wages of farm equipment mechanics ranged from about $3.50 to $6.35 in 1976, based on the limited information available. However, a few mechanics earned over $15,000 in 1976 because employees are paid time and a half for overtime. Farm equipment mechanics usually work a 44-hour week, which includes 4 hours on Saturday. During planting and harvesting seasons, however, they often work 6 to 7 days a week, 10 to 12 hours daily. In winter months, they may work fewer than 40 hours a week, and some may be laid off.

Mechanics often travel many miles to repair equipment in the field, and are exposed to all kinds of weather. They come in contact with grease, gasoline, rust, and dirt, and there is

danger of injury when they repair heavy parts supported on jacks or by hoists. Engine burns and cuts from sharp edges of machinery also are possible.

Very few farm equipment mechanics belong to labor unions, but those who do are members of the International Association of Machinists and Aerospace Workers.

Sources of Additional Information

Details about work opportunities may be obtained from local farm equipment dealers and local offices of the State employment service. For general information about the occupation, write to:

National Farm and Power Equipment Dealers Association, 10877 Watson Road, St. Louis, Mo. 63127.

INDUSTRIAL MACHINERY REPAIRERS

(D.O.T. 626. Through 631.)

Nature of the Work

When a machine breaks down in a plant or factory, not only is the machine idle, but raw materials and human resources are wasted. It is the industrial machinery repairer's job to prevent these costly breakdowns and to make repairs as quickly as possible.

Industrial machinery repairers—often called maintenance mechanics—spend much time doing preventive maintenance. This includes keeping machines well oiled and greased, and periodically cleaning parts. The repairer regularly inspects machinery and checks performance. Tools such as micrometers, calipers, and depth gauges are used to measure and align all parts. For example, on sewing machines in the apparel industry, treadles may need adjustment and gears and bearings may have to be aligned. By keeping complete and up-to-date records, mechanics can anticipate trouble and hopefully service machinery before

the factory's production is interrupted.

When repairs become necessary, the maintenance mechanic must first locate the specific cause of the problem. This challenge requires knowledge reinforced by instinct. For example, after hearing a vibration from a machine, the mechanic must decide whether it is due to worn belts, weak motor bearings, or any number of other possibilities. Repairers often follow blueprints and engineering specifications in maintaining and fixing equipment.

After correctly diagnosing the problem, the maintenance mechanic disassembles, and then repairs or replaces the necessary parts. Hand and power tools usually are needed. The repairer may use a screwdriver and a wrench to take the door off an oven or a crane to lift a printing press off the ground. Electronic testing equipment often is included in the mechanic's tools. Repairers use catalogs to order replacements for broken or defective parts. When parts are not readily available, or when a machine must be quickly returned to production, repairers may sketch a part that can be fabricated by the plant's machine shop.

The repairer reassembles and tests each piece of equipment after it has been serviced, for once it is back in operation, the machine is expected to work as if it were new.

Many of the industrial machinery repairer's duties, especially preventive maintenance, also are performed by millwrights.

Places of Employment

Industrial machinery repairers work in almost every industry that uses large amounts of machinery. Many of the 320,000 repairers employed in 1976 worked in the following manufacturing industries: food products, primary metals, machinery, chemicals, fabricated metal products, transportation equipment, paper, and rubber.

Because industrial machinery repairers work in a wide variety of plants, they are employed in every section of the country. Employment is concentrated, however, in heavily industrialized areas.

Training, Other Qualifications, and Advancement

Most workers who become industrial machinery repairers start as helpers and pick up the skills of the trade informally, through several years of experience. Others learn the trade through formal apprenticeship programs. Apprenticeship training usually lasts 4 years and consists of both on-the-job training and related classroom (or correspondence school) instruction in subjects such as shop mathematics, blueprint reading, welding, and safety. Upgrade examinations may be administered periodically to determine the repairer's ability to maintain more advanced machinery. Some repairers are promoted to machinists or tool and die makers. A few become master mechanics.

Mechanical aptitude and manual dexterity are important qualifications for workers in this trade. Good physical condition and agility also are necessary because repairers sometimes have to lift heavy objects or do considerable climbing to reach equipment located high above the floor.

High school courses in mechanical drawing, mathematics, and blueprint reading are recommended for those interested in entering this trade.

Employment Outlook

Employment of industrial machinery repairers is expected to increase much faster than the average for all occupations through the mid-1980's. In addition to jobs from employment growth, many openings will result from the need to replace experienced repairers who retire, die, or transfer to other occupations.

More repairers will be needed to take care of the growing amount of machinery used in manufacturing, coal mining, oil exploration, and other industries. In addition, as machinery becomes more complex, repair work and preventive maintenance will become more essential.

Earnings and Working Conditions

According to a survey of metropolitan areas, hourly wages for industrial machinery repairers averaged $6.47 in 1976—one-third higher than the average for all nonsupervisory workers in private industry, except farming. Average hourly earnings of industrial machinery repairers in 12 areas that represent various regions of the country are shown in the following tabulation:

Area	Hourly rate
Detroit	$7.66
Indianapolis	7.18
Baltimore	7.13
Chicago	6.89
Houston	6.80
New York	6.33
Cincinnati	6.27
Minneapolis—St. Paul	6.24
St. Louis	6.19
New Orleans	5.71
Worcester, Mass.	5.59
Greenville—Spartanburg, S.C.	4.76

Industrial machinery repairers usually are not affected by seasonal changes in production. During slack periods when some plantworkers are laid off, repairers often are retained to do major overhaul jobs.

Industrial machinery repairers may be called to the plant during off-duty hours, especially in emergencies. Thus they may have to work nights and weekends, depending on the maintenance necessary.

Repairers may work in stooped or cramped positions, to reach the underside of a generator, for example. They also may find it necessary to work from the top of ladders when repairing a large machine. These workers are subject to common shop injuries such as cuts and bruises. Goggles, metal-tip shoes, safety helmets, and other protective devices help prevent injuries.

Labor unions to which most industrial machinery repairers belong include the United Steelworkers of America; the International Union, United Automobile, Aerospace and Agricultural Implement Workers of America; the International Association of Machinists and Aerospace Workers; and the International

Union of Electrical, Radio and Machine Workers.

Sources of Additional Information

Information about employment and apprenticeship opportunities in this field may be available from local offices of the State employment service or the following organizations:

International Union, United Automobile, Aerospace, and Agricultural Implement Workers of America, 8000 East Jefferson Ave., Detroit, Mich. 48214.

International Union of Electrical, Radio, and Machine Workers, 1126-16th St. NW., Washington, D.C. 20036.

LOCKSMITHS

(D.O.T. 709.281)

Nature of the Work

Locksmithing is an ancient trade—so old, in fact, that archeologists have found evidence of key-operated wooden locks made for Egyptian royalty as early as 2000 B.C. For many centuries, the locksmith's talents were available to only the relatively few who could afford the locks of the day, which were sometimes elaborate, if none too foolproof. In 1861, the pin tumbler lock was invented and a mass-production method developed that made these locks nearly as common as doors themselves. The locksmith came into demand as never before.

Today's locksmiths spend much of their time helping people who have locked themselves out of their cars, homes, and businesses. If the key has been left inside the car or house, for example, they may simply pick the lock. If, on the other hand, the keys are lost, new ones must be made. To do this, locksmiths first will try to obtain identifying key code numbers so that they can cut duplicates of the original key. Code numbers for a car's keys, for example, may be obtained by consulting the dealer who sold the car, or by checking the owner's bill of sale. Keys also can be duplicated by impression. In this case, locksmiths place a blank key in the lock and, by following marks left on the blank, file notches in it until it works.

Combination locks offer a special challenge. Locksmiths sometimes open them by touch, that is, by rotating the dial and feeling the vibrations when the wheels come into place. If all else fails, a hole may be drilled through the lock to open it. Finally, locksmiths repair damaged locks by replacing tumblers, springs, and other parts.

An important part of the lock-smith's job is to recommend security measures to customers. For example, they may advise a firm to rekey its locks periodically. To rekey, locksmiths change the locking mechanism to fit new key codes, thus making the old keys useless. Rekeying a master system is one of the most complicated and time-consuming jobs handled by a locksmith. In a master system, some keys must open all doors; others open various combinations (for example, all doors on one floor); still others are individual keys for each door.

Some locksmiths install and repair electronic burglar alarms and surveillance systems that signal police or firefighters when break-ins or fires occur. A basic knowledge of electricity and electronics is needed to install and repair these systems. Much of the work is done by specialists called protective-signal repairers, rather than by locksmiths.

Locksmiths use screwdrivers, pliers, tweezers, and electric drills in their work, as well as special tools such as lockpicks. They make original and duplicate keys on keycutting machines. To guide them in their work, they refer to manuals that describe the construction of various locks.

Places of Employment

Most of the estimated 10,000 locksmiths in 1976 worked for locksmith shops. Many operated their own businesses. Locksmith shops typically employ one to three locksmiths; few employ more than five. Some locksmiths worked in hardware and department stores that offered locksmith services to the public; others worked in government agencies and large industrial plants. A small number worked for safe and lock manufacturers.

Although most jobs will be found in big cities, locksmiths work in virtually every part of the country. Locksmithing in small towns, however, is usually a part-time job, often combined with other work, such as fixing lawnmowers, guns, and bicycles.

Training, Other Qualifications, and Advancement

The skills of this trade are learned primarily through on-the-job training under experienced locksmiths. First, beginners may learn to duplicate keys and make keys from codes. Later, they learn to open, repair, and install locks, and finally, to work on safes. Generally, a beginner needs about 4 years of on-the-job training to qualify as a locksmith. Additional training is needed to service electronic security systems.

Formal training also is available in a few public and private schools that offer 1- to 2-year programs in locksmithing. Students are taught the basics of locksmithing such as repairing and opening locks. At some schools, students may specialize in safe repair or alarm systems. Completion of a course, however, does not assure a job; interested persons should check with local employers to make sure the school's training is acceptable.

Employers look for people who have mechanical aptitude, good hand-eye coordination, and manual dexterity. A neat appearance and a friendly, tactful manner also are important, since the locksmith has frequent contact with the public. Employers usually will not hire applicants who have been convicted of crimes.

Although high school graduates are preferred, many employers will hire applicants with less education. High school courses in machine shop, mechanical drawing, electronics, and mathematics are helpful. Completion of a correspondence school course in locksmithing increases the chances of getting a train-

ee job.

Many States and cities have licensing requirements. To obtain a license, the applicant generally must be fingerprinted and pay a fee. Some cities require that an individual pass a written or pratical examination. However, specific requirements vary from city to city. Information on licensing may be obtained from local governments.

To keep up with new developments in their field, locksmiths read monthly technical journals or attend training classes at the annual convention of Associated Locksmiths of America.

Locksmiths can advance to shop supervisors—positions found, however, only in the larger shops. Experienced locksmiths also can go into business for themselves with relatively little capital. Many do business from their homes.

Employment Outlook

Employment in this relatively small occupation is expected to grow faster than the average for all occupations through the mid-1980's. In addition to the need to fill new positions, a few hundred openings will arise each year as experienced locksmiths retire, die, or transfer to other occupations.

Employment of locksmiths is expected to increase as a result of population growth and a more security-conscious public. Also, many businesses feel that conventional locks and other security devices are not adequate and are having more complex equipment installed. Opportunities will be particularly favorable for locksmiths who know how to install and service electronic security systems. Use of such systems has expanded greatly in recent years, and still greater growth is expected in the future. Opportunities also will be favorable for locksmiths who are willing to work at night to handle emergencies.

Earnings and Working Conditions

Experienced locksmiths earned from about $4.60 to $7.50 an hour in early 1976, according to the limited information available; many self-employed locksmiths earned even more. Trainees usually started at about $2.50 an hour, with periodic raises during training.

Most locksmiths receive an hourly rate or weekly salary, although some work on a commission basis, receiving a percentage of the money they collect; their earnings depend on the amount of work available and how quickly they complete it.

Locksmiths generally work year round. Most work 40 to 48 hours a week; even longer hours are common among the self-employed. The locksmith may be called at night to handle emergencies, though in many shops the responsibility to be "on call" is rotated among the staff.

Locksmiths do considerable driving from job to job. At times, they must work outside in bad weather and occasionally work in awkward positions for long periods. However, locksmithing is cleaner work than that of most mechanical trades and is comparatively free from the danger of injury.

Sources of Additional Information

Details about training and work opportunities may be available from local locksmith shops and local offices of the State employment service. For a list of schools offering courses in locksmithing and general information about the occupation, contact:

Associated Locksmiths of America, Inc., 3003 Live Oak St., Dallas, Tex. 75204.

MAINTENANCE ELECTRICIANS

(D.O.T. 825.281 and 829.281)

Nature of the Work

Maintenance electricians keep lighting systems, transformers, generators, and other electrical equipment in good working order. They also may install new electrical equipment. Duties vary greatly, depending on where the electrician is employed.

Electricians who work in large factories may repair particular items such as motors and welding machines. Those in office buildings and small plants usually fix all kinds of electrical equipment. Regardless of location, electricians spend much of their time doing preventive maintenance—periodic inspection of equipment to locate and correct defects before breakdowns occur. When trouble occurs, they must find the cause and make repairs quickly to prevent costly production losses. In emergencies, they advise management whether continued operation of equipment would be hazardous.

Maintenance electricians make repairs by replacing items such as a fuse, switch, or wire. When replacing a wire, they first make sure the power is off. Workers then pull the old wire from the conduit (a pipe or tube) and pull the new wire through to replace the old. Once the new wire is connected, they test to make sure the circuit is complete and functioning properly.

Maintenance electricians sometimes work from blueprints, wiring diagrams, or other specifications. They use meters and other testing devices to locate faulty equipment. To make repairs they use pliers, screwdrivers, wirecutters, drills, and other tools.

Places of Employment

An estimated 300,000 maintenance electricians were employed in 1976. More than half of them worked in manufacturing industries; large numbers worked in plants that make automobiles, machinery, chemicals, aluminum, and iron and steel. Many maintenance electricians also were employed by public utilities, mines, railroads, and by Federal, State, and local governments.

Maintenance electricians are employed in every State. Large numbers work in heavily industrialized States such as California, New York, Pennsylvania, Illinois, and Ohio.

Training, Other Qualifications, and Advancement

Most maintenance electricians learn their trade on the job or through formal apprenticeship pro-grams. A relatively small number learn the trade in the Armed Forces. Training authorities generally agree that apprenticeship gives trainees more thorough knowledge of the trade and improved job opportunities during their working life. Because the training is comprehensive, people who complete apprenticeship programs may qualify either as maintenance or construction electricians.

Apprenticeship usually lasts 4 years, and consists of on-the-job training and related classroom instruction in subjects such as mathematics, electrical and electronic theory, and blueprint reading. Training may include motor repair, wire splicing, installation and repair of electronic controls and circuits, and welding and brazing.

Although apprenticeship is the preferred method of training, many people learn the trade informally on the job by serving as helpers to skilled maintenance electricians. Helpers begin by doing simple jobs such as replacing fuses or switches and, with experience, advance to more complicated jobs such as splicing and connecting wires. They eventually get enough experience to qualify as electricians. This method of learning the trade, however, may take more than 4 years.

Persons interested in becoming maintenance electricians can obtain a good background by taking high school or vocational school courses in electricity, electronics, algebra, mechanical drawing, shop, and science. To qualify for an apprenticeship program, an applicant must be at least 18 years old and usually must be a high school or vocational school graduate with 1 year of algebra.

Although physical strength is not essential, manual dexterity, agility, and good health are important. Good color vision is necessary because electrical wires frequently are identified by color.

All maintenance electricians should be familiar with the National Electric Code and local building codes. Many cities and counties require maintenance electricians to be licensed. Electricians can get a license by passing an examination that tests their knowledge of electrical theory and its application.

Some maintenance electricians become supervisors. Occasionally, they advance to jobs such as plant electrical superintendent or plant maintenance superintendent.

Employment Outlook

Employment of maintenance electricians is expected to increase about as fast as the average for all occupations through the mid-1980's. This growth will stem from increased use of electrical and electronic equipment by industry. In addition to the jobs from employment growth, a few thousand openings will arise each year to replace experienced electricians who retire, die, or transfer to other occupations.

Growth in the number of job openings is expected to be fairly steady in the years ahead since the demand for maintenance electricians is not very sensitive to ups and downs in the economy. At times when construction activity is depressed, however, beginners may face competition for job openings because some unemployed construction electricians apply for these openings.

Earnings and Working Conditions

Earnings of maintenance electricians compare favorably with those of other skilled workers. In 1976, based on a survey of metropolitan areas, maintenance electricians averaged about $6.95 an hour, ranging from $4.84 in Greenville, S.C., to $8.02 in Indianapolis. By comparison, all production and nonsupervisory workers in private industry, except farming, averaged $4.87.

Apprentices start at about 60 percent of the skilled electrician's hourly pay rate and receive increases every 6 months.

During a single day, an electrician may repair equipment both in a clean, air-conditioned office and on a factory floor, surrounded by the noise, oil, and grease of machinery. Electricians often climb ladders or work on scaffolds in awkward or cramped positions.

Because maintenance electricians work near high-voltage industrial equipment, they must be alert and accurate. Errors in wiring installations could endanger both the electrician and other employees. Safety principles, which are a part of all electrician training programs, have reduced the frequency of accidents. Electricians are taught to use protective equipment and clothing, to respect the destructive potential of electricity, and to fight small electrical fires.

Among unions organizing maintenance electricians are the International Brotherhood of Electrical Workers; the International Union of Electrical, Radio and Machine Workers; the International Association of Machinists and Aerospace Workers; the International Union, United Automobile, Aerospace and Agricultural Implement Workers of America (Ind.); and the United Steelworkers of America.

Sources of Additonal Information

Information about apprenticeships or other work opportunities in the trade is available from local firms that employ maintenance electricians, and from local union-management apprenticeship committees. In addition, the local office of the State employment service may provide information about training opportunities. Some State employment service offices screen applicants and give aptitude tests.

MOTORCYCLE MECHANICS

(D.O.T. 620.281 and .384)

Nature of the Work

In 1950 there were just over 500,000 motorcycles in the United States. Today there are over 5 million. Accompanying this rapid rise in the number of motorcycles has been a rapid increase in the number of motorcycle mechanics. For although many cycling enthusiasts repair their own vehicles, most rely on skilled mechanics.

Motorcycles, like automobiles, need periodic servicing to operate at peak efficiency. Spark plugs, ignition points, brakes, and many other parts frequently require adjustment or replacement. This routine servicing represents the major part of the mechanic's work.

The mark of a skilled mechanic is the ability to diagnose mechanical and electrical problems and to make repairs in a minimum of time. In diagnosing problems, the mechanic first obtains a description of the symptoms from the owner, and then runs the engine or test-rides the motorcycle. The mechanic may have to use special testing equipment and disassemble some components for further examination. After pinpointing the problem, the mechanic makes needed adjustments or replacements. Some jobs require only the replacement of a single item, such as a carburetor or generator, and may be completed in less than an hour. In contrast, an overhaul may require several hours, because the mechanic must disassemble and reassemble the engine to replace worn valves, pistons, bearings, and other internal parts.

Mechanics use common handtools such as wrenches, pliers, and screwdrivers, as well as special tools for getting at parts that are hard to remove such as flywheels and bearings. They also use compression gauges, timing lights, and other kinds of testing devices. Hoists are used to lift heavy motorcycles.

Most mechanics specialize in servicing only a few of the more than 30 brands of motorcycles and motor scooters. In large shops, some mechanics specialize in overhauling and rebuilding engines and transmissions, but most are expected to perform all kinds of repairs. Mechanics may occasionally repair mini-bikes, go-carts, snowmobiles, outboard motors, lawnmowers, and other equipment powered by small gasoline engines.

Places of Employment

About 12,000 persons had full-time jobs as motorcycle mechanics in

1976, and a few thousand more had part-time jobs. Most mechanics work for motorcycle dealers. Others work for city governments to maintain police motorcycles. A small number of mechanics work for firms that specialize in modifying or "customizing" motorcycles. Most shops employ fewer than five mechanics.

Motorcycle mechanics work in every State and major city. About half work in nine States: California, Michigan, Texas, Ohio, Pennsylvania, Illinois, Florida, Minnesota, and Indiana.

Mechanics who specialize in repairing motorcycles work mainly in metropolitan areas. In smaller cities, motorcycles frequently are repaired by owners or managers of motorcycle dealerships or by mechanics who repair all kinds of equipment powered by small gasoline engines, such as outboard motors and lawnmowers.

Training, Other Qualifications, and Advancement

Motorcycle mechanics usually learn their trade on the job, by picking up skills from experienced workers. Beginners usually start by learning to uncrate, assemble, and road-test new motorcycles. Next, they learn routine maintenance jobs such as adusting brakes and replacing spark plugs and ignition points. As trainees gain experience, they progress to more difficult tasks such as repairing electrical systems and overhauling engines and transmissions. Generally, 2 to 3 years of training on the job are necessary before trainees become skilled in all aspects of motorcycle repair.

Trainees usually accumulate handtools as they gain experience. Experienced mechanics often have several hundred dollars invested in tools.

Employers sometimes send mechanics and experienced trainees to special training courses conducted by motorcycle manufacturers and importers. These courses, which can last as long as 2 weeks, are designed to upgrade the worker's skills and provide information on repairing new models.

When hiring trainees, employers look particularly for cycling enthusiasts who have gained practical experience by repairing their own motorcycles. However, many employers will hire trainees with no riding experience if they have mechanical aptitude and show an interest in learning the work. Trainees must be able to obtain a motorcycle driver's license so they can deliver newly assembled motorcycles and test drive those brought in for repairs.

Most employers prefer high school graduates, but will accept applicants with less education. Courses in small engine repair—offered by some high schools and vocational schools—generally are helpful, as are courses in automobile mechanics, science, and mathematics. Many motorcycle dealers employ students to help assemble new motorcycles and perform minor repairs.

Public schools in some large cities offer postsecondary and adult education in small engine and motorcycle repair. Some technical schools have training programs for motorcycle mechanics. Many junior and community colleges offer courses in motorcycle repair.

Because all internal combustion engines are similar, skills learned through repairing motorcycles can be transferred to other fields of mechanical work. For example, motorcycle mechanics can become automobile, truck, or diesel mechanics after some additional training. However, transferring to one of these occupations would not necessarily mean higher earnings.

Motorcycle mechanics have limited advancement possibilities. Those with supervisory ability may advance to service manager and, eventually, to general manager in large dealerships. Those who have the necessary capital may become dealers.

Employment Outlook

Employment in this relatively small occupation is expected to grow faster than the average for all occupations through the mid-1980's. Openings arising from growth will fluctuate from year to year, however, as motorcycle sales and thus employment of motorcycle mechanics appear to be sensitive to dips in the business cycle. Additional openings will arise from the need to replace experienced mechanics who retire, die, or transfer to other fields of work.

Underlying the anticipated growth in the number of motorcyle mechanics is the continued growth in the number of motorcycles. Increases in the young adult population and in personal income levels will create a demand for more motorcycles, and additional mechanics will be needed to maintain these machines. Also, growth in the numbers of minibikes and snowmobiles will stimulate the demand for mechanics.

Opportunities for employment will be best in larger dealerships, most of which are located in the suburbs of metropolitan areas. Many motorcycle dealers in small cities do not have enough business to hire full-time trainees, but part-time or summer jobs may be available.

Earnings and Working Conditions

Earnings of motorcycle mechanics and trainees vary widely and depend on level of skill, geographic location, season of the year, and employer. Limited information indicates that experienced mechanics employed by motorcycle dealers earned between $4 and $10 an hour in late 1976. Generally, experienced mechanics earned 2 to 3 times as much as trainees.

Some mechanics receive an hourly rate or a weekly salary. Others receive a percentage—usually about 50 percent—of the labor cost charged to the customer. If a mechanic is paid on a percentage basis, income depends on the amount of work assigned and how rapidly the mechanic completes it. Frequently, trainees are paid on a piecework basis when uncrating and assembling new motorcycles. At other times, they are paid an hourly rate or weekly salary.

Motorcycling increases sharply as the weather grows warmer. As a result, most mechanics work more than 40 hours a week during the summer. Many temporary workers hired to help handle the increased work load work only part time, and are laid off in the fall. However, a large proportion of these are either students or workers with other jobs.

Motorcycle repair shops generally are well-lighted and ventilated, but are noisy when engines are being tested. The work is not hazardous, although mechanics are subject to cuts, bruises, burns, and other minor injuries. Since motorcycles are relatively lightweight and have easily accessible parts, mechanics rarely do heavy lifting or work in awkward positions.

A small percentage of motorcycle mechanics are members of the International Association of Machinists and Aerospace Workers.

Sources of Additional Information

For further information regarding employment opportunities and training, contact local motorcycle dealers or the local office of the State employment service.

SHOE REPAIRERS

(D.O.T. 365.381)

Nature of the Work

People like their shoes to look nice and be in good condition. Keeping them that way is the job of the shoe repairer.

Shoe repairers spend most of their time replacing worn soles and heels. They remove worn soles and old stitching, and "rough" the bottom of the shoes on sanding wheels. They select precut soles or cut them from pieces of leather; they then cement, nail, or sew the soles to the shoes. Finally, they trim the soles. To re-heel shoes, repairers pry off old heels, select replacement heels or cut them to shape, and cement and nail them into place. After the heels and soles have been replaced, repairers stain and buff them to match the color of the shoes.

Shoe repairers also replace insoles, restitch loose seams, and restyle old shoes by changing heels or dyeing uppers. Highly skilled repairers may design, make, or repair orthopedic shoes according to doctors' prescrip-

tions. Repairers also may mend handbags, luggage, tents, and other items made of leather, rubber, or canvas. They also replace zippers, dye handbags, and stretch shoes to conform to the foot.

In large shops, repair work sometimes is divided into a number of specialized tasks. For example, some repairers only remove and replace heels and soles; others only restitch torn seams.

Shoe repairers use power-operated sole-stitchers and heel-nailing machines, and manually operated sewing machines. Among the handtools they use are hammers, awls, nippers, and skivers (a special tool for splitting pieces of leather).

Self-employed shoe repairers have managerial responsibilities in addition to their regular duties. They estimate repair costs, keep records, and supervise other repairers.

Places of Employment

About 25,000 shoe repairers were employed in 1976. About one-half of them owned shoe repair shops, many of which were small, one-person operations. Most of the remaining repairers worked in large shoe shops. Some repairers worked in shoe stores, department stores, and drycleaning shops. A small number were employed in shoe manufacturing, to repair shoes damaged in production. These workers generally are less skilled than those who work in repair shops.

All cities and towns and many very small communities have shoe repair shops. Employment, however, is concentrated in large cities.

Training, Other Qualifications, and Advancement

Most shoe repairers learn on the job as helpers to experienced repairers. Helpers begin by assisting experienced repairers with simple tasks, such as staining, brushing, and shining shoes. As they gain experience, trainees learn to replace heels and soles, to estimate the cost of repairs, and to deal with customers. Helpers usually become fully skilled in 2 to 3 years.

Some repairers learn the trade at vocational schools. Applicants to vocational schools usually must have a high school diploma. In addition to learning shoe repairing, vocational school students attend classes in business administration. The programs last from 6 months to 2 years. Graduates often are encouraged to gain additional training by working with experienced shoe repairers.

Shoe repairers must have manual dexterity and mechanical aptitude to work with various machines and handtools. They must be able to work alone with little supervision. Shoe repairers need patience to perform the work and deal with customers. Repairers who own shops must have a working knowledge of basic arithmetic to maintain records.

Advancement opportunities for shoe repairers are limited. Many open their own shops and some who are employed in large shops become supervisors.

Employment Outlook

Employment of shoe repairers is not expected to change significantly through the mid-1980's. Nevertheless, numerous job openings are expected each year in this relatively small occupation, because of the need to replace experienced shoe repairers who retire, die, or leave the field for other reasons. Job opportunities should be very good because few people are attracted to this occupation. Opportunities should be especially good for experienced repairers who wish to open their own shops.

In recent years, employment of shoe repairers has declined because new shoes were relatively inexpensive and many people bought new shoes instead of having old ones fixed. This reduced the need for shoe repairs and repairers. The popularity of cushion-soled shoes and other casual footwear which usually are not practical to repair also limited the demand for these workers. However, shoe repairer employment is expected to remain about the same in the future. Expected shoe price increases should reduce the practice of replacing worn shoes with new shoes and should stimulate the demand for repairs.

Earnings and Working Conditions

Information from a limited number of employers indicates that shoe repairers earned between $3 and $4 an hour in 1976. Inexperienced trainees generally earned between $2.30 and $2.50 an hour. Some highly skilled repairers, including managers of shoe repair shops, earned more than $300 a week.

Shoe repairers generally work 8 hours a day, 5 days a week. The workweek for the self-employed is often longer, sometimes 10 hours a day, 6 days a week. Although shoe repair shops are busiest during the spring and fall, work is steady with no seasonal layoffs.

Because many shoe repairers own shops, working conditions are determined by the repairer. Large shops are usually comfortable, but small shops may be crowded and noisy and have poor light or ventilation. Strong odors from leather goods, dyes, and stains may be present.

The work is not strenuous and there are few hazards. However it does require stamina, because repairers must stand much of the time.

Sources of Additional Information

Information about training opportunities may be obtained from:

Shoe Service Institute of America, 222 W. Adams St., Chicago, Ill. 60606.

Information about work opportunities is available from State employment service offices, as well as shoe shops in the community.

TRUCK MECHANICS AND BUS MECHANICS

(D.O.T. 620.281)

Nature of the Work

Commercial vehicles serve an important function in the Nation's economy. Heavy trucks are used by industries, such as mining and construction to carry ore and building materials, while small trucks are used for local hauling. Buses are used for both local and transcontinental transportation, as well as for shipping some goods. Truck and bus mechanics perform the vital role of keeping these vehicles in good operating condition.

Truck and bus mechanics work on both diesel and gasoline engines. However, most mechanics usually repair only one type, because many of the engine components are different. (See the statement on diesel mechanics elsewhere.)

Mechanics who work for organizations that maintain their own vehicles may spend much time doing preventive maintenance to assure safe operation, to prevent wear and damage to parts, and to reduce costly breakdowns. During a maintenance check, they usually follow a regular check list that includes the inspection of brake systems, steering mechanisms, wheel bearings and other important parts. If a part is not working properly, they usually can repair or adjust it. If it cannot be fixed, it is replaced.

In many shops mechanics do all kinds of repair work. For example, they may work on a vehicle's electrical system one day and do major engine repair the next. In some large shops, however, mechanics specialize in one or two types of repair work. For example, one mechanic may specialize in major engine repair, another in transmission work, another in electrical systems and yet another in suspension or brake systems.

Truck and bus mechanics use a variety of tools in their work. They use power tools such as pneumatic wrenches to remove bolts quickly; machine tools such as lathes and grinding machines to rebuild brakes and other parts; welding and flame cutting equipment to remove and repair mufflers and other parts; common handtools such as screwdrivers, pliers, and wrenches to work on small parts and reach hard-to-get-to places; and jacks and hoists to lift and move large parts.

Truck and bus mechanics also use a variety of testing equipment. For example, when working on electrical systems, they may use ohmmeters, ammeters, and voltmeters; to locate engine malfunctions, they often use dynamometers.

For heavy work, such as removing engines and transmissions, two mechanics may work as a team, or a mechanic may be assisted by an apprentice or helper. Mechanics generally get their assignments from shop supervisors or service managers who may check the mechanics work or assist in diagnosing problems.

Places of Employment

A large proportion of the estimated 125,000 truck mechanics employed in 1976 worked for firms that owned fleets of trucks. Fleet owners include trucking companies and businesses that haul their own products such as dairies and bakeries. Other employers include truck dealers, truck manufacturers, truck repair shops, firms that rent or lease trucks, and Federal, State, and local governments.

Most of the estimated 20,000 bus mechanics employed in 1976 worked for local transit companies and intercity buslines. Bus manufacturers employed a relatively small number of mechanics.

Truck and bus mechanics are employed in every section of the country, but most work in large towns and cities where trucking companies, buslines, and other fleet owners have large repair shops.

Training, Other Qualifications, and Advancement

Most truck or bus mechanics learn their skills on the job. Beginners usually do tasks such as cleaning parts, fueling, and lubrication. They may also drive vehicles in and out of the shop. As beginners gain experience and as vacancies become available, they usually are promoted to mechanics' helpers. In some shops, beginners—especially those having prior automobile repair experience—start as mechanics' helpers.

Most helpers can make minor repairs after a few months experience and advance to increasingly difficult jobs as they prove their ability. Generally, 3 to 4 years of on-the-job experience are necessary to qualify as an all-round truck or bus mechanic.

Additional training may be necessary for mechanics who wish to specialize in diesel engines.

Most training authorities recommend a formal 4-year apprenticeship as the best way to learn these trades. Typical apprenticeship programs for truck and bus mechanics consist of approximately 8,000 hours of shop training in which trainees obtain practical experience working on transmissions, engines, and other components and at least 576 hours of classroom instruction in which trainees learn blueprint reading, mathematics, engine theory and safety. Frequently, these include training in both diesel and gasoline engine repair.

For entry jobs, employers generally look for applicants who have mechanical aptitude, are at least 18 years of age, and in good physical condition. Completion of high school is an advantage in getting an entry mechanic job because most employers believe it indicates that a person has at least some of the traits of a good worker, such as reliability and perseverance. Employers do not want to spend a lot of time and money training mechanics only to see them quit.

When the mechanic's duties include driving trucks or buses on public roads, applicants may need a State chauffeur's license. If the employer is engaged in interstate transportation, applicants also may have to meet qualifications for drivers established by the U.S. Department of Transportation. These applicants must be at least 21 years of age, in good physical condition, and have good hearing and 20/40 eyesight with or without glasses. They must read and speak English and have a good driving record, including 1 year's driving experience.

Persons interested in becoming truck or bus mechanics can gain valuable experience by taking high school or vocational school courses in automobile and diesel repair. Science and mathematics are helpful since they better one's understanding of how trucks and buses operate. Practical experience in automobile repair from working in a gasoline service station, the Armed Forces, or as a hobby also is valuable.

Most mechanics must buy their own handtools. Experienced mechanics often invest several hundred dollars in tools.

Employers sometimes send experienced mechanics to special training classes conducted by truck, bus, diesel engine, and parts manufacturers. In these classes, mechanics learn to repair the latest equipment or receive special training in subjects such as diagnosing engine malfunctions. Mechanics also may read service and repair manuals to keep abreast of engineering changes.

Experienced mechanics who have leadership ability may advance to shop supervisors or service managers. Truck mechanics who have sales ability sometimes become truck sales representatives. Some mechanics open their own gasoline service stations or repair shops.

Employment Outlook

Employment of truck mechanics is expected to increase about the same as the average for all occupations through the mid-1980's as a result of significant increases in the transportation of freight by trucks. More trucks will be needed for both local and intercity hauling due to the increased production of goods and the necessity of transporting them greater distances and to more places as both population and industrial centers spread out. In addition to the jobs created by employment growth, many openings will arise to replace truck mechanics who retire, die, or transfer to other occupations.

Bus mechanic employment is expected to increase slower than the average for all occupations through the mid-1980's because of offsetting factors affecting the demand for bus service. More buses will be needed for local travel due to increased emphasis on mass transit systems. Intercity bus travel, on the other hand, is expected to remain about the same. Most job openings will result from the need to replace bus mechanics who retire, die, or transfer to other occupations.

Earnings and Working Conditions

Truck and bus mechanics employed by trucking companies, buslines, and other firms that maintain their own vehicles had estimated average hourly earnings of $6.53 in 1976. By comparison, nonsupervisory workers in private industry, except farming, averaged $4.87.

Beginning apprentices usually earn one-half the rate of skilled workers and receive increases about every 6 months until a rate of 90 percent is reached.

Most mechanics work between 40 and 48 hours per week. Because many truck and bus firms provide service around the clock, mechanics who work for these firms may work evenings, nights, and weekends. When they do, they usually receive a higher rate of pay.

Truck mechanics and bus mechanics are subject to the usual shop hazards such as cuts and bruises. Mechanics handle greasy and dirty parts and may stand or lie in awkward or cramped positions when repairing vehicles. Work areas usually are well lighted, heated, and ventilated, and many employers provide locker rooms and shower facilities. Although most work is done indoors, mechanics occasionally work or make emergency repairs on the road.

Many truck and bus mechanics are members of labor unions, including the International Association of Machinists and Aerospace Workers; the Amalgamated Transit Union; the International Union, United Automobile, Aerospace and Agricultural Implement Workers of America; the Transport Workers Union of America; the Sheet Metal Workers' International Association; and the International Brotherhood of Teamsters, Chauffers, Warehousemen and Helpers of America (Ind.).

Sources of Additional Information

More details about work opportunities for truck or bus mechanics may be obtained from local employers such as trucking companies, truck dealers, or bus lines; locals of unions previously mentioned; or the local office of the State employment service. The State employment service also may have information about apprenticeship and other training programs.

For general information about the work of truck mechanics and apprenticeship training, write to:

American Trucking Associations, Inc., 1616 P St. NW., Washington, D.C. 20036.

The Outlook for Industries

MINING AND PETROLEUM

The mining and petroleum industry provides most of the basic raw materials and energy sources for industry and consumer use. Metal mines provide iron, copper, gold, and other ores. Quarrying and other non-metallic mining yield many of the basic materials such as limestone and gravel for building schools, offices, homes, and highways. Nearly all of the Nation's energy for industrial and personal use comes from oil, gas, and coal. Few products from mines reach the consumer in their natural state; nearly all require further processing.

The mining and petroleum industry employed about 770,000 workers in 1976. Almost half of these worked in the exploration for and removal of crude petroleum and natural gas. Coal mining accounted for over one-fourth of the industry's workers. The remaining workers were in metal mining and quarrying and nonmetallic mineral mining.

As shown in the accompanying chart, blue-collar workers (craft workers and operatives) account for nearly seven-tenths of the industry's employment. Operatives is the largest occupational group in the industry. Included in the operative group are oil well drillers, mining machinery operators, and truck and tractor drivers. Skilled craft workers constitute the second largest occupational group. Mechanics and repairers maintain the complex equipment and machinery used in mining and in oil well drilling. Many operators of heavy equipment, such as power shovels and bulldozers, work in open pit mining. Large numbers of pumpers, gaugers, and engine workers hold jobs in the production and transportation of petroleum and natural gas. Supervisors of blue-collar workers also constitute an important part of the craft worker group.

The industry's white-collar employees are divided among three occupational groups—professional and technical, clerical, and managerial workers. Taken together, these groups compose the remaining three-tenths of the industry's employment.

Professional and technical workers are concentrated largely in petroleum and gas extraction. Most are engineers, geologists, or technicians engaged in exploration and research. Two out of three clerical employees work in petroleum and gas extraction. Most are secretaries, office machine operators, and typists.

Employment in the mining and petroleum industry is expected to increase faster than the average for all industries through the mid-1980's, but different growth patterns are likely within the industry. Employment in coal mining and in petroleum and natural gas extraction should increase rapidly as the Nation strives to become self-sufficient in energy sources. Employment in metal mining also is expected to grow. Employment in quarrying and nonmetallic mining, on the other hand, is expected to decline as laborsaving equipment leads to higher output with fewer workers.

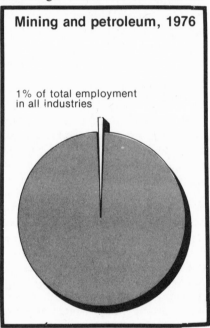

Mining and petroleum, 1976

1% of total employment in all industries

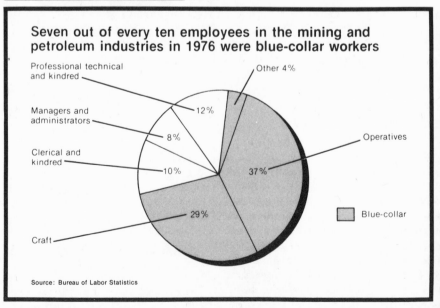

Seven out of every ten employees in the mining and petroleum industries in 1976 were blue-collar workers

Professional technical and kindred 12%

Managers and administrators 8%

Clerical and kindred 10%

Craft 29%

Other 4%

Operatives 37%

Blue-collar

Source: Bureau of Labor Statistics

COAL MINING

Nature of the Industry

Coal has played a vital role in the development of this Nation. Originally used only as a source of heat, coal grew rapidly as a source of power with the coming of the steam engine. By the beginning of the 20th century, coal had become vital, not only for heating homes and powering locomotives, but also as a source of energy for producing electric power and a necessary ingredient for making steel. Although coal has been largely replaced by other fuels for heating and transportation, it is used in products ranging from lipstick to chemicals, and most importantly as a source of electric power.

Coal usually is divided into two classes, bituminous and anthracite. Bituminous, or "soft" coal, is the most widely used and the most plentiful, and accounts for most coal production. Production of anthracite, or "hard" coal, on the other hand, is steadily declining due to dwindling reserves and difficulty of recovery. Other forms of coal, such as lignite and peat, are used in only limited amounts.

Most of the Nation's coal is mined in the Appalachian area that extends from Pennsylvania through Eastern Ohio, West Virginia, Virginia, Kentucky, Tennessee, and Alabama. Large amounts of coal also are mined in Indiana, Illinois, and in the Rocky Mountain States.

Types of Mines

Coal is either mined underground or extracted from the earth's surface. Underground mines employ most of the workers in the industry but produce less than half of all bituminous coal. Surface mining, a more productive type than underground mining, employs fewer miners to produce more coal.

The type of mine a company decides to open depends on the geological formation and the depth and location of the coal seam. Underground mines are used to reach coal that lies deep below the surface. A series of entries must be constructed so that air, miners, and equipment can reach the seam and coal can be carried out. Depending on the depth of the coal seam, the entry may be vertical (shaft mine), horizontal (drift mine), or at an angle (slope mine). (See chart.) Shaft mines are used to reach coal lying far below the surface. Drift and slope mines are usually not as far underground as shaft mines.

After the coal seam has been reached, nearly all underground mines are constructed the same way. Miners make a network of interconnecting tunnels so that the mine resembles a maze with passageways going off in predetermined directions, sometimes extending over many miles. As coal is removed, the tunnels become longer and longer. Throughout this process, a significant amount of coal (pillars) is left between the tunnels to support the roof. When miners reach the end of the company's property, they start working back toward the entrance, mining most of the remaining coal as they retreat. This is called retreat mining.

If the coal seam is not too far below ground, surface mining is practiced. Two types of surface mines are strip and auger. At strip mines, huge machines remove the earth and expose the coal. Auger mining is used to remove coal from extremely steep hillsides. A large auger (drill) bores into the hill and pulls the coal out.

Occupations in the Industry

In 1976 about 210,000 people worked in the bituminous coal and lignite mining industry. An additional 4,000 people were employed by companies producing anthracite coal. About 85 percent of all persons in these industries were production workers who mined and processed coal.

Mining jobs range from apprentice miners who usually act as helpers in several occupations to highly skilled and experienced miners who operate equipment worth several hundred thousand dollars. Jobs available in a mine vary by type and method of mining.

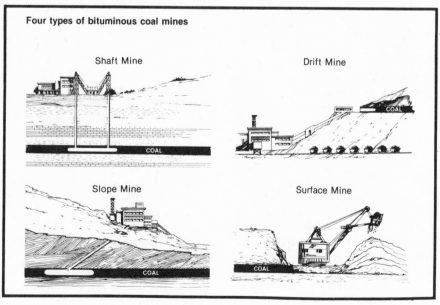

Four types of bituminous coal mines

Shaft Mine

Drift Mine

Slope Mine

Surface Mine

Mining Occupations. Two basic methods of mining underground coal, conventional and continuous, account for 95 percent of total underground production. A third method, longwall, makes up most of the remaining production and is increasing in importance. The hand loading method is rarely used.

Conventional mining is the oldest method and requires the most workers and procedures. This type of mining, however, is rapidly being phased out. In conventional mining, the *cutting machine operator* (D.O.T. 930.883) uses a huge electric chain saw, with a cutter ranging in length from 6 to 15 feet, to cut a strip, or kerf, underneath the coal seam to control the direction of the coal as it falls after it has been blasted. Next the *drilling machine operator* (D.O.T. 930.782) drills holes into the coal where the *shot firer* (D.O.T. 931.281) places explosives. This work can be dangerous and must be timed very carefully. The shot firer, for example, must allow enough time for miners to leave the area before the blast.

After the blast, the *loading machine operator* (D.O.T. 932.883) scoops up and dumps the coal into small rubber-tired cars, which are run by the *shuttle car operator* (D.O.T. 932.883). Depending on the type of haulage system used, these cars take the coal to a conveyor belt for shipment to the main entry or to the surface, or onto mine cars that are transported on tracks to the surface.

The continuous mining method eliminates the drilling and blasting operations of conventional mining. The *continuous-mining machine operator* (D.O.T. 930.883) sits or lies in a cab and operates levers to cut or rip out the coal and load it directly onto a conveyor or shuttle cars.

Longwall mining is basically an extension of continuous mining. In this method, the *longwall machine operator* runs a huge machine with drums which shear and automatically load coal onto a conveyor. At the same time hydraulic jacks reinforce the roof. As the coal is cut and the face progresses, the jacks are hydraulically winched forward and the roof is allowed to cave behind.

Many other workers are required to run a safe and efficient underground mine. Before miners are allowed underground, the *fire boss* or preshift examiner (D.O.T. 939.387) inspects the work area for loose roof, dangerous gases, and adequate ventilation. If safety standards are not met, the fire boss will not allow the miners to enter. The *rock-dust machine operator* (D.O.T. 939.887) sprays limestone on the mine walls and ground to hold down dust since coal dust is extremely explosive and interferes with breathing.

The *roof bolter* (D.O.T. 930.883) operates a machine to install roof support bolts. This operation is extremely important because of the ever-present threat of roof cave-ins, the biggest cause of mine injuries. The *stopping builder* (D.O.T. 869.884) constructs doors, walls, or partitions in the passageways to force air through the tunnels to working areas. The supervisor, called a *face boss* (D.O.T. 939.138), is in charge of all operations at the work site where coal is actually mined.

Teamwork is very important in all types of underground mining. Miners are dependent upon each other when accidents occur for first aid and, if necessary, assistance in leaving the mine. A simple slip around a continuous mining machine, for example, could result in severed limbs.

Most surface miners operate the large machines that either remove the earth above the coal or dig and load the coal. The number of workers required to operate a surface mine depends on the types of machines used and the amount of overburden above the coal seam. The more overburden present, the greater the number of workers usually required.

In many strip mines, the overburden is first drilled and blasted. Then the *overburden stripping operator* or *dragline operator* (D.O.T. 859.883) scoops the earth away to expose the coal. Sometimes, a dragline is so huge and complicated to run that a team of persons is required to operate the levers.

Once the overburden is removed, the *coal loading machine operator* (D.O.T. 932.883) rips coal from the seam and loads the coal into trucks to be driven to the preparation plant. In auger mines, the *rotary auger operator* (D.O.T. 930.782) runs the machine that pulls the coal from sides of hills. *Tractor operators* (D.O.T. 929.883) drive bulldozers to move materials or pull out imbedded boulders or other objects. Helpers assist in operating these machines.

Other workers, not directly involved in the mining processes, work in and around coal mines. For example, skilled repairers, called *fitters* (D.O.T. 801.281), fix all types of mining machinery, and electricians check and install electrical wiring. Carpenters construct and maintain benches, bins, and stoppings. Many mechanics and electricians assemble, maintain, and repair the machines used in mines. While these workers generally need the same skills as their counterparts in other industries, they require additional training to work under the unusual conditions in the mines. Mechanics, for example, may have to repair machines while on their knees with only their headlamp to illuminate the working area. Truckdrivers haul coal to railroad sidings or preparation plants and supplies to the mine.

Preparation Plant Occupations. Rocks and other impurities must be removed before coal is crushed, sized, or blended to meet the buyer's wishes. These processes take place at the preparation plant.

Many preparation plants are located next to the mine. The plant's size and number of employees vary by the amount of coal processed and degree of mechanization. Some plants have all controls centrally located and require few workers to oversee all washing, separating, and crushing operations. Among these workers is the *preparation plant central control operator* (D.O.T. 549.138) who oversees all operations. Plants that are not as mechanized, however, need workers at each step, such as the *wash box attendant* (D.O.T. 541.782) and *separation tender* (D.O.T. 934.885). Wash box attendants operate equipment that sizes and separates impurities from coal. The separation tender operates a device that further cleans coal with currents of water. Most jobs in the preparation plant are very repetitive.

Training, Other Qualifications, and Advancement

Most miners start out as helpers to experienced workers and learn skills on the job. Formal training, however, is becoming more important due to the growing use of technologically advanced machinery and mining methods. As a result, most companies supplement on-the-job training with formal programs and actively seek recent graduates of high school vocational programs in mining, or junior college or technical school programs in mine technology.

Mine technology programs are available in a few colleges throughout the country, mostly in coal mining areas. The programs lead either to a certificate in mine technology after 1 year, or an associate degree after 2 years. Courses cover areas such as mine ventilation, roof bolting, and machinery repairs. Prospective students do not need a high school education but must pass an entrance examination in basic math and English.

The type of formal training administered by coal companies varies. For example, some companies have training mines where skills are taught; others give classroom instruction for a few weeks before allowing workers into a mine. All miners working at mines covered by the United Mine Workers of America contract, however, must receive both preservice and annual retraining sessions from their employers. These programs include subjects such as machine operation, first aid, and health and safety regulations. The U.S. Mining Enforcement and Safety Administration also conducts classes on health, safety, and mining methods, and mine machinery manufacturers offer courses in machine operation and maintenance.

As miners gain more experience, they can move to higher paying jobs. When a vacancy occurs, an announcement is posted and all workers qualified may bid for the job. A mining machine operator's helper, for example, may become an operator. The position is filled on the basis of seniority and ability. A small number of miners advance to supervisory positions and, in some cases, to administrative jobs in the office.

Miners must be at least 18 years old and in good physical condition. A high school diploma is not required. All miners should be able to work in close areas and have quick reflexes in emergencies.

Requirements for scientific and engineering, administrative, and clerical jobs are similar to those in other industries. College graduates are preferred for jobs in advertising, personnel, accounting, and sales. For clerical and secretarial jobs, employers usually hire high school graduates who have training in stenography and typing.

Employment Outlook

Coal is expected to play an increasingly important role as a basic energy source. Rising demand for electric power coupled with greater emphasis on developing domestic energy supplies should result in accelerated coal production. The extent of growth in production, however, is uncertain. Oil, natural gas, and nuclear energy also are used to generate electricity, and the demand for coal will be determined, to some extent, by the price and availability of these fuels. Growth in production also depends on how quickly economical methods of coal gasification and liquification are developed. Environmental standards relating to strip mining and the use of high sulfur content coal, which causes air pollution, may also affect coal output. More coal, however, will be needed to make steel, chemicals, and other products.

Employment is expected to increase but the amount of growth will depend on the level of production, on the types of mines opened, and the mining methods and machinery used. In addition to openings due to growth, several thousand openings will occur each year as experienced miners retire, die, or transfer to other fields of work.

Earnings and Working Conditions

In 1976, union wage rates for miners ranged from $48.62 to $58.92 a day; workers in underground mines generally earned slightly more than those in surface mines or preparation plants. In comparison, production workers in manufacturing averaged $41.52 a day.

Because underground miners spend time traveling from the mine entrance to their working areas, they have a slightly longer day than surface miners. Those in surface occupations work a 7 1/4-hour shift (36-1/2-hour week), while underground miners work an 8-hour day (40-hour week).

Union miners receive 10 holidays and 14 days of paid vacation each year. As their length of service increases, they gain extra vacation days up to a total of 29. Union workers also receive benefits from a welfare and retirement fund, and workers suffering from pneumoconiosis (black lung) receive Federal aid.

Miners have unusual and harsh working conditions. Underground mines are damp, dark, noisy, and cold. At times, several inches of water may be on tunnel floors. Although mines have electric lights, many areas are illuminated only by the lights on the miners' caps. Workers in mines with very low roofs have to work on their hands and knees, backs, or stomachs in cramped areas.

Though safety conditions have improved considerably, miners must constantly be on guard for hazards. There also is the risk of developing pneumoconiosis from coal dust and silicosis from the rock dust generated by the drilling in the mines. Surface mines and preparation plants are usually less hazardous than underground mines.

Sources of Additional Information

For details about job opportunities in mining, contact individual coal companies. General information on mining occupations is available from:

United Mine Workers of America, 900 15th St. NW., Washington, D.C. 20005.

National Coal Association, 1130 17th St. NW., Washington, D.C. 20036.

Mining Enforcement and Safety Administration, Department of Interior, Washington, D.C. 20240.

CONSTRUCTION

The activities of the construction industry touch nearly every aspect of our daily lives. The houses and apartments in which we live; the factories, offices, and schools in which we work; and the roads on which we travel are examples of some of the products of this industry. The industry includes not only new construction, but also additions, alterations, and repairs to existing structures.

In 1976, about 3.6 million people worked in contract construction. An additional 1.4 million workers not in contract construction are estimated to be either self-employed—mostly owners of small building firms—or are Federal, State, or local government employees who build and maintain our Nation's vast highway systems.

The contract construction industry is divided into three major segments. About half of the jobholders work for electrical, air-conditioning, plumbing, and other special trade contractors. Almost one-third work for the general building contractors that do most residential, commercial, and industrial construction. The remaining one-fifth build dams, bridges, roads, and similar heavy construction projects.

As illustrated in the accompanying chart, craft and kindred workers account for 55 percent of the total employment in this industry—a much higher proportion than in any other major industry. Some examples of craft workers are carpenters, painters, plumbers, and bricklayers. Laborers are the next largest occupational group and account for 14 percent of employment. They provide materials, scaffolding, and general assistance to skilled workers. Semiskilled workers (operatives), such as truckdrivers and welders, represent about 8 percent of the industry's work force. Managers and administrators—mostly self-employed—account for about 12 percent of employment. Clerical workers, largely typists, secretaries, and office machine operators, constitute another 7 percent of the industry's employment. Professional and technical workers, mostly engineers and engineering technicians, drafters, and surveyors, make up the remaining 3 percent of the work force.

Construction industry employment is expected to rise faster than the average for all industries through the mid-1980's, as population and income growth create a demand for more houses, schools, factories, and other buildings. However, employment may fluctuate from year to year

workers in private industry, except farming. Yearly earnings of construction workers generally are lower than the hourly rate would indicate, however, because the annual number of hours they work can be adversely affected by poor weather and fluctuations in construction activity.

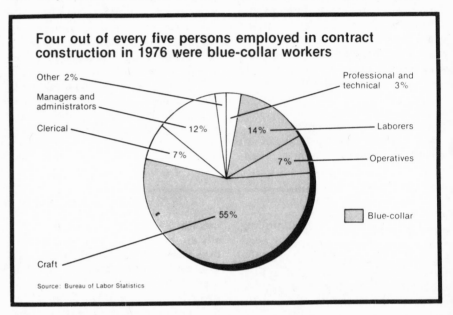

Four out of every five persons employed in contract construction in 1976 were blue-collar workers

Source: Bureau of Labor Statistics

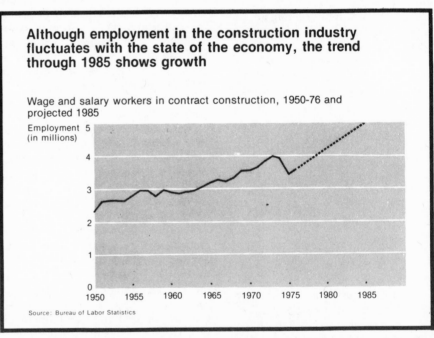

Although employment in the construction industry fluctuates with the state of the economy, the trend through 1985 shows growth

Wage and salary workers in contract construction, 1950-76 and projected 1985

Source: Bureau of Labor Statistics

because construction activity is sensitive to changes in economic conditions.

Construction trade workers in the industry earned an average of $7.68 per hour in 1976. This was about 50 percent more than the hourly average of production or nonsupervisory

Contract construction is the major source of employment for skilled craft workers such as bricklayers, painters, and carpenters. For information on these and other construction crafts, see the chapter on construction occupations elsewhere.

MANUFACTURING

Our Nation's economy is composed of nine major industry divisions that provide us with a wide variety of goods and services. These nine divisions are agriculture; mining; contract construction; manufacturing; transportation and public utilities; wholesale and retail trade; finance, insurance, and real estate; services; and government. In terms of the impact it has on our lives, manufacturing may well be the most important.

Almost everything we use in our work, leisure, and even in our sleep is a product of a manufacturing industry. Factories produce goods that range in complexity from simple plastic toys to intricate electronic computers, and in size from miniature electronic components to gigantic aircraft carriers. Workers in the many diverse manufacturing industries process foods and chemicals, print books and newspapers, spin textiles and weave them, make clothing and shoes, and produce the thousands of other products needed for our personal and national welfare.

In terms of employment, manufacturing, with almost 20 million workers in 1976, was the largest of the major industry divisions. About three-fifths of all manufacturing employees worked in plants that produced durable goods, such as steel, machinery, automobiles, and household appliances. The rest worked in plants that produced nondurable goods, such as processed food, clothing, and chemicals.

The occupational distribution of the major industry divisions differs according to each industry's particular needs. Industries such as wholesale and retail trade, for example, require large numbers of sales and service workers while the mining industry needs very few workers in these occupational groups. Like all industries, manufacturing has its own unique occupational composition.

As illustrated in the accompanying table, blue-collar workers (craft workers, operatives, and laborers) make up about two-thirds of manufacturing employment. Operatives, who are needed to run the machines used to manufacture goods, account for over four-tenths of total employ-

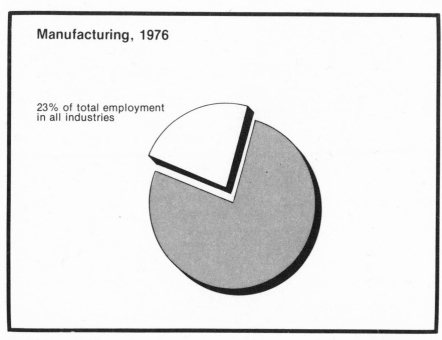

Manufacturing, 1976

23% of total employment in all industries

ment in manufacturing. Many are spinners and weavers, sewing machine operators, machine tool operators and welders, or operators of the specialized processing equipment used in the food, chemical, paper, and petroleum industries.

Craft and kindred workers make up the next largest group and account for nearly one-fifth of employment in manufacturing. Many of these skilled workers help support the production processes by installing and maintaining the wide assortment of machinery and equipment

required in all factories. Others are directly involved in production. Machinists, for example, are especially important in the metalworking industries, as are skilled inspectors and assemblers. In the printing and publishing industries, compositors, typesetters, photoengravers, lithographers, and pressworkers make up a large share of the work force. The craft group also includes supervisors of blue-collar workers.

Laborers account for about 1 out of every 20 jobs in manufacturing. Many of these workers help support

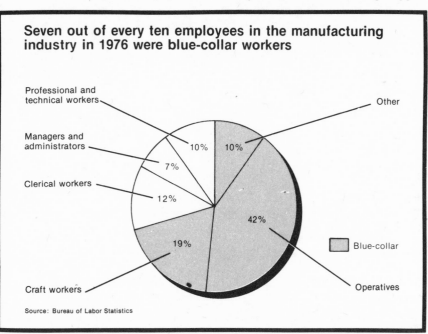

Seven out of every ten employees in the manufacturing industry in 1976 were blue-collar workers

Professional and technical workers — 10%
Other — 10%
Managers and administrators — 7%
Clerical workers — 12%
Blue-collar — 42%
Craft workers — 19%
Operatives

Source: Bureau of Labor Statistics

the production process by moving and storing raw materials and by helping more skilled workers prepare equipment for use.

Population growth, rising personal income, and expanding business activity will create a substantial increase in the demand for manufactured products through the mid-1980's. Employment in manufacturing, however, is expected to increase at a slower pace than production as technological advances and improvements in manufacturing methods increase the amount of goods each worker can produce.

The employment outlook for individual manufacturing industries, however, will vary widely. Employment in the industries manufacturing rubber and miscellaneous plastic products, medical and dental instruments, and computers and peripheral equipment, for example, should increase faster than the average. While employment in most manufacturing industries is expected to increase through the mid-1980's, employment in some—including tobacco, food, and radio and television sets—is expected to decline.

Aluminum was once considered a specialty metal having limited applications. Today it is produced in quantities second only to iron and steel. It is used in products that range from household appliances and cooking utensils to automobiles, aircraft, and missiles. In recent years, many new uses for aluminum have been developed, including house siding, food and beverage containers, and electrical cables. In 1976, the industry produced about 12.9 billion pounds of primary aluminum, or about twice the output of only 10 years earlier.

This statement describes occupations in plants that produce ingots (bars) of primary aluminum. It also describes occupations in plants that shape the ingots into sheets, wire, and other forms by rolling, stretching, or forcing the aluminum through an opening. Occupations concerned with casting, forging, stamping, machining, and fabricating aluminum are discussed separately in the *Handbook* statements dealing with forge shop, foundry, and metalworking occupations.

More than 93,000 persons worked in the aluminum industry in 1976. Approximately one-third helped make primary aluminum; the remainder helped convert large pieces into sheets, cables, and other industrial products.

Since the huge machinery necessary for making aluminum is very expensive, the production of primary aluminum is concentrated in a relatively small number of plants. These plants generally are located near abundant sources of alumina and electricity. Many are in Arkansas, Louisiana, Texas, Alabama, and Tennessee, where bauxite ore is mined locally or imported from the Caribbean area, and electricity is obtained from the Tennessee Valley Authority or generated from local deposits of natural gas or oil. About two-fifths of the employees who make aluminum work in these States. Another one-fifth work in the State of Washington, where plants obtain electricity from the Bonneville Power Authority and serve customers on the West Coast. A significant number of employees also work in plants located in Ohio, Indiana, and New York.

Plants that shape aluminum into sheets, wire, and other products are more dispersed geographically. Over one-half of the employment in these plants is in California, Pennsylvania, Tennessee, Illinois, Alabama, New York, and Ohio. The remainder is widely scattered throughout a large number of States.

Occupations in the Industry

Employment in the aluminum industry falls into several categories. The largest group of workers—about three-fourths—are the production workers directly involved in operating or maintaining the industry's production equipment. The remaining one-fourth are in professional, technical, administrative, clerical, and supervisory positions.

Production Occupations. To illustrate the production occupations found in the industry, a description of the major steps in making and shaping aluminum follows.

Making Aluminum. Aluminum is obtained from alumina by using electricity to create chemical changes that separate pure aluminum from other materials. Alumina—a fine, white powder processed from bauxite ore—is placed in large containers called "pots" that are filled with a special liquid. Suspended in the liquid are poles (anodes); electric cables are attached to the pots and poles. When the process is in operation, electricity flows from the poles, through the liquid containing the alumina, to the walls and floors of the pots. As the electricity passes through the liquid, it heats and chemically changes the alumina to pure, liquid aluminum. Because the aluminum is heavier, it settles to the bottom of the pot; waste materials go to the top of the liquid. Periodically, pure aluminum is removed from the bottom of the pot.

Pot tenders (D.O.T. 512.885) see that the pots operate continuously. Each is responsible for a number of pots. As a result of the chemical changes, the alumina in each pot is slowly used up. Instruments monitor the level of alumina and signal the tender when to add alumina from the overhead storage compartment.

Every 24 to 72 hours, molten aluminum is drawn from the bottom of the pots into huge brick-lined, steel containers or "crucibles." The *tapper* (D.O.T. 514.884) and *tapper helper* (D.O.T. 514.887) signal the *hot-metal crane operator* (D.O.T. 921.883 place the overhead crane near the pot. Using automatic equipment, they break a hole in the crust of waste materials that forms on the top of the liquid. One end of a curved, cast iron tube is inserted into the pot; the other end is placed into a crucible and the molten metal is drawn from the pot into the crucible.

After aluminum has been taken from several pots and the crucible is full, *charge gang weighers* (D.O.T. 502.887) weigh and sample the molten metal for laboratory analysis. Weighers also select chemicals that the analysis indicates should be blended with the molten aluminum. Then, workers operating overhead cranes pour the molten metal from the crucible into a remelting furnace. A *remelt operator* (D.O.T. 512.885) adds portions of aluminum scrap, other molten metal, or chemicals that will produce metal with the desired properties. Finally, hand skimmers remove waste products that have been forced to the surface of the molten metal.

The metal is then transferred to the second or holding compartment of the furnace until a sufficient supply is obtained for pouring. The *d.c. casting operator* (D.O.T. 514.782) has charge of the pouring station where the molten metal is cast into ingots—large blocks of metal. The operator controls the cooling conditions of the casting unit by keeping the molds full of metal and spraying water against the molds to produce ingots of uniform size and quality.

After a pot has been operating for a number of months, the heat and chemical reactions make holes in the pot's lining so that the liquid metal contacts the steel container. When this happens, the pot is shut down and the liquid drained so that *pot liners* (D.O.T. 519.884) can make repairs. Depending on the condition of the pots liners may patch holes in the lining or may completely remove and replace the lining.

Shaping aluminum. The large

ingots must be reduced in size before the aluminum is useful to customers. Depending on the final product desired, several methods may be used to shape the ingot. Aluminum products such as plate, sheet, and strip are produced by rolling.

The first step in rolling is to remove surface impurities from the ingot. The *scalper operator* (D.O.T. 605.782) manipulates levers of a scalper machine and cuts thin layers of the rough metal from the ingots so that the surfaces are smooth. Then, the ingots are heated to proper working temperatures for rolling. Workers operating overhead cranes lower the ingots into furnaces, or "soaking pits," where they are kept sealed for 12 to 18 hours. *Soaking pit operators* (D.O.T. 613.782) manage the furnace and control the temperature and heating time.

After being heated, the huge ingots are positioned on the "breakdown" or hot rolling mill where they are converted into elongated slabs. *Rolling mill operators* (D.O.T. 613.782) manipulate the ingots back and forth between powerful rollers until they are reduced in thickness to about 3 inches. The slabs then move down the line on the rollers to additional hot mills that work them down to a thickness of about one-eighth of an inch. At the end of the hotline, a *coiler operator* (D.O.T. 613.885) tends a coiler that automatically winds the metal onto reels.

The coiled aluminum cools at room temperature before being cold-rolled still thinner. Cold-rolling produces a better surface finish and increases the metal's strength and hardness. Since continuous cold-rolling could make the metal too brittle, an *annealer* (D.O.T. 504.782) occasionally heats (anneals) the metal.

To relieve internal stress created during the rolling process or surface contours the metal may be stretched. *Stretcher-level-operators* (D.O.T. 619.782) and *stretcher-level-operator helpers* (D.O.T. 619.886) position the finished plate or sheet in clamps, determine the stretch required to remove surface contours, and operate the machine that pulls the metal from end to end to stretch it.

Sometimes ingots are melted and cast in molds to produce "billets."

Besides being smaller and easier to handle than ingots, billets can be molded into shapes which make it easier to produce the final product.

In the rod and bar factory, billets are heated to make them softer and then are rolled through progressively smaller openings, until the desired size is obtained. To produce wire, hot-rolling continues until the rod is about three-eighths of an inch in diameter. Then, *wire draw operators* (D.O.T. 614.782) operate machines that pull the cold wire through a series of holes (dies) that gradually reduce its size. The machines also automatically coil the wire on revolving reels.

Structural products such as I-beams and angles may be hot-rolled or extruded. Hot-rolled products are made by passing a square billet with rounded corners between grooved rolls that gradually reduce the thickness and change the shape of the metal.

Extruding of metal often is compared with squeezing toothpaste from a tube. Extruded aluminum shapes are produced by placing hot billets (bars) inside a cylinder in a powerful press. A hydraulic ram that usually has a force of several million pounds pushes the metal through a hole (die) at the other end of the cylinder. The metal takes the shape of the die and then may be cut into desired lengths. By using dies of varying design, almost any shape of aluminium product may be formed. *Extrusion press operators* (D.O.T. 614.782) regulate the rate at which the metal is forced through the press.

Of increasing importance in shaping aluminum is the continuous casting process. This process uses a tall, curved mold that is wider at the top than at the bottom. The mold has an opening at the bottom that is the shape of the final product—for example, it is square if billets are being made. As space becomes available, molten aluminum is added to the top of the mold and moves down through the mold while being cooled by water sprays. When the now solid aluminum comes out of the mold, it moves onto a conveyor belt where it is cut to the desired lengths.

During both the production and the shaping process, workers and machines inspect the metal to assure quality. *Radiographers* (D.O.T. 199.381) operate various types of X-ray equipment to inspect the metal. Computers monitor operations and automatically adjust metal temperature and mill speed.

Other production workers in the aluminum industry keep machines and equipment operating properly. Some move materials, supplies, and finished products throughout the plants; still others are in service occupations such as guard and custodian.

Since electricity is vital to making aluminum, the industry needs many electricians to install and repair electrical fixtures, apparatus, and control equipment. Other employees, such as millwrights and maintenance machinists, make and repair mechanical parts for plant machinery. Stationary engineers operate and maintain the powerplants, turbines, steam engines, and motors used in aluminum plants.

Other important groups are the diemakers who assemble and repair dies used in aluminum metalworking operations; the bricklayers who build and reline furnaces, soaking pits, and similar installations; and the welders who join metal parts together with gas or electric welding equipment. In addition, plumbers and pipefitters lay out, install, and maintain piping and piping systems for steam, water, and other materials used in aluminum manufacturing.

Employment Outlook

Employment in the aluminum industry is expected to grow about as fast as the average for all industries through the mid-1980's. In addition to openings created by growth of the industry, many job opportunities will arise from the need to replace workers who retire, die, or leave the industry for other reasons. The number of job opportunities may vary from year to year, however, because the demand for aluminum fluctuates with the ups and downs in the economy.

Over the long run, the demand for aluminum is expected to grow as population increases and aluminum is substituted for other materials. In dustries that represent major markets for aluminum are growing industries with potential for new product development. For example, aluminum studs are replacing wood studs in the construction of large buildings and for residential construction and remodeling. With the growing emphasis on fuel economy, car and truck manufacturers are expected to use more aluminum in the future to reduce the weight of vehicles.

Employment, however, will grow more slowly than the demand for aluminum. Furthermore, the aluminum industry supports a strong research and development program and an aggressive marketing program which should continue to develop new alloys, processes, and products. As a result, the number of engineers, scientists, and technical personnel is expected to increase as a proportion of total employment. Technological developments, such as continuous casting and computer-controlled rolling operations, will limit employment growth among some production occupations.

Earnings and Working Conditions

Hourly earnings of plantworkers in the aluminum industry are higher than the average for manufacturing industries. In 1976, production workers in plants which make aluminum averaged $7.29 an hour, and those in aluminum rolling and drawing plants averaged $6.27. In comparison, production workers in manufacturing industries as a whole averaged $5.19 an hour.

Skilled operators and skilled maintenance and craft workers hold the highest paying plant jobs. Hourly rates in 1976 for selected occupations in a number of plants covered by one major union-management contract are shown below.

Making Aluminum:

Anode rebuilder	$7.09
Pot liner	6.57
Pot tender	6.74
Head tapper	7.00
Charge weigher	6.30

Shaping Aluminum:

Scalper operator	6.74
Soaking pit operator	6.48
Hot mill operator, junior	7.35

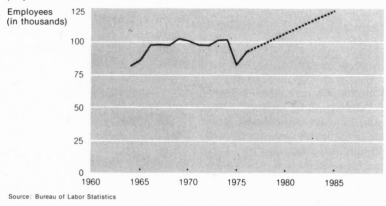

Although long-term employment growth is expected in the aluminum industry, the number of job openings each year will fluctuate with economic conditions

Wage and salary workers in aluminum industry, 1964-76, and projected 1985

Source: Bureau of Labor Statistics

Continuous mill operator	7.61
Annealer	6.30
Stretcher and flattener operator	6.39
Inspector	6.57
Extrusion press operator	7.00

Maintenance:

Boiler operator	6.57
Brickmason	7.44
Welder	7.35
Pipefitter	7.35
Millwright (maintenance mechanic)	7.35
Electrician	7.61
Machinist	7.61

Aluminum workers receive many fringe benefits, such as paid vacations and holidays, retirement benefits, life and health insurance, shift differentials, supplemental jury-duty pay, and supplemental unemployment benefits. Most workers receive paid vacations ranging from 1 to 4 weeks, depending on length of service. In addition, there are extended vacation plans that provide a 10-week vacation with 13 week's pay every 5 years.

Making aluminum requires high temperatures and some potrooms may be hot, dusty, and smoky. However, working conditions in plants have been improved as a result of control programs and other projects. Because making aluminum is a con-

Making aluminum requires high temperatures and some potrooms may be hot, dusty, and smoky. However, working conditions in plants

have been improved as a result of control programs and other projects. Because making aluminum is a continuous process, some production employees have to work nights and weekends.

The shaping sector of the industry generally offers more favorable working conditions, although workers in certain jobs are subjected to heat and loud noises.

The industry stresses safe working conditions and conducts safety education programs. Plants where aluminum is made have had a lower rate of injuries than the average for all metal industries, while the rate for aluminum rolling and drawing mills has been about the same as the average. However, the average number of workdays lost for each injury in the aluminum industry has been greater than the average for all metal industries.

Most process and maintenance workers in the aluminum industry belong to labor unions. In addition, labor organizations represent some office and technical personnel. The unions having the greatest number of members in the industry are United Steelworkers of America; Aluminum Workers International Union; and International Union, United Automobile, Aerospace and Agricultural Implement Workers of America.

OCCUPATIONS IN FOUNDRIES

Metal castings produced by foundry workers are essential parts of thousands of products ranging from missiles to cooking utensils. The strength of metal that has been cast makes it suitable for many household and industrial items, and the development of improved alloys, or combinations of metals, has widened the range of products made by casting.

In 1976, about 300,000 people worked in the foundry industry producing bath tubs, tubing, plumbing fixtures, and thousands of other products. Thousands of other workers were employed in the foundry departments of other industries that make castings to use in their final product, such as crank shafts and engine blocks for automobiles and compressors for refrigerators.

Casting is a method of forming metal into intricate shapes. To cast metal, a mold is created that has a cavity exactly shaped like the object to be produced. Molten metal, usually iron, is poured into the mold where it cools and solidifies.

Nature and Location of the Foundry Industry

Nearly three-fourths of the foundry industry's employees work in iron and steel foundries. The remainder work in plants that cast nonferrous metals, such as aluminum, bronze, and zinc. Foundries usually specialize in a limited number of metals, because different methods and equipment are needed to melt and cast different alloys.

There are six principal methods of casting, each named for the type of mold used. In the most common method, green-sand molding, a special sand is packed around a pattern in a boxlike container called a flask. The pattern is withdrawn and molten metal is poured into the mold cavity to form the desired shape. Because

sand molds can be used only once, a second method, called permanent molding, was developed which employs a metal mold that can be used many times. Permanent molding is used chiefly for casting nonferrous metals.

Precision investment casting, a third method (often called the lost wax process), uses ceramic molds. A wax or plastic pattern is coated with clay; after the coating hardens, the wax or plastic is melted and drained so that a mold cavity is left. Unlike the first two methods, castings produced from these molds are precise and require little finishing.

Shell molding, a fourth process, is becoming increasingly important because castings produced from these molds not only are precise but also have a smooth surface that requires almost no finishing. In this method, a heated metal pattern is covered with a mixture of sand and resin. The sand forms a thin shell mold that, once hardened, is peeled from the pattern.

Diecasting, a fifth process, is done mostly by machines. Dies are impressions that are carved by machines into metal blocks or plates. Molten metal is forced under high pressure into dies from which the castings are later automatically ejected or removed by hand.

A sixth method, centrifugal casting, is used to make pipe and other products that have cylindrical cavities. In this process, molten metal is poured into a mold that is spinning at a very high speed. The spinning motion forces the metal against the walls of the mold where it then hardens.

Most foundries are small. More than 90 percent employ fewer than 250 workers, although several of the largest employ more than 5,000 workers.

Small foundries generally produce a variety of castings in small quanti-

ties. They employ hand and machine molders and coremakers (the key foundry occupations) and a substantial number of unskilled laborers. Large foundries often are highly mechanized and produce great quantities of identical castings. These shops employ relatively few unskilled laborers because cranes, conveyors, and other types of equipment replace manual labor in the moving of materials, molds, and castings. Since much of the casting in large shops is mechanized, they also employ proportionately fewer skilled molders and coremakers than small shops. However, many skilled maintenance workers, such as millwrights and electricians, are employed to service and repair the large amount of machinery.

Though foundries are located in many areas, jobs are concentrated in States that have considerable metalworking activity, such as in Michigan, Ohio, Pennsylvania, Illinois, Indiana, and Wisconsin.

Foundry Occupations

Most of the industry's 300,000 employees in 1976 were plant workers. To illustrate more clearly the duties of these workers, a brief description of the jobs involved in the most common casting process—sand molding—follows:

After the casting is designed, a *patternmaker* (D.O.T. 600.280 and 661.281), following the design blueprint, makes a wood or metal pattern in the shape of the casting. Next, a *hand molder* (D.O.T. 518.381) makes sand molds by packing and ramming sand, specially prepared by a *sand mixer* (D.O.T. 579.782), around the pattern. A *molder's helper* (D.O.T. 519.887) may assist in these operations. If large numbers of identical castings are to be made, machines may be used to make the molds at a faster speed than is possible by hand. The operator of this equipment is called a *machine molder* (D.O.T. 518.782).

A *coremaker* (D.O.T. 518.381 and .885) shapes sand into cores (bodies of sand that make hollow spaces in castings). *Core-oven tenders* (D.O.T. 518.885) bake most cores in ovens to harden and strengthen them so that they can be handled without breaking. When a sufficient number of cores are assembled, they are placed in the molds by *core setters* (D.O.T. 518.884) or molders. Now the molds are ready for the molten metal.

A *furnace operator* (D.O.T. 512.782) controls the furnace that melts the metal which a *pourer* (D.O.T. 514.884) lets flow into molds. When the castings have solidified, a *shakeout worker* (D.O.T. 519.887) removes them from the sand and sends them to the cleaning and finishing department.

Dirty and rough surfaces of castings are cleaned and smoothed. A *shotblaster* (D.O.T. 503.887) operates a machine that cleans large castings by blasting them with air mixed with metal shot or grit. Smaller castings may be smoothed by tumbling. In this process, the castings, together with sand or another abrasive material, are placed in a barrel that is rotated at high speed. The person who controls the barrel is called a *tumbler operator* (D.O.T. 599.885). Sandblasters and tumbler operators may also operate a machine that both tumbles and blasts the castings. A *chipper* (D.O.T. 809.884) and a *grinder* (D.O.T. 809.884) use pneumatic chisels, power abrasive wheels, powersaws, and handtools, such as chisels and files, to remove excess metal and to finish the castings.

Castings frequently are heat-treated in furnaces to strengthen the metal; a *heat treater*, or *annealer* (D.O.T. 504.782), operates these furnaces. Before the castings are packed for shipment, a *casting inspector* (D.O.T. 514.687) checks them to make sure they are structurally sound and meet specifications. Often, the inspection involves X-raying the casting to check for separations in the metal.

Many foundry workers are employed in occupations that are common to other industries. For example, maintenance mechanics, machinists, carpenters, and millwrights maintain and repair foundry equipment. Crane and derrick operators and truckdrivers move materials from place to place. Machine tool operators finish castings. Foundries also employ thousands of workers in unskilled jobs, such as guard, janitor, and laborer.

About one-sixth of all foundry workers are employed in professional, technical, administrative, clerical, and sales occupations. Of these personnel, the largest number are clerical workers, such as secretaries, typists, and accounting clerks.

Foundries employ engineers and metallurgists to do research, design machinery and plant layout, develop improved alloys, control the quality of castings, and supervise plant operations and maintenance. In recent years, many of these workers have been hired to sell castings and to assist customers in designing cast parts. Most foundry technicians are concerned with quality control. For example, they may test molding and coremaking sand, make chemical analyses of metal, and operate machines that test the strength and hardness of castings. Administrative workers employed in foundries include office managers, personnel workers, purchasing agents, and plant managers.

Detailed discussions of three principal foundry occupations—patternmakers, coremakers, and molders—appear elsewhere.

Training, Other Qualifications, and Advancement

Most workers start in unskilled jobs, such as laborer or helper, and, after receiving on-the-job training from a supervisor or experienced worker, gradually learn more skilled jobs. This is the usual practice in training workers for casting process jobs such as melter, chipper, and grinder.

Some skilled foundry workers—particularly hand molders, hand coremakers, and patternmakers—learn their jobs through formal apprenticeship. Apprentices receive supervised on-the-job training for 2 to 4 years, usually supplemented by classroom instruction. High school graduates are preferred for most apprenticeship programs, but applicants with less education sometimes are hired. For some apprenticeship programs, especially those for patternmaking, a high school education is the minimum requirement. Management prefers workers who have completed an apprenticeship, because they have a greater knowledge of all foundry operations and therefore are better qualified to fill supervisory jobs.

Skilled foundry workers also can learn their trades informally on the job or through a combination of trade school and on-the-job training. In some cases, trade school courses may be credited toward completion of formal apprenticeships. Some foundries and the American Foundry Society Cast Metals Institute conduct training programs to update and upgrade the skills of experienced workers.

Employment Outlook

Over the long run, population growth and higher incomes will create a demand for more automobiles, household appliances, and other consumer products that have cast parts. More castings also will be needed for industrial machinery as factories expand and modernize. Despite the increasing demand for castings, employment in the foundry industry is expected to grow only about as fast as the average for all industries through the mid-1980's. Technological developments will enable foundries to meet the increased demand for castings with only a moderate increase in employment. Continued improvements in production methods will result in greater output per worker. In addition to those job openings that result from employment growth, many other openings will arise due to the need to replace experienced workers who die, retire, or transfer to other fields of work. The number of openings fluctuates greatly from year to year, since demand for castings is very sensitive to ups and downs in the economy.

Much of the employment increase in the foundry industry will be in production jobs. However, employment will increase in other occupations, as

Employment in foundries is very sensitive to year-to-year fluctuations in the business cycle

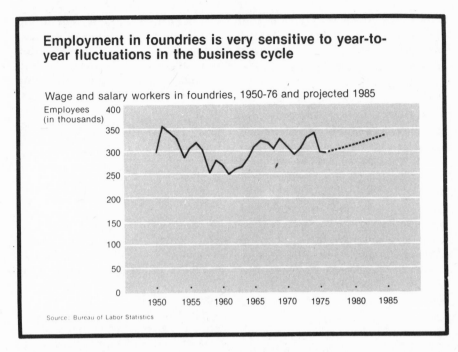

Wage and salary workers in foundries, 1950-76 and projected 1985

Source: Bureau of Labor Statistics

well. For example, employment of scientists and engineers is expected to increase because of expanding research and development activities. Technicians also will be needed in greater numbers to help improve quality control and production techniques. More maintenance workers will be hired to keep the industry's growing amount of machinery in working order. In contrast, machine molding and coremaking will be substituted for hand processes, and will limit the need for additional hand molders and hand coremakers. Improved molding techniques, such as quick set molding in which the mold hardens quickly and without baking in an oven, also will limit employment of molders. As more machinery for materials handling is introduced, employment of laborers and other unskilled workers may decline.

Earnings and Working Conditions

Production workers in foundries have higher average earnings than those in manufacturing as a whole. In 1976, production workers in iron and steel foundries averaged $6.16 an hour, and those in nonferrous foundries averaged $5.22. By comparison, production workers in all manufacturing industries averaged $5.19 an hour.

Most foundry industry employees work under union contracts that provide periodic pay increases. In those foundries that operate 24 hours a day, 7 days a week, contracts generally provide for extra pay for shift work and work done on weekends and holidays. Also, most contracts provide paid vacations according to length of service. Typically, an employee receives 1 week of vacation after 1 year of service, 2 weeks after 2 years, and 3 weeks after 10 years. In addition, many employees are covered by paid sick leave plans, group insurance, accident and death benefits, and retirement and disability pensions.

Working conditions in foundries have improved in recent years. Many foundries have changed plant layouts

and installed modern ventilating systems to reduce heat, fumes, dust, and smoke. The injury rate in foundries is higher than the average for manufacturing; foundry workers are subject to burns from hot metal and cuts and bruises from handling metal castings. However, employers and unions are attempting to reduce injuries by promoting safety training.

Foundry workers belong to many unions, including the International Molders' and Allied Workers' Union; the United Steelworkers of America; and the International Union of Electrical, Radio and Machine Workers. Many patternmakers are members of the Pattern Makers' League of North America.

Sources of Additional Information

Further information about work opportunities in foundry occupations may be obtained from local foundries, the local office of the State employment service, the nearest office of the State apprenticeship agency, or the Bureau of Apprenticeship and Training, U.S. Department of Labor. Information also is available from the following organizations:

American Foundrymen's Society, Golf and Wolf Rds., Des Plaines, Ill. 60016.

Foundry Educational Foundation, 1138 Terminal Tower, Cleveland, Ohio 44113.

International Molders' and Allied Workers' Union, 1225 E. McMillan St., Cincinnati, Ohio 45206.

OCCUPATIONS IN THE IRON AND STEEL INDUSTRY

Steel is the backbone of any industrialized economy. Few products in daily use are not made from steel or processed by machinery made of steel. For example, steel sheets are made into automobile bodies, appliances, and furniture; steel bars are used to make parts for machinery and to reinforce concrete in building and highway construction; steel plates become parts of ships, bridges, railroad cars, and storage tanks; strip steel is used to make pots and pans, razor blades, and toys.

To satisfy the country's need for steel, the iron and steel industry employed about 540,000 persons in 1976. Employees work in a broad range of jobs that require a wide variety of skills; many of these jobs are found only in iron and steelmaking.

Characteristics of the Industry

The iron and steel industry, as discussed in this chapter, consists of the firms that operate blast furnaces, steel furnaces, and finishing mills. Blast furnaces make iron from iron ore, coke, and limestone. Steel furnaces refine the iron and scrap steel into steel. Primary rolling mills and continuous casting operations shape the steel into semifinished products called blooms, billets, and slabs, which other rolling mills shape into steel sheets, bars, plates, strips, wire, pipe, and various other finished products.

The types of operations performed in the more than 900 steel plants in the United States vary throughout the industry. Fully integrated steel plants, which are so large they may cover several square miles, contain blast furnaces, steel furnaces, and rolling mills. These plants perform all the operations necessary to convert processed iron ore into finished steel products. Other plants only perform finishing operations such as making steel wire and pipe from billets.

The number of people employed in the plants of the iron and steel industry also varies greatly. Individual plants typically employ a large number of workers because the production of iron and steel products is a monumental task. It requires the handling and use of thousands of tons of raw materials, and involves enormous facilities and equipment such as blast furnaces that may be 12 stories high and rolling mills that may be several city blocks long. About 65 percent of the industry's employees work in plants that have more than 2,500 employees; fully integrated plants may have more than 10,000. Many plants, however, have fewer than 100 employees.

Iron and steel plants are located mainly in the northeastern part of the United States near the abundant iron deposits of the Great Lakes area and the nearby coal deposits. About 7 out of 10 of the industry's workers are employed in five States—Pennsylvania, Ohio, Indiana, Illinois, and New York. Nearly 3 out of 10 are employed in Pennsylvania alone. The largest steel-producing plants are located in Indiana Harbor and Gary, Ind.; Sparrows Point, Md. (near Baltimore); Chicago; and Pittsburgh.

Occupations in the Industry

Workers in the iron and steel industry hold more than 2,000 different types of jobs. About 80 percent of all workers are directly engaged in moving raw materials and steel products about the plants, making iron and steel products, and maintaining the vast amount of machinery used in the industry. In addition, other workers are needed to do clerical, sales, professional, technical, administrative, and supervisory work.

Processing Occupations. The majority of the workers in the industry are employed in the many processing operations involved in converting iron ore into steel and then into semifinished and finished steel products. Because of the extensive use of automated control equipment in making steel from iron ore, most processing jobs are found in the rolling mills where the steel is shaped into semifinished and finished products. Following are brief descriptions of the major iron and steelmaking and finishing operations and some of the occupations connected with them.

Blast furnaces. The blast furnace, a large steel cylinder lined with heat-resistant (refractory) brick, is used to separate the iron from other elements in the iron ore. A mixture of ore, coke, and limestone (called a "charge") is fed into the top of the furnace. As this material works its way down through the furnace, hot air blown into the bottom from giant stoves causes the coke to burn at a high temperature. At this high temperature a chemical reaction takes place between the coke and the iron ore, freeing the iron from other elements in the ore.

The iron, which now is a liquid, trickles down through the burning coke and collects in a pool 4 to 5 feet deep at the bottom of the furnace. As the liquid iron passes through the coke, the intense heat causes another chemical reaction between the limestone, the burned-out coke, and any other materials to form a waste product called "slag". The slag also trickles down through the coke and floats on top of the heavier iron. In a typical furnace liquid iron is removed from the furnace every 3 or 4 hours; slag may be removed more frequently.

A blast furnace operates continuously, 24 hours a day, 7 days a week, unless it is shut down for repairs or for other reasons. A single furnace may produce up to 10,000 tons of iron in a 24-hour period.

The raw materials used in blast furnaces are transferred from storage areas on railroad cars. Moving on

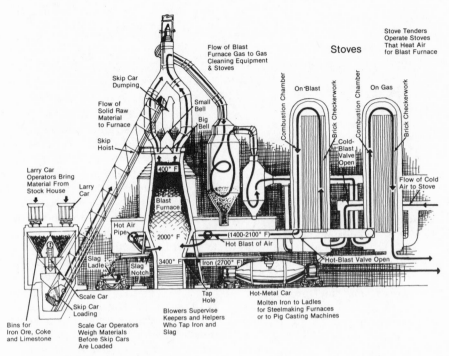

Source: American Iron and Steel Institute

elevated tracks to the furnace, the cars are positioned over an open grate. The raw materials are dumped through the grate and into a large funnel-shaped bin called a hopper. *Scale car operators* (D.O.T. 921.883) drive other railroad cars on tracks in tunnels underneath the hoppers. Positioning their car under one of these bins, they fill it with raw material, weigh the loaded car, and then dump the material into skip cars where the ore, limestone, or coke is automatically carried up a steep ramp to the top of the blast furnace and dumped. Scale car operators must keep records of what they put in the furnace. In blast furnace operations without automatic controls, a *skip car operator* (D.O.T. 921.883) uses electric and pneumatic controls to operate the cars.

Stove tenders (D.O.T. 512.782) operate the gas-fired stoves that heat air for the blast furnace. They observe controls that show the temperature of the air inside the stove. When air reaches the correct temperature, the tender opens valves on the stove that allow the heated air to pass to the furnaces. Stove tenders also keep the stove flues clean of carbon and dirt.

Blowers (D.O.T. 519.132) oversee the operation of one or more blast furnaces and are responsible for the quantity and quality of the iron produced. They coordinate the addition of raw materials by stockhouse workers with the operation of the furnace and supervise *keepers* (D.O.T. 502.884) and their *helpers* (D.O.T. 502.887) in removing (tapping) the liquid iron and slag from the furnace. If the iron is not forming correctly in the furnace, blowers may have the stove tenders change the temperature and flow of air into the furnace.

When the blower has determined that the iron is ready to be removed, the keeper and a helper use power drills, air hoses, or small explosive charges to remove the clay that is plugging a taphole above the liquid iron, allowing the slag to flow down a sand-lined channel into huge containers called ladles, which have been positioned under the channel by crane operators. Helpers open gates to divert the slag into other ladles when the first one is filled. After removing the slag, the keeper removes the clay from a lower taphole that allows the iron to flow down another channel into special railroad tank cars called "hot metal cars".

After the slag and iron have been removed, the keeper uses a "mud gun" to shoot clay into the tapholes. The keeper and helpers use tongs to remove solidified iron and slag from the channels and shovels to line the channels with special heat-resistant sand.

Some of the iron taken from the blast furnace is made into finished products such as automobile engine blocks and plumbing pipes. Most of it, however, is used to make steel.

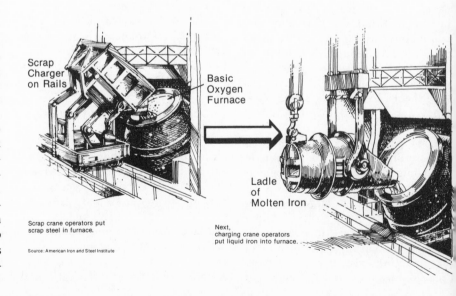

Scrap crane operators put scrap steel in furnace.

Next, charging crane operators put liquid iron into furnace.

Source: American Iron and Steel Institute

Because steel is stronger than iron and can be hammered and bent without breaking, it can be used for many more products.

Steel furnaces. Steel is made by heating iron or scrap steel to remove some of the carbon and other impurities and adding chemical agents such as silicon and manganese. By varying the amount of carbon and chemical agents contained in the final product, thousands of different types of steel can be made—each with specified properties that are suited for a particular product. For example, stainless steel is rust-resistant and heat-resistant and is used in products, which need those qualities such as razor blades.

Steel is made in three types of furnaces: basic oxygen, open hearth, and electric. More than 60 percent of all domestic steel is made in basic oxygen furnaces (BOF's) and about 20 percent in open hearth furnaces. Both produce similar kinds of steel, but BOF's do the job faster and are expected to replace many of the open hearths now in operation. For many years electric furnaces were used mainly to produce high quality steels such as stainless and tool steel. They now produce large quantities of regular steel and account for about 20 percent of total U.S. steel output.

Although the steelmaking procedure varies with the type of furnace used, the jobs associated with the various processes are similar. Since basic oxygen furnaces account for most of the U.S. steel, the jobs connected with them will be used as an illustration of those in other steel furnace operations.

A *melter* (D.O.T. 512.132) supervises workers at a steel furnace. Melters receive information on the characteristics of the raw materials they will be using and the type and quality of steel they are expected to produce. The melter makes the steel according to the desired specifications by varying the proportions of iron, scrap steel, and limestone in the furnace, and by adding small amounts of other materials such as manganese, silicon, copper, or chrome. The melter directs the workers who load furnaces with these raw materials and supervises the taking of

a sample of liquid steel that is tested to insure the steel has the desired qualities. The melter must coordinate the loading and melting of the raw materials with the steel molding operation to avoid delays in production.

A basic oxygen furnace is a giant, pear-shaped steel container lined with heat-resistant brick. The furnace can be tilted from side to side to receive raw materials and discharge steel and slag. The *furnace operator* (D.O.T. 512.782), under the direction of the melter, controls the operation of the furnace. To begin the operation, the furnace operator's first assistant uses controls to tilt the furnace to receive a load or "charge" of steel scrap and molten iron. A *scrap crane operator* (D.O.T. 921.883) adds scrap steel and is followed by a *charging crane operator* (D.O.T. 921.883) who adds the liquid iron made by the blast furnace. After the assistant rights the furnace, the furnace operator, who works in a control room overlooking the furnace, uses levers and buttons to lower the oxygen lance, a pipe that blows oxygen into the furnace at supersonic speeds. The furnace operator also controls the addition of lime, which combines with impurities in the iron to form slag, and the addition of any chemical agents that are required to

give the steel the desired properties. If the chemical reactions in the furnace become too violent, the furnace may overheat, causing slag and iron to splash out the top. Thus, the furnace operator must pay close attention to conditions in the furnace, regulate the oxygen flow, and, if the furnace does overheat, direct the rocking of the furnace to cool it.

By observing the various instruments in the control room, the furnace operator knows when the steel has almost the correct composition. The first assistant then tilts the furnace while the second assistant and helpers, working from behind a heat shield, use a long-handled spoon to take a sample. The sample is sent up to the lab where metallurgists determine how close the steel is to the product desired. Based on this information, the furnace operator determines how much longer and at what temperature the furnace should operate. When the furnace operator has determined that the steel has the specified qualities, the first assistant tilts the furnace towards a waiting ladle. The steel flows through a taphole in the side of the furnace and into the ladle. The second assistant and helpers may add chemical agents to the ladle while the steel is poured. By continually tilting the furnace at a steeper angle the first assistant can

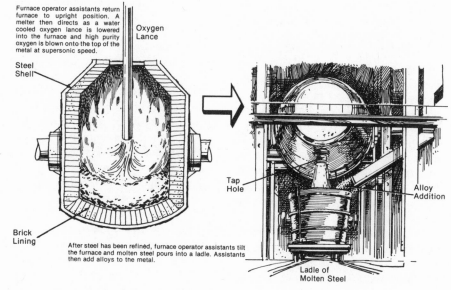

Furnace operator assistants return furnace to upright position. A melter then directs as a water cooled oxygen lance is lowered into the furnace and high purity oxygen is blown onto the top of the metal at supersonic speed.

Oxygen Lance

Steel Shell

Brick Lining

After steel has been refined, furnace operator assistants tilt the furnace and molten steel pours into a ladle. Assistants then add alloys to the metal.

Tap Hole

Alloy Addition

Ladle of Molten Steel

Source: American Iron and Steel Institute

keep the slag above the taphole, preventing it from flowing into the ladle. Eventually, the slag is poured through the taphole into the slag pot. The assistants and helpers then use handtools to clean out the taphole and furnace lip.

The liquid steel usually is solidified into large blocks called "ingots." A *hot metal crane operator* (D.O.T. 921.883) controls an overhead crane which picks up the ladle of liquid steel and moves it over a long row of iron ingot molds resting on railroad flatcars (ingot buggies). The *steel pourer* (D.O.T. 514.884) operates a stopper at the bottom of the ladle to let the steel flow into these molds. The steel pourer also examines the molds to see that they are clean and smooth and directs a helper in taking a sample of the steel for chemical analysis. As soon as the steel has solidified sufficiently, an *ingot stripper* (D.O.T. 921.883) operates an overhead crane, which removes the molds from the ingots. The steel now is ready to be shaped into semifinished and finished products.

Rolling and finishing. The three principal methods of shaping steel are rolling, casting, and forging. (Forged steel usually is made in forging shops. Occupations in those shops are described elsewhere.)

About 90 percent of the steel processed in steel mills is shaped by rolling. In this method, heated steel ingots are squeezed into longer and flatter shapes between two massive cylinders or "rolls." Before ingots of steel are rolled, they are heated to the temperature specified by plant metallurgists. The heating is done in large furnaces called "soaking pits" located in the plant floor. A *soaking pit crane operator* (D.O.T. 921.883) maneuvers an overhead crane to lift the ingots from small railcars and place them in the soaking pit. A *heater* (D.O.T. 613.782) and *helper* (D.O.T. 613.885) control the soaking pit operation. They adjust controls, which regulate the flow of air and fuel to the burners, to maintain the correct temperature in each pit, and by watching dials they determine when the ingot is uniformly heated to the required temperature.

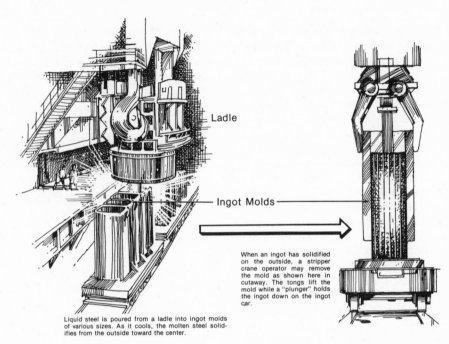

Ladle

Ingot Molds

When an ingot has solidified on the outside, a stripper crane operator may remove the mold as shown here in cutaway. The tongs lift the mold while a "plunger" holds the ingot down on the ingot car.

Liquid steel is poured from a ladle into ingot molds of various sizes. As it cools, the molten steel solidifies from the outside toward the center.

Source: American Iron and Steel Institute

When the ingots are needed in the mill, the crane operator places them on an ingot buggy, which carries them to the first rolling mill, sometimes called a "primary" mill. Here, the ingots are rolled into smaller, more easily handled semifinished products called blooms, billets, and slabs. Blooms generally are between 6 and 12 inches wide and 6 and 12 inches thick. Billets, which are rolled from blooms, have a smaller cross-section and are longer than blooms. Slabs are much wider and thinner than blooms.

Rolling ingots into blooms and slabs are similar operations; in fact some rolling mills can do both. In the mill, the ingot moves along on a roller conveyor to a machine that resembles a giant clothes wringer. A "two-high" rolling mill has two grooved rolls that revolve in opposite directions. The rolls grip the approaching red hot ingot and pull it between them, squeezing it thinner and longer. When the ingot has made one such pass, the rolls are reversed, and the ingot is fed back through them. Throughout the rolling operation, the ingot periodically is turned 90 degrees by mechanical devices called "manipulators," and passed between the rolls again so that all sides are rolled. This operation is repeated until the ingot is reduced to a

slab or bloom of the desired size. It is then ready to be cut to specified lengths.

A *roller* (D.O.T. 613.782), the worker in charge of the mill, works in a glass-enclosed control booth, located above or beside the conveyor line. This employee's duties, which appear to consist principally of moving levers and pushing buttons, look relatively simple. However, the quality of the product and the speed with which the ingot is rolled depend upon the roller's skill. The roller regulates the opening between the rolls after each pass. If the opening is set too wide, more passes will be needed to get the required shape, and production will be slowed. If the opening is too narrow, the rolls or gears may be damaged. Long experience and a knowledge of steel characteristics are required for a worker to become a roller. A *manipulator operator* (D.O.T. 613.782) sits in the booth beside the roller and operates controls that correctly position the ingot on the roller conveyor before each pass.

Upon leaving the rolling mill, the red-hot slab, billet, or bloom moves along a conveyer to a place where a *shear operator* (D.O.T. 615.782) controls a heavy hydraulic shear that cuts the steel into desired lengths. In a rolling mill that has automatic controls, a rolling mill attendant is given a card that has been punched with a series of holes. The holes represent coded directions as to how the ingot is to be rolled. The attendant inserts the card into a card "reader" and presses a button to start the automatic rolling sequence. When this process is used, the roller's job is shifted from operating the controls to directing and coordinating the rolling process.

Of increasing use in shaping steel into slabs, blooms, and billets is the continuous casting process; which eliminates the necessity of producing large ingots that in turn must be reheated and then put through the primary mill. In one type of continuous casting, a ladle of liquid steel, a water-cooled mold of the desired product shape (for example, a bloom) and a cooling chamber are set above the plant floor. A series of rolls descend from the cooling chamber to the floor. Liquid steel is poured into the mold. The steel cools and solidifies along the bottom and lower sides of the mold. Passing down through the chamber, the steel is further cooled by a water spray. The rolls control the molded steel's descent, support its weight, and straighten it as it moves toward the plant floor. The molded steel is cut to the desired lengths as it emerges from the rolls. Continuous casting requires fewer workers than the pouring and rolling of ingots require.

After the steel is rolled or cast into primary shapes, most of it is put through finishing operations. Slabs, for example, can be reduced and shaped into sheets, and billets can be made into wire and pipe.

Steel sheet is the most important finished product made by the iron and steel industry. To make sheets, a slab is first heated in a furnace similar to the soaking pits described earlier, and then run through a hot strip mill. The hot strip mill is a continuous series of pairs of rolls, similar to the two at the primary mill. As the slab moves through each pair of rolls, it becomes thinner and longer. Edge guides control its width. After passing through the last pair of rolls, the sheet is wound into a coil. If the customer prefers a thinner sheet or an

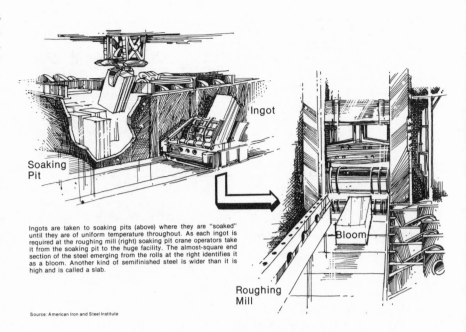

Ingots are taken to soaking pits (above) where they are "soaked" until they are of uniform temperature throughout. As each ingot is required at the roughing mill (right) soaking pit crane operators take it from the soaking pit to the huge facility. The almost-square end section of the steel emerging from the rolls at the right identifies it as a bloom. Another kind of semifinished steel is wider than it is high and is called a slab.

Source: American Iron and Steel Institute

improved surface, the product may be cold rolled in another mill.

Having obtained information on the characteristics of the sheet desired, the roller at the hot strip mill refers to a printed guide to determine the necessary gauge between each pair of rolls, and the speed at which the slab should travel. Working in a pulpit, the roller uses controls to set the gauge on the last series of rolls, while the *speed operator* (D.O.T. 613.782) works controls that adjust the speed of the rolls and conveyor. Unless problems develop, the jobs of these two workers are repetitive. However, if the sheet should begin to buckle between rolls, due to the steel's composition or temperature, these two employees must readjust the gauge and speed of the rolls in an attempt to avoid damage to the sheet.

Under the direction of the roller, a *rougher* (D.O.T. 613.782) and assistant use handtools to adjust the gauge and edge guides for the first series of rolls (called the roughing mill). A *rougher pulpit operator* (D.O.T. 613.782), following the rougher's instructions, signals the furnace crew for additional slabs and operates controls to position the slab on the conveyor and guide it into the rolls.

Other important steel mill products include various types of wire and pipe. These products are made from

billets. To make drawn wire, the billet is rolled into a long, thin, round product called a rod. A *wire drawer* (D.O.T. 614.782) operates equipment that pulls the steel rod through a die. The die has a tapered hole, one end of which is smaller than the rod. As the rod passes through the hole, it is made thinner and longer and becomes wire. The wire drawer positions the rod in the die, sets the speed for drawing the rod through the die, lubricates the rod and checks the wire for scratches and defects.

A *piercing-mill operator* (D.O.T. 613.885) controls machinery that makes seamless pipe. The operator moves levers that drop the hot billet from a conveyer into a trough and pass it between two barrel-shaped rolls that spin the billet and force an end of it against a sharp plug or "mandrel." The mandrel smooths the inside wall of the billet and makes the diameter of the hole uniform. The operator uses controls to remove the mandrel and drop the billet on a conveyor for further processing.

Maintenance, Transportation, and Plant Service Occupations. Large numbers of workers are required in steel plants to support processing activities. Some maintain and repair machinery and equipment, while others operate the equipment that provides power, steam, and water.

Machinists and machine tool op-

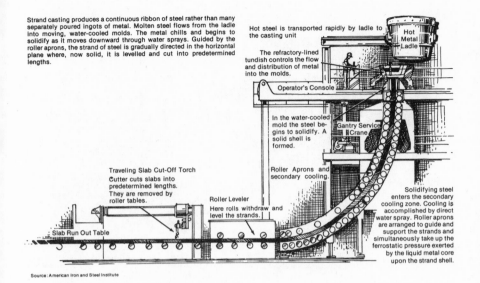

Strand casting produces a continuous ribbon of steel rather than many separately poured ingots of metal. Molten steel flows from the ladle into moving, water-cooled molds. The metal chills and begins to solidify as it moves downward through water sprays. Guided by the roller aprons, the strand of steel is gradually directed in the horizontal plane where, now solid, it is levelled and cut into predetermined lengths.

Hot steel is transported rapidly by ladle to the casting unit

Hot Metal Ladle

The refractory-lined tundish controls the flow and distribution of metal into the molds.

Operator's Console

In the water-cooled mold the steel begins to solidify. A solid shell is formed.

Gantry Service Crane

Roller Aprons and secondary cooling.

Solidifying steel enters the secondary cooling zone. Cooling is accomplished by direct water spray. Roller aprons are arranged to guide and support the strands and simultaneously take up the ferrostatic pressure exerted by the liquid metal core upon the strand shell.

Traveling Slab Cut-Off Torch Cutter cuts slabs into predetermined lengths. They are removed by roller tables.

Roller Leveler Here rolls withdraw and level the strands.

Slab Run Out Table

Source: American Iron and Steel Institute

erators make and repair metal parts for production equipment. Diemakers use machine tools to form dies, such as those used to make wire. *Roll turners* (D.O.T. 801.884) use lathes, grinders, and other machine tools to refinish the steel rolls used in the rolling mills.

Millwrights overhaul machinery and repair and replace defective parts. Electricians install wiring and fixtures and hook up electrically operated equipment. Electrical repairers (motor inspectors) keep wiring, motors, switches, and other electrical equipment in good operating condition.

Electronic repairers install and maintain the increasing number of electronic devices and systems used in steel manufacturing plants. Typically, this equipment includes communication systems such as closed-circuit television; electronic computing and data recording systems; and measuring, processing, and control devices such as X-ray measuring or inspection equipment.

Bricklayers repair and rebuild the brickwork in furnaces, soaking pits, ladles, and coke ovens, as well as mill buildings and offices. Pipefitters lay out, install, and repair piping that is used to carry the large amounts of liquids and gases used in steelmaking. Boilermakers test, repair, and rebuild heating units, storage tanks, stationary boilers, and condensers. Locomotive engineers and other train crew members operate trains that transport materials and products

in the vast yards of iron and steel plants. Other skilled workers operate the various boilers, turbines, and switchboards in factory powerplants.

Other types of maintenance and service workers include carpenters, oilers, painters, instrument repairers, scale mechanics, welders, loaders, riggers, janitors, and guards. Many laborers are employed to load and unload materials and do a variety of cleanup jobs.

Training, Other Qualifications, and Advancement

New workers in processing operations usually are hired as unskilled laborers. Openings in higher rated jobs usually are filled by promoting workers from lower grade jobs. Length of service with the company is the major factor considered when selecting workers for promotion. Promotions to first level supervisory positions, such as blower and melter, differ among companies. Some firms determine these promotions solely on seniority while others also consider ability to do the job.

Training for processing occupations is done almost entirely on the job. Workers move to operations requiring progressively greater skill as they acquire experience. A crane operator, for example, first is taught how to operate relatively simple cranes, and then advances through several steps to cranes much more difficult to run, such as the hot-metal crane.

Workers in the various operating units usually advance along fairly well-defined lines of promotion within their departments. For example, to become a blast furnace blower, a worker generally starts as a laborer, advancing to second helper, first helper, keeper, and finally blower. At a basic oxygen furnace, a worker may begin by doing general cleanup work and then advance to furnace hand, second assistant, first assistant, furnace operator, and eventually to melter. A possible line of job advancement for a roller in a finishing mill might be assistant rougher, rougher pulpit operator, rougher, speed operator, and finish roller. Workers can be trained for skilled jobs, such as blower, melter, and roller, which are among the highest rated steelmaking jobs, in a minimum of 4 or 5 years, but they may have to wait much longer before openings occur.

To help them advance in their work, many employees take part-time courses in subjects such as chemistry, physics, metallurgy and management. Steel companies sometimes provide this training—often within the plant. Other workers take evening courses in high schools, trade schools, or universities or enroll in correspondence courses.

Apprenticeship is the best way to learn a maintenance trade. Apprenticeship programs usually last 3 or 4 years and consist mainly of shop training in various aspects of the particular jobs. In addition, classroom instruction in related technical subjects usually is given, either in the plant, in local vocational schools, or through correspondence schools.

Steelmaking companies have different qualifications for apprentice applicants. Generally, employers require applicants to have the equivalent of a high school or vocational school education. In most cases, the minimum age for applicants is 18. Some companies give aptitude and other types of tests to applicants to determine their suitability for the trades. Apprentices generally are chosen from among qualified workers already employed in the plant.

The minimum requirement for administrative, engineering, and scientific jobs usually is a bachelor's degree with an appropriate major. Practically all the larger companies have formal training programs for college-trained workers and recruit these workers directly from college campuses. In these programs, trainees work for brief periods in various operating and maintenance divisions to get a broad picture of steelmaking operations before they are assigned to a particular department. In other companies, the newly hired professional worker is assigned directly to a specific research, operating, maintenance, administrative, or sales unit. Engineering graduates frequently are hired for sales work and many of the executives in the industry have engineering backgrounds. Engineering graduates, as well as graduates of business administration and liberal arts colleges, are employed in sales, accounting, and labor-management relations, as well as in managerial positions.

Completion of a business course in high school, junior college, or business school is preferred for entry into most of the clerical occupations. Clerical jobs requiring special knowledge of the steel industry generally are filled by promoting personnel already employed in the industry.

Employment Outlook

Employment in the iron and steel industry is not expected to change significantly through the mid-1980's. Nevertheless, many workers will be hired to replace those who retire, die, or leave their jobs for other reasons. The total number hired may fluctuate from year to year because the industry is sensitive to changes in business conditions and defense needs.

Production of iron and steel is expected to increase as population and business growth create a demand for more automobiles, household appliances, industrial machinery, and other products that require large amounts of these metals. Because of laborsaving technology, however, employment is not expected to keep pace with increases in production. Giant blast furnaces are being built that make more iron per worker than the smaller furnaces they are replac-

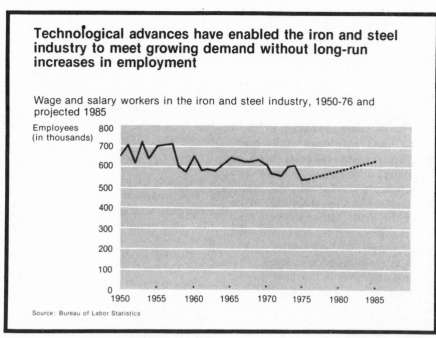

Technological advances have enabled the iron and steel industry to meet growing demand without long-run increases in employment

Wage and salary workers in the iron and steel industry, 1950-76 and projected 1985

Source: Bureau of Labor Statistics

ing. Some blast furnaces now have conveyor systems that automatically weigh and transfer raw materials from the storage areas to the furnace. Such systems will eliminate stockhouse jobs such as the scale car operator. Open hearth furnaces will continue to be replaced with more efficient basic oxygen furnaces, increasing the amount of steel produced per worker. Older primary rolling mills will be replaced by continuous casters, which use fewer employees to produce slabs, billets, and blooms. Greater use of computers to control plant equipment, as in hot finishing mills, and to process business records also will increase productivity.

Employment trends will differ among occupations. The number of job opportunities for engineers, metallurgists, laboratory technicians, and other technical workers will increase as the industry's research and development programs expand. Employment of computer systems analysts and programmers also will increase because computers will perform more of the work in the steelmaking operations. Some maintenance workers such as electronic repairers will be needed in greater numbers to maintain the increasingly complex machinery used by the steel mills. Employment of other maintenance workers—for example, bricklayers and carpenters, who work ex-

tensively on open hearth furnaces— will decline because they work on equipment that is being replaced. Employment in processing occupations is expected to decline slightly as more efficient plant machinery and equipment are introduced.

Earnings and Working Conditions

Earnings of production workers in iron and steelmaking are among the highest in manufacturing. In 1976, they averaged $7.68 an hour, while production workers as a whole averaged $4.87. To show how earnings vary by occupation and department, wage rates for employees in some of the principal occupations are presented in table 1. However, most steelworkers are paid on an incentive basis—that is, the more they produce the more they earn—and often earn more than the table would indicate.

Most production workers in the iron and steel industry are members of the United Steelworkers of America. Agreements between steel companies and the union include some of the most liberal fringe benefits in industry. Most workers receive vacation pay ranging from 1 to 5 weeks, depending on length of service. A worker in the top 50 percent of a seniority list receives a 13-week vacation every 5 years; the remaining workers receive 3 extra weeks of va-

Approximate basic straight-time hourly earnings [1] of workers in selected occupations in basic iron and steel establishments, mid-1976

	Hourly earnings
Blast furnaces:	
Larry or scale car operators	$6.55
Keepers	6.95
Basic oxygen furnaces:	
Second assistants (Second helper)	6.95
Furnace operators	7.80
Open hearth furnaces:	
Charging machine operators	7.20
Furnace operators (First helper)	8.15
Bloom, slab and billet mills:	
Soaking pit crane operators	7.05
Rollers	8.35
Continuous hot-strip mills:	
Roughers	7.20
Rollers	8.90
Maintenance:	
Bricklayers	7.30
Millwrights	7.20

[1] Excludes premium pay for overtime and for work on weekends, holidays, and late shifts and incentive pay.

cation once in a 5-year period. Professional and executive personnel receive similar benefits.

Workers may retire on company-paid pensions after 30 years of service, regardless of age. Employees having 2 years or more of service are eligible to receive supplemental unemployment benefits for up to 52 weeks. Other benefits include health and life insurance, and education and scholarship assistance.

Working conditions vary by department. Work in almost all professional and clerical jobs and many maintenance jobs is done in comfortable surroundings. Workers near the blast and steel furnaces and in the rolling mills, however, are subject to extreme heat and noise. For example, when raw materials such as scrap steel are loaded into a steel furnace a thunderous roar occurs. The temperature in the building which surrounds the blast furnace remains extremely high even in the middle of winter. Many plants have developed methods to reduce job discomfort. The use of remote control, for example, enables some employees, such as furnace operators, to work outside the immediate vicinity of processing operations. In other instances, the cabs in which the workers sit while operating mechanical equipment, such as cranes, may be air-conditioned. Because certain processes are continuous, many employees are on night shifts or work on weekends.

Sources of Additional Information

For additional information about careers in the iron and steel industry, contact:

American Iron and Steel Institute, 1000 16th St. NW., Washington, D.C. 20036.

United Steelworkers of America, Five Gateway Center, Pittsburgh, Pa. 15222.

TRANSPORTATION AND COMMUNICATIONS

Transportation, communications and public utility firms are commonly grouped together because they provide a public service and are owned or regulated by government or other public agencies. The purpose of this regulation varies from industry to industry, but in general the goals have been to ensure fair prices and to see that the public interest is served.

In 1976, almost 5.7 million people worked in this group of industries, almost one million of them in Federal, State, and local governments owning or regulating part of the industry. The two largest industries were communications, which employed 1.2 million workers, and motor freight transportation and warehousing (including local and long-distance trucking), which employed over 1 million workers. Close behind were electric, gas, and sanitary services with 750,000 workers, and railroads with 525,000.

As shown in the accompanying tabulation, blue-collar workers (craft workers, operatives, and laborers) accounted for three-fifths of the total employment in these industries in 1976. The remaining two-fifths were white-collar workers (professional, managerial, clerical, and sales). However, the occupational pattern differed among the various industries.

In the transportation industries, blue-collar operatives constitute the largest group of workers, almost three times as large as the next largest occupational group. Among the operatives are the thousands of bus and taxi drivers who provide public transportation. But over half of the total number of drivers are local and long-distance truck drivers who move goods throughout the country. Other operative workers include rail-

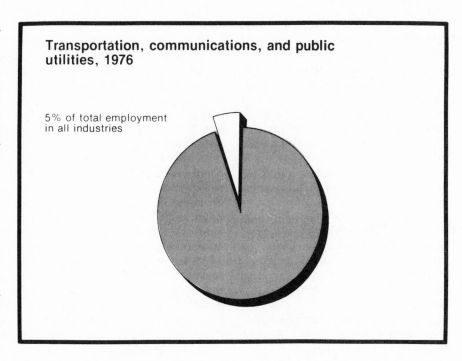

Transportation, communications, and public utilities, 1976

5% of total employment in all industries

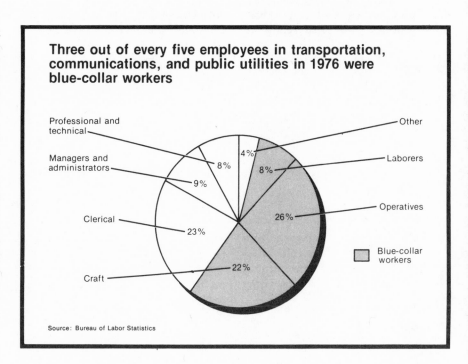

Three out of every five employees in transportation, communications, and public utilities in 1976 were blue-collar workers

Professional and technical — 8%
Managers and administrators — 9%
Clerical — 23%
Craft — 22%
Other — 4%
Laborers — 8%
Operatives — 26%
Blue-collar workers

Source: Bureau of Labor Statistics

137

road brake operators and sailors. Many craft workers also are needed in the transportation industries, such as the railroad shop workers who repair locomotives, and airplane mechanics. Also needed are numerous clerical employees, such as reservation and ticket clerks, yard clerks, and secretaries.

The communications industries employ many clerical workers to help provide vital public services such as the telephone, newspapers, and television. Secretaries, bookkeepers, stenographers, and payroll clerks keep records and prepare statistical reports. These workers, for example, ensure that customers are billed correctly for telephone and telegraph services. Also included are switchboard operators and messengers. The communications industries also employ entertainers, writers, interpreters, and other professionals. Many craft workers are employed to install, maintain, and repair the equipment used in the telephone industry and in radio and television studios.

Electric, gas, and water utilities, and sanitary services need a large number of craft workers to provide prompt and efficient service to consumers. In the electric power industry, for example, these employees install powerlines and run cables underground. They also repair all equipment, including the machinery in the powerplants and the meters in customers' homes. The need to record the use of these utilities and to bill customers promptly accounts for the large number of clerical employees that also are found in this industry group.

Employment in the transportation, communications, and public utility industries is expected to increase about as fast as the average for all industries through the mid-1980's. In addition to openings resulting from growth, many thousands of jobs will be available each year because of the need to replace workers who die, retire, or transfer to other industries.

Employment growth in the transportation industries will vary. Rising population and business expansion will stimulate growth in interurban transit at a faster than average rate. Average growth is expected in air transportation, trucking, and some local passenger transportation (subways and local buses). On the other hand, taxicab service employment is expected to remain about the same. The long-run decline in railroad employment is expected to continue, but at a decreasing rate.

Employment in communications is expected to grow at about the same rate as the average for all industries through the mid-1980's Although demand for the services provided by the communications industries will increase rapidly, advances in technology are expected to limit employment growth in some occupations, particularly in telephone communications. Computers and other electronic equipment are expected to be applied increasingly to work previously done by wage earners. For example, when long-distance phone calls are dialed directly, the length of the call and billing information can be recorded automatically. This reduces the need for telephone operators.

Employment in electric and gas utilities also will be affected strongly by advancing technology, so that while the demand for these utilities will increase greatly, the number of workers will grow at about the average rate. Most of the employment increase will be for scientific, engineering, and other technical workers as research accelerates in the development of more efficient ways of using energy.

The statements that follow cover major industries in the transportation and communications fields.

OCCUPATIONS IN THE RAILROAD INDUSTRY

Trains are one of the most efficient methods of transporting large amounts of freight over distances exceeding several hundred miles. Locomotives can pull thousands of tons of cargo using fewer employees and far less fuel than trucks and airplanes. In 1976, the railroads hauled 1.4 billion tons of freight, and carried 271 million passengers as well.

With 531,000 workers in 1976, the railroads were one of the Nation's largest employers. Railroad workers operate trains, build and repair equipment and facilities, provide services to customers, and collect and account for revenue. In most nonprofessional jobs, seniority systems prevail—workers start at the bottom and work their way up.

Nature and Location of the Industry

The railroad industry is made up of "line-haul" railroad companies that transport freight and passengers and switching and terminal companies that provide line-haul railroads with services at some large stations and yards.

About 95 percent of all railroad employees work for line-haul companies that handle about 99 percent of the industry's business. The remainder work for switching and terminal companies. Most railroad revenue and employment comes from freight. Passenger service has declined substantially in the past 30 years, because the railroads have not been able to compete with the speed of the airlines or the convenience of private automobiles.

Railroad workers are employed in every State except Hawaii. Large numbers work at terminal points where the railroads have central offices, yards, and maintenance and repair shops. Chicago, the hub of the Nation's railroad network, has more railroad employees than any other area, but many employees also work at the major railroad operations centered near New York, Los Angeles, Philadelphia, Minneapolis, Pittsburgh, and Detroit.

Railroad Occupations

Railroad workers can be divided into four main groups: Operating employees; station and office workers; equipment maintenance workers; and property maintenance workers.

Operating employees make up almost one-third of all railroad workers. This group includes locomotive engineers, conductors, and brake operators. Whether on the road or at terminals and railroad yards, they work together as traincrews. Also included are switchtenders who help conductors and brake operators by throwing track switches in railroad yards and hostlers who fuel, check, and deliver locomotives from the engine house to the crew.

One-fourth of all railroad workers are *station and office employees* who direct train movements and handle the railroads' business affairs. Professionals such as managers, accountants, statisticians, and systems analysts do administrative and planning work. Clerks keep records, prepare statistics, and handle business transactions such as collecting bills and adjusting claims. Agents manage the business affairs of the railroad stations. Telegraphers and telephoners pass on instructions to traincrews and help agents with clerical work.

More than one-fifth of all railroad employees are *equipment maintenance workers*, who service and repair locomotives and cars. This group includes car repairers, machinists, electrical workers, sheet-metal workers, boilermakers, and blacksmiths.

Property maintenance workers, who make up about one-sixth of all railroad employees, build and repair tracks, tunnels, signals, and other railroad property. Track workers repair tracks and roadbeds. Bridge and building workers construct and repair bridges, tunnels, and other structures along the right-of-way. Signal workers install and service the railroads' vast network of signals, including highway-crossing protection devices.

The accompanying chart shows the 1976 distribution of railroad employment among the four occupational groups.

Training, Other Qualifications, and Advancement

Most beginning railroad workers are trained on the job by experienced employees. Training for some office and maintenance jobs is available in high schools and vocational schools. Universities and technical schools offer courses in accounting, engineering, traffic management, transportation, and other subjects that are valuable to professional and technical workers.

New employees in some occupations, especially those in operating service jobs such as locomotive engineer, start as "extra board" workers. They substitute for regular workers who are on vacation, ill, or absent for other reasons. They also may be called when railroad traffic increases temporarily or seasonally.

Extra board workers with enough seniority move to regular assignments as they become available. The length of time a new worker spends on the extra board varies according to the number of available openings. Some workers do not receive regular assignments for many years.

Beginners in shop trades usually are high school graduates with no previous experience, although some shop laborers and helpers are pro-

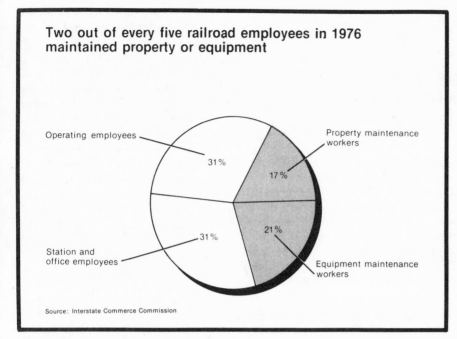

Two out of every five railroad employees in 1976 maintained property or equipment

Operating employees — 31%

Property maintenance workers — 17%

Station and office employees — 31%

Equipment maintenance workers — 21%

Source: Interstate Commerce Commission

moted to the trades. Shopworkers serve apprenticeships that last 3 to 4 years, depending on how much previous work experience the apprentice has.

Most applicants for railroad jobs must pass physical examinations. Those interested in traincrew jobs need excellent hearing and eyesight. Color-blind persons are not hired as locomotive engineers or brake operators or for any other jobs that involve interpreting railroad signals.

Railroad workers are promoted on the basis of seniority and ability. Job openings are posted on bulletin boards and workers may bid for them. The worker who is highest on the seniority list usually gets the job. To be promoted, however, workers may have to qualify by passing written, oral, and practical tests. Advancement in train and engine jobs is along established lines. All conductors, for example, are chosen from qualified brake operators.

Besides determining advancement procedures, seniority also gives workers some choice of working conditions. A telegrapher, for instance,

may have to work several years on the night shift at out-of-the-way locations before finally getting a day shift assignment near home.

Employment Outlook

The long-run decline in railroad employment is expected to continue through the mid-1980's, but at a decreasing rate. Nevertheless, thousands of job opportunities will develop each year as the industry replaces some experienced workers who retire, die, or transfer to other fields of work.

Despite an expected increase in freight traffic, railroad employment will decline as technical innovations increase worker productivity. For example, as automatic classification systems are installed in more yards, fewer yard workers will be needed to assemble and disassemble trains. The installation of wayside scanners, which identify cars electronically, will reduce the need for clerical workers.

Most people working in passenger

service may eventually work for AM-TRAK, the National Railroad Passenger Corporation, created in 1971 to revive train passenger service.

Earnings and Working Conditions

Nonsupervisory railroad employees averaged $6.88 an hour in 1976, about two-fifths higher than the average for all nonsupervisory workers in private industry, except farming. Earnings of railroad workers vary widely, however, depending on the occupation. For example, in 1976 average hourly earnings for locomotive engineers in passenger service were $12.71; for freight service brake operators $7.96; for railway clerks, $6.39; and for track gang members, $5.89. Regional wage differences are much less in railroading than in other industries because of nationally negotiated labor contracts.

Most railroad employees work a 5-day, 40-hour week, and receive premium pay for overtime. However, operating employees often work nights, weekends, and holidays. Extra board workers may be called to duty on short notice and at any time. Bridge and building workers, signal installers, and track workers may work away from home for days at a time.

Sources of Additional Information

Additional information about occupations in the railroad industry may be obtained from local railroad offices. For general information about the industry, write to:

Association of American Railroads, American Railroads Building, 1920 L St. NW., Washington, D.C. 20036.

OCCUPATIONS IN THE TELEPHONE INDUSTRY

Just about everyone has a telephone. Many households have two or more, and large businesses and organizations have hundreds. Some people have telephones in their cars and on their boats. A few even have portable telephones that they carry with them like briefcases. There also are thousands of public telephones on street corners and in airports, restaurants, and stores. Altogether, more than 155 million telephones were in use in the United States in 1976, and people made over 600 million local and long-distance calls every day.

To provide all this service, telephone companies employed approximately 920,000 persons in 1976. Most worked in telephone craft occupations, in clerical occupations, or as telephone operators.

The telephone industry offers steady, year-round employment in jobs requiring a variety of skills and training. Most require a high school education; some can be learned on the job. Many require particular skills that may take several years of experience, in addition to 9 months of training, to learn completely.

Telephone jobs are found in almost every community, but most telephone employees work in cities that have large concentrations of industrial and business establishments. The nerve center of every local telephone system is the central office that contains the switching equipment through which one telephone may be connected with any other telephone. When a call is made, the signals travel from the caller's telephone through wires and cables to the cable vault in the central office. Here thousands of pairs of wires, including a pair for the caller's telephone, fan out to a distributing frame where each pair is attached to switching equipment. As the number is dialed, electromechanical and electronic switching equipment make the connection automatically, and, in seconds, the caller hears the telephone ringing. Only in a few remaining switchboards and in unusual situations does an operator make the connection.

Because some customers make and receive more calls than a single telephone line can handle, a system somewhat similar to a miniature central office may be installed on the customer's premises. This system is the private branch exchange (PBX), usually found in office buildings, hotels, department stores, and other business firms.

Another type of service for businesses is called CENTREX, in which incoming calls can be dialed to any extension without an operator's assistance, and outgoing and interoffice calls can be dialed by the extension users. This equipment can be located either on telephone company premises or on the customer's premises. CENTREX has replaced PBX in popularity among business and industrial users that handle a very large volume of calls. However, PBX is still more popular with smaller users.

Other communications services provided by telephone companies include conference equipment installed at a PBX to permit conversations among several telephone users simultaneously; mobile radio-telephones in automobiles, boats, airplanes, and trains; and telephones equipped to answer calls automatically and to give and take messages by recordings.

Besides providing telephones and switching equipment, telephone companies build and maintain most of the vast network of cables and radio-relay systems needed for communications services, including those that join the thousands of broadcasting stations around the country. These services are leased to networks and their affiliated stations. Telephone companies also lease data and private wire services to business and government offices.

The Bell System owns more than 4 out of 5 of the Nation's telephones. Independent telephone companies own the remainder. There are approximately 1,600 independent telephone companies in the United

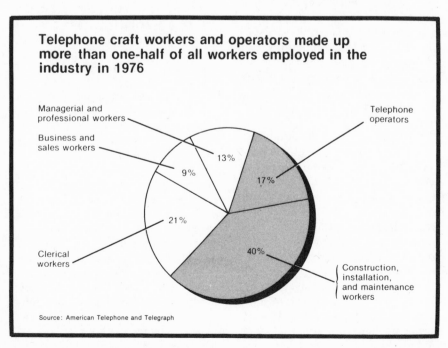

Telephone craft workers and operators made up more than one-half of all workers employed in the industry in 1976

Managerial and professional workers — 13%

Business and sales workers — 9%

Telephone operators — 17%

Clerical workers — 21%

Construction, installation, and maintenance workers — 40%

Source: American Telephone and Telegraph

States. General Telephone and Electronics Corp., United Utilities, Inc., and Continental Telephone Corp., service about 2 out of every 3 telephones owned by independent companies.

Telephone Occupations

Although the telephone industry requires workers in many different occupations, telephone craft workers and operators make up more than one-half of all workers. (See accompanying chart.)

Telephone craft workers install, repair, and maintain telephones, cables, switching equipment, and message accounting systems. These workers can be grouped by the type of work they perform. Construction workers place, splice, and maintain telephone wires and cables; installers and repairers place, maintain, and repair telephones and private branch exchanges (PBX) in homes and offices and other places of business; and central office craft workers test, maintain, and repair equipment in central offices.

Operators make telephone connections; assist customers in specialized services, such as reverse-charge calls; and provide information.

More than one-fifth of all telephone industry employees are clerical workers. They include stenographers, typists, bookkeepers, office machine and computer operators, keypunch operators, cashiers, receptionists, file clerks, accounting and auditing clerks, and payroll clerks. Clerical workers keep records of services, make up and send bills to customers, and prepare statistical and other reports.

About one-tenth of the industry's employees are professional workers. Many of these are scientific and technical personnel such as engineers and drafters. Engineers plan cable and microwave routes, central office and PBX equipment installations, new buildings, and the expansion of existing structures, and solve other engineering problems.

Some engineers also engage in research and development of new equipment, and persons with engineering backgrounds often advance to fill top managerial and administrative positons. Other professional and technical workers are accountants, personnel and labor relations workers, public relations specialists and publicity writers, computer systems analysts, computer programmers, and lawyers.

About 1 in every 12 of the industry's employees is a business and sales representative. These employees sell new communications services and directory advertising and handle requests for installing or discontinuing telephone service.

About 3 percent of the industry's workers maintain buildings, offices, and warehouses; operate and service motor vehicles; and do other maintenance jobs in offices and plants. Skilled maintenance workers include stationary engineers, carpenters, painters, electricians, and plumbers. Other workers employed by the telphone industry are janitors, porters, and guards.

Employment Outlook

Telephone industry employment is expected to increase about as fast as the average for all industries through the mid-1980's. In addition to the jobs from employment growth, tens of thousands of openings will arise each year because of the need to replace experienced workers who retire, die, or leave their jobs for other reasons.

Employment will grow primarily because higher incomes and a larger and more mobile population will increase the use of telephone service. Greater demand for transmission of computer-processed data and other information via telephone company lines also will stimulate employment growth. Laborsaving innovations, however, will keep employment from growing as rapidly as telephone service.

Employment of telephone operators is expected to decline. As the number of telephone companies charging customers for directory assistance calls increases, more people will dial numbers directly and use telephone directories to locate needed numbers, thus reducing the need for operators. Also, improved switching equipment will allow more calls to be connected without an operator's assistance, and more advanced billing systems will automatically relay billing information to computerized files that are used in preparing customer's billing statements. Technological innovations will restrict employment growth in some skilled crafts. For example, mechanical improvements, such as pole-lifting equipment and earth-boring tools, have limited the employment of line installers by increasing their efficiency.

New technology, however, is expected to increase the demand for engineering and technical personnel, especially electrical and electronic engineers and technicians, computer programmers, and systems analysts. Employment in administrative and sales occupations will rise as telephone business increases.

Earnings and Working Conditions

In 1976, earnings for nonsupervisory telephone employees averaged $6.46 an hour. In comparison, nonsupervisory workers in all private industries, except farming, averaged $4.87 an hour.

In late 1975, basic rates ranged from an average of $3.75 an hour for telephone operator trainees to $10.76 for professional and semiprofessional workers other than drafters.

A telephone employee usually starts at the minimum wage for the particular job. Advancement from the starting rate to the maximum rate generally takes 5 years, but operators and clerical employees of some companies may reach the maximum rate in 4 years.

More than two-thirds of the workers in the industry, mainly telephone operators and craft workers, are members of labor unions. The two principal unions representing workers in the telephone industry are the Communications Workers of America and the International Brotherhood of Electrical Workers, but many other employees are members of the 15 independent unions that form the Telecommunications International Union.

Union contracts govern wage rates, wage increases, and the amount of time required to advance from one step to the next for most telephone workers. The contracts

Although employment in the telephone industry will fluctuate due to economic cycles, moderate long-term growth is expected

Wage and salary workers in telephone communication, 1950-76 and projected 1985

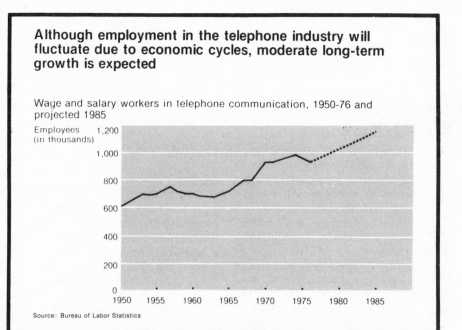

Source: Bureau of Labor Statistics

also call for extra pay for work beyond the normal 8 hours a day, or 5 days a week, and for all Sunday and holiday work. Most contracts provide a pay differential for night work.

Overtime work sometimes is required, especially during emergencies, such as floods, hurricanes, or bad storms. During an "emergency call-out," which is a short-notice request to report for work during non-scheduled hours, workers are guaranteed a minimum period of pay at the basic hourly rate. Travel time between jobs is counted as worktime for craft workers under some contracts.

Paid vacations are granted according to length of service. Usually, contracts provide for a 1-week vacation beginning with 6 months of service; 2 weeks for 1 to 7 years; 3 weeks for 8 to 15 years; 4 weeks for 16 to 24 years; and 5 weeks for 25 years and over. Depending on locality, holidays range from 9 to 11 days a year. Most telephone workers are covered by paid sick leave plans and group insurance which usually provide sickness, accident, and death benefits and retirement and disability pensions.

The telephone industry has one of the best safety records in American industry. The number of disabling injuries has been well below the average.

Sources of Additional Information

More details about employment opportunities are available from the telephone company in your community or local offices of the unions that represent telephone workers. If no local union is listed in the telephone directory, write to:

Telecommunications International Union, P.O. Box 5462, Hamden, Conn. 06518.

International Brotherhood of Electrical Workers, 1200 15th St. NW., Washington, D.C. 20005.

United States Independent Telephone Association, 1801 K St. NW., Suite 1201, Washington, D.C. 20006.

OCCUPATIONS IN THE TRUCKING INDUSTRY

In 1976, the trucking industry employed approximately 1.2 million workers—more than the rival rail, air, and pipeline transportation industries combined. It is a major employer of persons not planning to attend college, since nearly 90 percent of its employees are freight handlers, drivers, truck maintenance personnel, or clerical workers—occupations which only require a high school education.

Nature and Location of the Industry

The trucking industry is made up of companies that sell transportation and storage services. Although many trucking companies serve only a single city and its suburbs, and others carry goods only between distant cities, most large trucking firms provide both types of service. Some firms operate one type of truck and specialize in one type of product. For example, they may carry steel rods on flat trailers or grain in open top vans. In addition, trucking companies may operate as either contract or common carriers. Contract carriers haul commodities of one or a few shippers exclusively; common carriers offer transportation services to businesses in general.

Trucking companies vary widely in size. Almost half of the industry's workers are employed by less than 10 percent of the companies. But a large proportion of companies are small, particularly those which serve a single city. Many companies are owner-operated, and the owner does the driving.

Trucking industry employees work in cities and towns of all sizes and are distributed much the same as the Nation's population.

Occupations in the Industry

About four-fifths of all trucking industry employees have blue-collar jobs, including about 620,000 truckdrivers. Other large blue-collar occupations are material handlers, mechanics, washers and lubricators, and supervisors. Most white-collar employees are clerical workers, such as secretaries and rate clerks, and administrative personnel, such as terminal managers and accountants.

The duties and training requirements of some of these occupations are described briefly in the following sections.

Truckdriving Occupations. More than half of the industry's employees are drivers. *Long-distance truckdrivers* (D.O.T. 904.883) spend nearly all their working hours driving large trucks or tractor trailers between terminals. Some drivers load and unload their trucks, but the usual practice is to have other employees do this work. *Local truckdrivers* (D.O.T. 906.883) operate trucks over short distances, usually within one city and its suburbs. They pick up goods from, and deliver goods to, trucking terminals, businesses, and homes in the area.

Material Handling Occupations. About 1 out of 12 employees moves freight into and out of trucks and warehouses. Much of this work is done by *material handlers* (D.O.T. 929.887) who work in groups of three or four under the direction of a dock supervisor or gang leader. Material handlers load and unload freight with the aid of handtrucks, conveyors, and other devices. Heavy items are moved by *power truck operators* (D.O.T. 922.883) and *crane operators* (D.O.T. 921.280). Gang leaders determine the order in which items will be loaded, so that the cargo is balanced and items to be unloaded first are near the truck's door. *Truckdrivers' helpers* (D.O.T. 905.887) travel with drivers to unload and pick up freight. Occasionally, helpers may do relief driving.

Truck Maintenance Occupations. About 1 out of every 20 employees takes care of the trucks. *Truck mechanics* (D.O.T. 620.281) keep trucks and trailers in good running condition. Much time is spent in preventive maintenance to assure safe operation, to check wear and damage to parts, and to reduce breakdowns. When breakdowns do occur, these workers determine the cause and make the necessary repairs. *Truck mechanic helpers* (D.O.T. 620.884) and apprentices assist experienced mechanics in inspection and repair work. *Truck lubricators* and *washers* (D.O.T. 915.887 and 919.887) clean, lubricate, and refuel trucks, change tires, and do other routine maintenance.

Training, Other Qualifications, and Advancement

Workers in blue-collar occupations usually are hired at the unskilled level, as material handlers, truckdrivers' helpers, lubricators, and washers. No formal training is required for these jobs, but many employers prefer high school graduates. Applicants must be in good physical condition. New employees work under the guidance of experienced workers and supervisors while learning their jobs; this usually takes more than a few weeks. As vacancies occur, workers advance to more skilled blue-collar jobs, such as power truck operator and truckdriver. The ability to do the job and length of service with the firm are the primary qualifications for promotion. Material handlers who demonstrate supervisory ability can become gang leaders or dock supervisors.

Qualifications for truckdriving jobs vary and depend on individual employers, the type of truck, and other factors. In most States, drivers must have a chauffeur's license, which is a commercial driving permit obtained from State motor vehicle departments. The U.S. Department of Transportation establishes minimum qualifications for drivers who transport goods between States. They must be at least 21 years old, be able-bodied, have good hearing, and have at least 20/40 vision with or without glasses. However, many firms will not hire long-distance drivers under 25 years of age. Drivers also must be able to read, speak, and write English well enough to complete required reports. Drivers must have good driving records.

People interested in professional driving should take the driver-training courses offered by many high schools. A course in automotive mechanics also is helpful. Private truck-driving training schools offer another opportunity to prepare for a driving job; however, completion of such a course does not assure employment as a driver.

Most truck mechanics learn their skills informally on the job as helpers to experienced mechanics. Others complete formal apprenticeship programs that generally last 4 years and include on-the-job training and related classroom instruction. Unskilled workers, such as lubricators and washers, frequently are promoted to jobs as helpers and apprentices. However, many firms will hire inexperienced people, especially those who have completed courses in automotive mechanics, for helper or apprentice jobs.

Completion of commercial courses in high school or in a private business school is usually adequate for entry into general clerical occupations such as secretary or typist. Additional on-the-job training is needed for specialized clerical occupations such as claims adjuster.

Generally, no specialized education is needed for dispatcher jobs. Openings are filled by truckdrivers, claims adjusters, or other workers who know their company's operations and are familiar with State and Federal driving regulations. Candidates may improve their qualifications by taking college or technical school courses in transportation.

Administrative and sales positions frequently are filled by college graduates who have majored in busi-

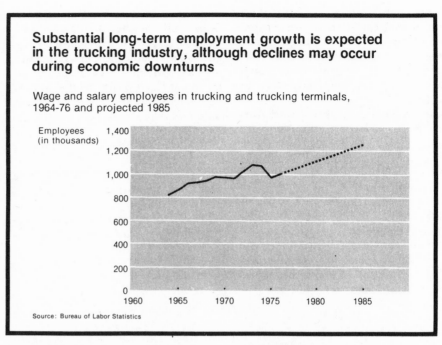

Substantial long-term employment growth is expected in the trucking industry, although declines may occur during economic downturns

Wage and salary employees in trucking and trucking terminals, 1964-76 and projected 1985

Source: Bureau of Labor Statistics

ness administration, marketing, accounting, industrial relations, or transportation. Some companies have management training programs for college graduates in which trainees work for brief periods in various departments to get a broad understanding of trucking operations before they are assigned to a particular department. High school graduates may be promoted to administrative and sales positions.

Employment Outlook

Employment in the trucking industry is expected to grow about as fast as the average for all industries through the mid-1980's. In addition to the large number of job openings created by employment growth, thousands more will arise as experienced workers retire, die, or transfer to other fields. The number of jobs may vary from year to year, however, because the amount of freight fluctuates with ups and downs in the economy.

Trucks carry virtually all freight for local distribution and a great deal of freight between distant cities. As the volume of freight increases with the Nation's economic growth, employment in the trucking industry will rise. More employees also will be needed to serve the many factories, warehouses, stores, and homes being built where railroad transportation is

not available.

Employment will not increase as fast as the demand for trucking services because technological developments will increase output per worker. For example, more efficient freight-handling methods—such as conveyors and draglines to move freight in and out of terminals and warehouses—will increase the efficiency of material handlers. Larger trucks as well as more efficient packaging techniques will allow truckdrivers to carry more cargo.

Earnings and Working Conditions

In 1976, nonsupervisory workers in the trucking industry averaged $6.57 an hour, compared with $4.87 an hour for their counterparts in all private industry, except farming. Earnings are relatively high in the trucking industry, because highly paid drivers represent a large proportion of employment; many long-distance drivers earn more than $300 a week.

Most employees are paid an hourly rate or a weekly or monthly salary. However, truckdrivers on the longer runs generally are paid on a mileage basis while driving. For all other worktime, they are paid an hourly rate.

Working conditions vary greatly among occupations in the industry.

While maneuvering large trucks in fast-moving traffic can cause tension, more comfortable seating, power steering, and air-conditioned cabs have reduced physical strain. Long-distance drivers frequently work at night and may spend time away from home; local drivers usually work during the day. Material handlers and truckdrivers' helpers have strenuous jobs, although conveyor systems and other freight handling equipment have reduced some of the heavier lifting, making the work easier and safer. Truck mechanics and other maintenance personnel may have to work in awkward or cramped positions while servicing vehicles, and frequently get dirty because of the grease and oil on the trucks. In addition, most maintenance shops are hot in summer and drafty in the winter. Mechanics occasionally make repairs outdoors when a truck breaks down on the road.

Many large organizations operate around the clock and require some material handling and maintenance personnel to work evenings, nights, and weekends.

A large number of trucking industry employees are members of the International Brotherhood of Teamsters, Chauffeurs, Warehousemen and Helpers of America (Ind).

Sources of Additional Information

For general information about career opportunities in the trucking industry, write to:

American Trucking Associations, Inc., 1616 P St. NW., Washington, D.C. 20036.

Information about specific jobs may be available from the personnel departments of local trucking companies or the local office of your State employment service.

WHERE TO GO FOR MORE INFORMATION

Whether you have questions about a particular job or are trying to compare various fields, *A Guide to Job Opportunities* is a good place to begin. The *Guide* will introduce you to some of the important aspects of an occupation and answer many of your initial questions. But the *Guide* is only one of many available sources of information about jobs and careers. After reading a few *Guide* statements, you may decide that you want more detailed information about a particular occupation. Or you may want to find out where you can find this kind of work in your community or where you can go for appropriate training. If you are willing to make an effort, you will discover a wealth of occupational information — much of it available at little or no cost.

Sources of Career Information

Much information on careers is put out by government, industry, trade unions, schools, professional associations, private guidance services, and other organizations. You should be careful in assessing any single piece of career guidance material. Keep in mind the date and source, in particular. Material that is too old may contain obsolete or even misleading information. Be especially cautious about accepting information on employment outlook, earnings, and training requirements if it is more than 5 years old. You also need to consider the source — and thus the intent — of the career guidance material you obtain.

Although some occupational materials are produced solely for the purpose of objective vocational guidance, others are produced for recruitment purposes. You should be wary of biased information, which may tend to leave out important items, over-glamorize the occupation, overstate the earnings, or exaggerate the demand for workers.

School counselors can be a very important source of guidance information. Counselors should be able to refer you to the different types of career materials available in your school or community. They are likely to be familiar with the job market. They also can discuss entry requirements and costs of the schools or training programs that offer preparation for the kind of work in which you are interested. Most important of all, your counselor can help you consider the occupational information you obtain in relation to your own abilities, personal aspirations, and career goals.

Libraries have books, brochures, magazines, and audiovisual materials that contain information about jobs and careers. Check your school library or media center, of course — but don't forget the public library. Many libraries have pamphlet files devoted to specific occupations. Some libraries also have collections of filmstrips, records and tapes, and microfilms with occupational information. The reference shelf undoubtedly contains one di-

rectory or more that you will find useful if you want to get the names of specific schools or business concerns. The library staff can direct you to the information best suited to your needs.

Trade unions, business firms, trade associations, professional societies, and educational institutions all publish career information, and much of this is available for the asking.

The **Sources of Additional Information** section at the end of most *Guide* statements lists organizations you can write to. This is a good way to begin. For the names and addresses of other organizations, consult the directories on your library's reference shelf. There, you are likely to find directories that list:

—trade associations.
—professional associations.
—business firms.
—home study and correspondence programs.
—business, trade, and technical schools.
—sources of scholarships and financial aid.

Your school library or career center may have one directory or more put out by commercial publishers that list sources of career information by occupation.

Computer-assisted occupational information systems have been installed in some schools and career centers. These systems allow users to obtain career information stored in a computer by entering specific requests and receiving immediate answers. Through the occupational information systems, users are able to examine the ways in which different personal abilities, interests, and preferences are related to different occupations. The U.S. Department of Labor is currently providing funds for such systems in eight States.

Don't overlook the importance of **personal contacts**. An interview with someone in a particular job can often tell you much more than a booklet or brochure can. By asking the right questions, you find out what kind of training is really important, how workers got their first jobs as well as the one they're in now, and what they like and dislike about the work.

State employment security agencies in many States publish career briefs for dozens of different occupations and industries. These briefs usually describe earnings and job outlook information for a particular State — and sometimes for a city or metropolitan area. By contrast, the *Guide* gives information for the Nation as a whole. In addition, a number of States publish brochures on writing resumes, finding job openings, preparing for interviews, and other aspects of a job search. To find out what materials are available for your State, consult the U.S. Employment and Training Administration's *Guide to Local Occupational Information*. Or write directly to the chief information officer in your State employment security agency. Following is a list of their titles and addresses:

Alabama

Public Information Officer, Department of Industrial Relations, Industrial Relations Bldg., 649 Monroe St., Montgomery, Ala. 36130.

Alaska

Information Officer, Employment Security Division, Department of Labor, P.O. Box 3-7000, Juneau, Alaska 99811.

Arizona

Chief of Information and Education, Arizona State Employment Security Commission, P.O. Box 6123, Phoenix, Ariz. 85005.

Arkansas

Public Information Officer, Employment Security Division, P.O. Box 2981, Little Rock, Ark. 72203.

California

Public Information Section, Employment Development Department, 800 Capitol Mall, Sacramento, Calif. 95814.

Colorado

Public Information Officer, Division of Employment, Department of Labor and Employment, 251 East 12th Ave., Denver, Colo. 80203.

Connecticut

Public Information Supervisor, Connecticut Employment Security Division, 200 Folly Brook Blvd., Weatherfield, Conn. 06109.

Delaware

Secretary, Department of Labor, 801 West 14th St., Wilmington, Del. 19899.

District of Columbia

Chief, Community Relations and Information Office, D.C. Department of Manpower, Room 601, 500 C St. NW., Washington, D.C. 20212.

Florida

Information Director, Florida Department of Commerce, Collins Bldg., Tallahassee, Fla. 32304.

Georgia

Chief of Public Relations and Information, Georgia Department of Labor, 254 Washington St. SW., Atlanta, Ga. 30334.

Hawaii

Information Specialist, Department of Labor and Industrial Relations, 825 Mililani St., Honolulu, Hawaii 96813.

Idaho

Public Information Coordinator, Department of Employment, P.O. Box 35, Boise, Idaho 83707.

Illinois

Director, Communications and Public Information, Illinois Department of Labor, State Office Bldg., Room 705, Springfield, Ill. 62706.

Indiana

Director of Information and Education, Employment Security Division, 10 North Senate Ave., Indianapolis, Ind. 46204.

Iowa

Chief of Information Services, Employment Security Commission, 1000 East Grand Ave., Des Moines, Iowa 50319.

Kansas

Public Relations Director, Department of Human Resources, 401 Topeka Ave., Topeka, Kans. 66603.

Kentucky

Supervisor, Public Information, Department of Human Resources, 592 East Main St., Frankfort, Ky. 40601.

New Jersey

Director of Public Information, Division of Employment Security, Department of Labor and Industry, John Fitch Plaza, Trenton, N.J. 08625.

New Mexico

Information Officer, Employment Security Commission, P.O. Box 1928, Albuquerque, N. Mex. 87103.

New York

Director, Division of Research and Statistics, Department of Labor, 2 World Trade Center, New York, N.Y. 10047.

North Carolina

Communications and Information Specialist, Employment Security Commission, P.O. Box 25903, Raleigh, N.C. 27602.

North Dakota

Public Information Section, Employment Security Bureau, 145 South Front St., Bismarck, N. Dak. 58501.

Ohio

Public Information Officer, Bureau of Employment Services, 145 South Front St., Columbus, Ohio 43216.

Oklahoma

Information Director, Employment Security Commission, Will Rogers Memorial Office Bldg., Oklahoma City, Okla. 73105.

Oregon

Information Officer, Employment Division, 875 Union St. NE., Salem, Oreg. 97310.

Pennsylvania

Director of Public Relations, Bureau of Employment Security, Department of Labor and Industry Bldg., 7th and Forster Sts., Harrisburg, Pa. 17121.

Puerto Rico

Information Officer, Bureau of Employment Security, 414 Barbosa Ave., Hato Rey, P.R. 00917.

Rhode Island

Information Officer, Department of Employment Security, 24 Mason St., Providence, R.I. 02903.

South Carolina

Public Information Director, Employment Security Commission, P.O. Box 995, Columbia, S.C. 29202.

South Dakota

Public Information Director, Department of Labor, Office Bldg. No. 2, Pierre, S. Dak. 57501.

Tennessee

Chief of Public Relations, Department of Employment Security, 519 Cordell Hull Bldg., Nashville, Tenn. 37219.

Texas

Public Information Officer, Texas Employment Commission, TEC Bldg., 15th and Congress Ave., Austin, Tex. 78778.

Utah

Public Relations Director, Department of Employment Security, P.O. Box 11249, Salt Lake City, Utah 84111.

Vermont

Public Information Officer, Department of Employment Security, P.O. Box 488, Montpelier, Vt. 05602.

Virginia

Director, Information Services, Virginia Employment Commission, P.O. Box 1358, Richmond, Va. 23211.

Washington

Information Officer, Employment Security Department, P.O. Box 367, Olympia, Wash. 98504.

West Virginia

Information Representative, Department of Employment Security, 4407 McCorkle Ave. SE., Charleston, W. Va. 25305.

Wisconsin

Director of Information, Department of Industry, Labor, and Human Relations, P.O. Box 2209, Madison, Wis. 53701.

Wyoming

Information Officer, Employment Security Commission, P.O. Box 2760, Casper, Wyo. 82601.

Information on Finding a Job

Do you need help in finding a job? For information on job openings, follow up as many leads as possible. Parents, neighbors, teachers, and counselors may know of jobs. Check the want ads. Investigate the local office of your State employment service. And find out whether private or nonprofit employment agencies in your community can help you. The following section will give you some idea of where you can go to look for a job and what sort of help to expect.

Informal job search methods. Informal methods of job search are the most popular, and also the most effective. Informal methods include direct application to employers with or without referral by friends or relatives. Jobseekers locate a firm that might employ them and file an application, often without certain knowledge that an opening exists.

You can find targets for your informal search in several ways. The Yellow Pages and local chambers of commerce will give you the names and addresses of appropriate firms in the community where you wish to work. You can also get listings of most firms in a specific industry by consulting one of the directories on the reference shelf in your public library. Friends and relatives may suggest places to apply for a job, and people you meet in the course of your job search are also likely to give you ideas.

Want ads. The "Help Wanted" ads in a major newspaper contain hundreds of job listings. As a job search tool, they have two advantages: They are cheap and easy to acquire, and they often result in successful placement. There are disadvantages as well. Want ads give a distorted view of the local labor market, for they tend to underrepresent small firms. They also tend to overrepresent certain occupations. How helpful they are to you will depend largely on the kind of job you seek.

Bear in mind that want ads do not provide complete information; many ads give little or no description of the job, working conditions, and pay. Some ads omit the identity of the employer. In addition, firms often run multiple listings. Some ads offer jobs in other cities (which do not help the local worker); others advertise employment agencies rather than employment.

Public employment service. The public employment service, also called the Job Service, can be a good source of information about job openings in your community. Employment security (ES) agencies in each of the 50 States and the District of Columbia are affiliated with the U.S. Employment Service, and provide their services without charge. Operating through a network of 2,500 local offices, State agencies help jobseekers find employment and help employers find qualified workers. To find the office nearest you, look in the State government telephone listings under "Job Service" or "Employment." If the local office does not provide the information or services you are looking for, write to the information officer in your State capital. Addresses are given in the first section of this chapter.

General services. Assuming you come to your local employment service office because you're looking for a job, the first step is to fill out an application that asks for general background and work history. To speed up the process, you should bring along complete information on previous jobs, including dates of employment, names and addresses of employers, and pay levels.

You may also talk at length with occupational counselors. These counselors, or interviewers, can assist in a wide range of areas. They can help you pinpoint a suitable field of interest, suggest training programs and other means of preparing for a particular occupation, or simply advise you on compiling a resume.

One other aspect of your local office's services deserves particular attention — the occupational registers. Employment service offices often maintain files of resumes of qualified workers for use by employers seeking such workers. Ask to have your resume filed in the appropriate register.

Special services. Serving people with job market disadvantages is an important function of the employment service, and many local offices have specially trained counselors who advise veterans, youth, handicapped, or older workers.

By law, veterans are entitled to priority in interviewing, counseling, testing, job development, and job placement. Special counselors called veterans reemployment representatives are trained to deal with the particular problems of veterans, many of whom find it difficult to readjust to civilian life. While such veterans often face multiple problems, joblessness alone is a major barrier to resuming an ordinary life. Special help for disabled veterans begins with outreach units in each State, whose job it is to identify disabled veterans and make them aware of the many kinds of assistance available to them.

As part of the effort to reduce excessive youth unemployment, local employment service offices test and counsel young people, and refer them to training programs or jobs whenever possible. These offices also manage summer youth programs. Youthful jobseekers from very poor families receive information on the various kinds of federally funded job programs for young people, including part-time and work-experience projects and the Job Corps.

For people with mental or physical disabilities, the employment service provides assistance in making realistic job choices, and in overcoming problems related to getting and holding jobs. Job openings for handicapped workers are listed as well. Often, these openings are with government contractors and other firms that are making a positive effort to employ handicapped workers.

Older worker specialists in many local employment service offices assist middle-aged and older workers, whose job search generally differs from that of younger workers. Both counseling and placement services are tailored to the unique needs of older workers. Jobseekers over 55 who have very low incomes may be referred to one of the thousands of part-time, community service jobs for the elderly funded by the Federal Government.

Private employment agencies. In the appropriate section of the classified ads or the telephone book you can find numerous advertisements for private employment agencies. All are in business to make money, but some offer higher quality service and better chances of successful placement than others.

The three main places in which private agencies advertise are newspaper want ads, the Yellow Pages, and trade journals. Telephone listings give little more than the name, address, phone number, and specialty of the agency, while trade journals only list openings for a particular occupation. Want ads, then, are the best source of general listings of agencies.

These listings fall into two categories — those offering specific openings and those offering general promise of employment. You should concentrate on the former, using the latter only as a last resort. With a specific opening mentioned in the ad, you have greater assurance of the agency's desire to place qualified individuals in suitable jobs.

When responding to such an ad, you may learn more about the job over the phone. If you are interested, visit the agency, fill out an application, present a resume, and talk with an interviewer. The agency will then arrange an interview with the employer if you are qualified, and perhaps suggest alternative openings if you are not.

Most agencies operate on a commission basis, with the fee contingent upon a successful match. Agencies advertising "no fees, no contracts" are paid by the employer and charge the applicant nothing. Many other agencies, however, do charge their applicants. You should find out before using them exactly what the services will cost you.

Community agencies. A growing number of nonprofit organizations throughout the Nation provide counseling, career development, and job placement services. These agencies generally concentrate on services for a particular labor force group — women, the elderly, youth, minorities, or ex-offenders, for example.

Community employment agencies serve an important function in providing the extensive counseling that many disadvantaged jobseekers require. They often help their clients resolve personal, family, or other fundamental problems that may stand in the way of finding a suitable job. Some agencies provide necessary job training, while others refer their clients to training programs elsewhere. For the most part, these community agencies take a strong active interest in their clients, and provide an array of services designed to help people find and keep jobs.

It's up to you to discover whether there are such agencies in your community — and whether they can help you. The State employment service should be able to tell you whether such an agency has been established in your community. If the local office cannot help, write the State information officer. Your church, synagogue, or local library may have the information, too. The U.S. Department of Labor is another possible source of information, for many of these agencies receive some or all of their funding from the Federal Government, through the Comprehensive Employment and Training Act (CETA). Among its many and varied provisions, CETA authorizes Federal money for local organizations that offer job counseling, training, and placement help to unemployed and disadvantaged persons. For further information, write:

Office of Comprehensive Employment Development, Employment and Training Administration, U.S. Department of Labor, Room 6000, 601 D St. NW., Washington, D.C., 20213; or the Office of Information, Room 10406, at the same address.

Another likely source of information is the U.S. Department of Labor's *Directory for Reaching Minority Groups.* Although the 1973 directory is out of print, a revised edition is being prepared, and will list organizations that provide job information, training, and other services to minorities. For information, write to:

Bureau of Apprenticeship and Training, U.S. Department of Labor, 601 D St. NW., Washington, D.C., 20213.

A directory that lists employment counseling and advocacy organizations for women is available for a nominal charge from

Wider Opportunities for Women (WOW), 1649 K St. NW., Washington, D.C., 20006.

Labor Market Information

All State employment security agencies develop detailed labor market data needed by employment and training specialists and educators who plan for local needs. Such information helps policymakers decide whether or not to expand a vocational training program, for example — or drop it altogether. Jobseekers and counselors also may find these studies helpful. Typically, State agencies publish reports that deal with future occupational supply, characteristics of the work force, changes in State and area economic activities, and the employment structure of important industries. For all States, and for nearly all Standard Metropolitan Statistical Areas (SMSA's) of 50,000 inhabitants or more, data are available that show current employment as well as estimated future needs. This information is very detailed; generally, each State issues a report covering current and future employment for as many as 200 industries and 400 occupations. In addition, major statistical indicators of labor market activity are released by all of the States on a monthly, quarterly, and annual basis. For information on the various labor market studies, reports, and analyses available in a specific State, contact the chief of research and analysis in the State employment security agency.

TOMORROW'S JOBS

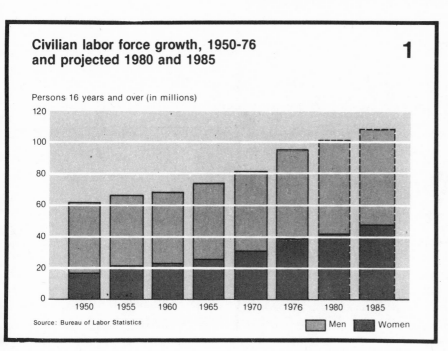

Civilian labor force growth, 1950-76 and projected 1980 and 1985 **1**

Persons 16 years and over (in millions)

1950 1955 1960 1965 1970 1976 1980 1985

Source: Bureau of Labor Statistics

Men   Women

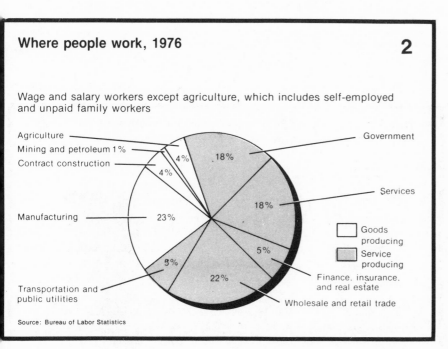

Where people work, 1976 **2**

Wage and salary workers except agriculture, which includes self-employed and unpaid family workers

Agriculture
Mining and petroleum 1%
Contract construction — 4%
Government 18%
4%
Services 18%
Manufacturing — 23%
Goods producing
Service producing
5%
Finance, insurance, and real estate
5%
22%
Transportation and public utilities
Wholesale and retail trade

Source: Bureau of Labor Statistics

Employment Projections in a Changing Economy

The demand for workers in any occupation depends on the consumer. If a product is unwanted, no workers will be needed to produce or provide it. In addition, technology has created or eliminated hundreds of thousands of jobs.

Fortunately, most of the factors that alter the demand for workers do not change overnight. Shifts generally occur in an orderly, fairly predictable fashion. It is possible to make useful industry and occupation employment projections.

Job Openings

The total number of job openings expected results from retirements, deaths, and transfers, as well as from employment growth. Jobs go to the best qualified persons available, but this does not necessarily mean those with the most education. There are numerous well-paying occupations that do not require a college degree. Workers in the construction crafts and in mechanic and repairer occupations are generally high school graduates, yet many earn more than workers in some jobs that require a college degree.

The demand for workers in occupations requiring technical, vocational, or apprenticeship training is expected to rise through the mid-1980s. No matter what the goal, early planning allows time to consider all the choices available for tomorrow's jobs.

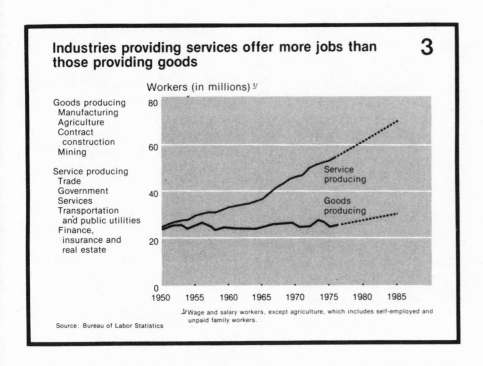

Industries providing services offer more jobs than those providing goods   3

Workers (in millions) [1]

Goods producing
  Manufacturing
  Agriculture
  Contract
    construction
  Mining

Service producing
  Trade
  Government
  Services
  Transportation
    and public utilities
  Finance,
    insurance and
    real estate

Service
producing

Goods
producing

80

60

40

20

0
1950   1955   1960   1965   1970   1975   1980   1985

[1] Wage and salary workers, except agriculture, which includes self-employed and unpaid family workers.

Source: Bureau of Labor Statistics

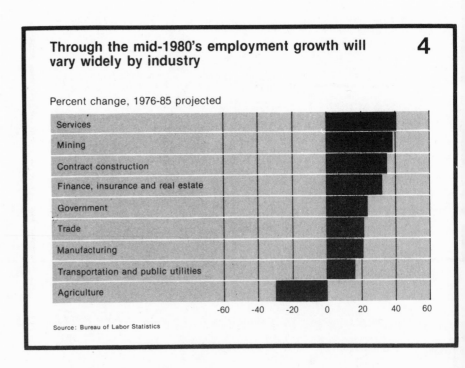

Through the mid-1980's employment growth will vary widely by industry   4

Percent change, 1976-85 projected

Services
Mining
Contract construction
Finance, insurance and real estate
Government
Trade
Manufacturing
Transportation and public utilities
Agriculture

-60   -40   -20   0   20   40   60

Source: Bureau of Labor Statistics

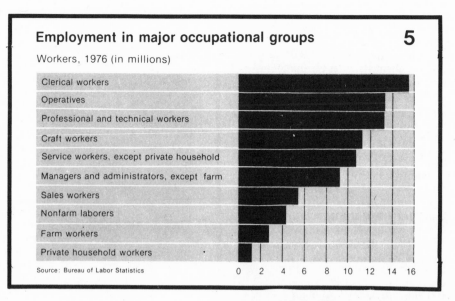

Employment in major occupational groups   5

Workers, 1976 (in millions)

Clerical workers	
Operatives	
Professional and technical workers	
Craft workers	
Service workers, except private household	
Managers and administrators, except farm	
Sales workers	
Nonfarm laborers	
Farm workers	
Private household workers	

0 2 4 6 8 10 12 14 16

Source: Bureau of Labor Statistics

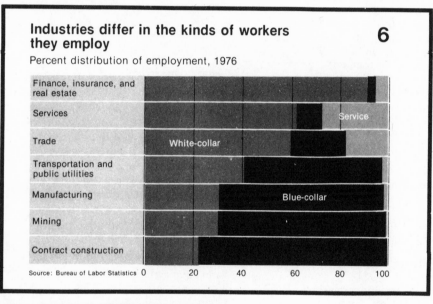

Industries differ in the kinds of workers they employ   6

Percent distribution of employment, 1976

Finance, insurance, and real estate	
Services	Service
Trade	White-collar
Transportation and public utilities	
Manufacturing	Blue-collar
Mining	
Contract construction	

Source: Bureau of Labor Statistics   0   20   40   60   80   100

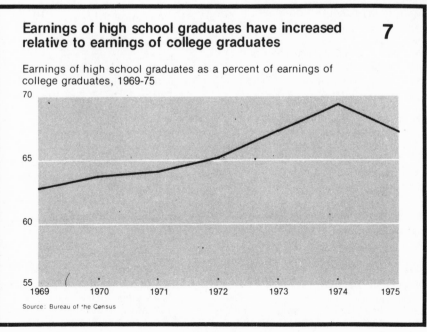

Earnings of high school graduates have increased relative to earnings of college graduates   7

Earnings of high school graduates as a percent of earnings of college graduates, 1969-75

70

65

60

55
1969   1970   1971   1972   1973   1974   1975

Source: Bureau of the Census

DICTIONARY OF OCCUPATIONAL TITLES
(D.O.T.) INDEX

D.O.T. numbers classify each job according to the type of work performed, training required, physical demands, and working conditions. The index is useful as a cross-reference to show where in the *Guide* the occupation is mentioned and under what industries.